STATUE OF JOGUES, AT DUNWOODIE.

PIONEER PRIESTS

OF

NORTH AMERICA

1642-1710

BY THE

REV. T. J. CAMPBELL, S.J.

FORDHAM UNIVERSITY PRESS,
FORDHAM UNIVERSITY,
NEW YORK.
1908.

As all of the priests whose work is here described labored for
a long time in what is now New York territory, this
volume is properly and with the profoundest respect

DEDICATED

TO

HIS GRACE, THE MOST REVEREND JOHN M. FARLEY, D.D.,
ARCHBISHOP OF NEW YORK.

Nibil Obstat

REMIGIUS LAFORT, S.T.L.,
Censor Deputatus.

Imprimatur

JOHN M. FARLEY, D.D.,
Archbishop of New York.

CONTENTS.

	PAGE
INTRODUCTION	
ISAAC JOGUES	i
JOSEPH BRESSANI	42
JOSEPH PONCET	61
SIMON LE MOYNE	75
CLAUDE DABLON	101
JOSEPH CHAUMONOT	125
PAUL RAGUENEAU	141
RÉNE MÉNARD	158
JAMES FRÉMIN	172
JAMES BRUYAS	190
JOHN PIERRON	205
JOHN DE LAMBERVILLE	226
PETER MILLET	246
STEPHEN DE CARHEIL	262
PETER RAFFEIX	276
FRANCIS BONIFACE	285
JAMES DE LAMBERVILLE	298
JULIEN GARNIER	312

ILLUSTRATIONS.

Statue of Jogues, at Dunwoodie Seminary . *Frontispiece*

Orleans . . . . . . Facing page 2

Anne of Austria, Queen Regent of
    France . . . . . . " " 30

Lake of the Blessed Sacrament . . " " 34

Isaac Jogues, S.J . . . . . " " 38

Governor de Montmagny (Onontio) . " " 42

Pope Innocent X . . . . . " " 54

Mme. de la Peltrie . . . . " " 62

Ven. Marie de l'Incarnation . . . " " 72

Peter Stuyvesant . . . . " " 89

As Seen by Le Moyne . . . . " " 92

The Saguenay . . . . . " " 110

The Saguenay . . . . . " " 115

Loretto in Italy . . . . . " " 126

Lorette in Canada . . . . " " 137

Paul Ragueneau, S.J. . . . . " " 141

Old Quebec . . . . . " " 155

Dieppe . . . . . . " " 158

Mgr. Laval . . . . . " " 165

Caughnawaga Indians . . . . " " 181

Street in Caughnawaga . . . " " 187

Lord Bellomont . . . . . " " 203

Rouen (de Lamberville's Birthplace) . " " 226

Niagara . . . . . . " " 251

Bishop de Saint-Vallier . . . " " 280

Sir William Johnson, Bart . . " " 295

Tegakwitha . . . . . . " " 302

INTRODUCTION.

The Pioneers.

THE Pioneer Priests whose lives are sketched in this volume, are not *all* the " Pioneer Priests of North America." Only those have been chosen who had to do with the Iroquois Indians. The reason of this selection is that, although nearly all of the missionaries who labored among those savages were very remarkable men, yet they are, with one or two exceptions, practically unknown. It is true that they appear at intervals in the general history of the period, but that is not sufficient to give us an adequate idea of their greatness. Not only were they wonderful apostles, but some of them were conspicuous figures in the political events of the colonies, yet even their names are now forgotten. The desire to revive the memory of their heroism and holiness is the motive of these individual studies of their lives. The chronological order has been followed, as far as possible, so as to correspond with the general history of the missions.

Their work began in 1642, when Father Jogues was taken prisoner on the St. Lawrence, and carried down to what is now Auriesville, on the Mohawk. In 1644, Father Bressani was captured and brought to the same place; as was Father Poncet, in 1655. The two latter were released, after being tortured, but Father Jogues was put to death there in 1646.

In 1654, Father Le Moyne visited the Onondagas, and in 1655, Fathers Dablon and Chaumonot established a mission near the present site of Syracuse. They were subsequently joined by Fathers Frémin, Ménard, Ragueneau, and Le Mercier. A French colony was also attempted there, but to avoid a general massacre, an exodus took place on the night of March 20, 1658.

In 1661, a deputation of Indians was sent to Montreal to ask for the return of the Black Gowns. Le Moyne went

INTRODUCTION.

with them and remained a year among the Onondagas and Cayugas, but on the outbreak of hostilities, he was compelled to withdraw.

In 1667, after the punitive expedition of de Tracy, the missions were reorganized by Fathers Frémin, Bruyas, de Carheil, John and James de Lamberville, Millet, Raffeix, de Gueslis, Julien Garnier, Pierron and Boniface. The work was continued with more or less interruption until about 1686, when the impolitic measures of the Governors of Canada precipitated a war and ruined the missions. These nineteen years are in reality the only time in which it was possible to evangelize the New York Indians.

It was not until 1702 that Bruyas succeeded in inducing the Iroquois to recall the priests. Julien Garnier and James de Lamberville went down a second time among them, and were assisted by Mareuil and d'Heu; but by 1709, the English had succeeded in driving them out. When they came back, it was usually in the disguise of Indians.

Forty years afterwards, the Sulpitian Picquet established a settlement near where Ogdensburg now stands, but it was destroyed in 1760. Meantime, the Scotch Jesuit, Mark Anthony Gordon, had founded St. Regis, on what is now the border line of Canada and the United States. It still exists as a Catholic Reservation.

THE PLACE.

A very remarkable map of the old Iroquois mission sites was published in 1879 by the distinguished cartographer, General Clark, who in the following year began a series of laborious investigations to determine the exact place where the first missionary, Father Jogues, met his death. He fixed it beyond any possibility of doubt at what is now known as Auriesville. Twenty-five years afterwards, he affirmed that he was so sure of the identification of the site that he felt he could plant his spade on the very spot where the stake was fixed which held the head of Father Jogues.

INTRODUCTION.

By means of the two charts, which we owe to him, it is possible to follow every step of the missionaries in their apostolic journeys from the Hudson to Lake Erie. The name of every chapel is given, along with the date of its erection; the various trails are indicated, and every creek, and river, and bay is most carefully traced. The work involved must have been prodigious, not only in the collating of the old manuscripts and the consultation of books, but in the years of field work which were required to unearth and determine the remains of the aboriginal villages. General Clark has put all students of history under great obligations to him; but he especially deserves the gratitude of American Catholics.

We had at first intended to add these two maps to the present volume, but as the work of the Iroquois missionaries extended after their expulsion from New York far up into the region near Hudson Bay and westward to the wilderness of Michigan and Wisconsin, it will be necessary in order to properly appreciate the work accomplished to have before our eyes a view of the entire territory. We are thus obliged to refer the reader to the general atlas of North America.

THE PEOPLE.

The Iroquois were descendants of the Indians whom Jacques Cartier had met on the St. Lawrence, in 1634. How, when, or why they drifted down to New York is still largely a matter of speculation. They gradually formed into five distinct tribes or nations. They were called by the English, Mohawks, Oneidas, Onondagas, Cayugas, and Senecas; and by the French, Agniers, Onneyuts, Onontagués, Goyogouins, and Tsonnontouans; in their own language they were the *Ganeagono,* or People of the Flint; *Oneyotekeano,* or Granite People; *Onundagono,* or Hill People; *Gwengwhehono,* or Muck Land People, and *Nundawono,* or Great Hill People. The localities in which they lived are still indicated by the river and lakes which bear their names.

INTRODUCTION.

Collectively they were designated by the French as "The Iroquois;" by the English, as "The Five Nations," while they styled themselves the *Hodenosaunee,* or People of the Long House, because of the shape of their lodges. The name Iroquois is said by Charlevoix to have been given to them because of their fashion of ending their discourses by the word "hero" or "hiro,"—"I have spoken," with the suffix "que," or something equivalent in sound, which was uttered as a sign of pleasure or pain; its meaning being determined by the intonation. The Bureau of American Ethnology, however, derives it from the Algonquin word *Iriakhoiw,* which means "real adders." They were joined by the Tuscaroras, about 1722, and from that out they were called by the English, "The Six Nations."

When Father Jogues was among them, in 1646, they claimed the territory from the Hudson to the Genesee, but between 1650 and 1655, they drove out the Eries or Cats, and extended their domain to Lake Erie. They were united in a Confederacy or League, whose character seems to have been more deliberative than executive, as separate tribes or families, or even individuals, could go to war when they considered themselves aggrieved. It is said to have been formed about 1570. Its central seat was at Onondaga.

As their language was an offshoot of the Huron, it was possible for the missionary who had labored in Canada to make himself more or less intelligible in New York. Thus we find Le Moyne addressing the council at Onondaga in Huron, immediately on his arrival. They were not numerous and scarcely ever exceeded sixteen or seventeen thousand. La Hontan's estimate of seventy thousand is generally regarded as absurd. But few as they were they struck terror into the Dutch, French, and English, as well as all their Indian foes. Dablon was in dread of them, far up the Saguenay; they organized expeditions against the Illinois; they annihilated the Hurons near the Great Lakes; and went to war with the Andastes of Pennsylvania,

INTRODUCTION.

and the Crees of Tennessee. This constant warfare, of course, drained their strength, and disease and drunkenness helped the work of destruction; but they kept up their numbers by adopting many of the captives whom they had seized in their raids.

They were an intelligent race, but unfortunately having determined to destroy or assimilate all the other nations, they directed all their energies to the prosecution of war. They knew nothing of agriculture, and were satisfied with the maize, beans and squash raised by their squaws. The mystery of well-digging was too deep for them, so they had to keep close to the lakes and river courses to live. They have left no pottery of any value, and being ignorant of the textile arts, made their clothing of the skins of wild beasts. They lived in towns, which were protected by two or three lines of palisades, but they quickly adopted, in their rude fashion, the European methods of defense. Their houses were arched constructions, sometimes 120 feet in length, and were covered with bark, and shaped something like a grape arbor. Of course, they were swarming with vermin and reeking with disease. They were divided off into sections or stalls, to accommodate the several families that occupied them, but without any pretense or possibility of privacy. The fires were built in a line down the middle of the lodge, and the smoke escaped from the top.

Their personal habits were filthy in the extreme. Bruyas speaks of that as one of his tortures. They ate the most disgusting things, and boasted of their prowess in that regard. Yet, though voracious gluttons, they starved uncomplainingly when food was lacking—which was often. They knew nothing of the laws of health, though Lafitau tells us of their use of lotions and poultices, and attributes to them some skill in setting bones, and in making incisions with their stone knives, but the reader of the *Relations* will find such medical treatment rare. Incantations are mostly in evidence, and some of the results achieved by the medicine-

INTRODUCTION.

men, as well as some of their predictions, were so startling that they were attributed by the missionaries to diabolical intervention. Mostly, however, their sorcerers were ridiculous charlatans.

Morally, the Iroquois were very degraded, and the abominations of the villages are only hinted at in the *Relations*. They were thieves and gamblers, of course. There was no reason for their being polygamists, because their marriages, which the mothers of the parties concerned generally arranged, could be broken at will. The women were corrupt from girlhood, and after a few years became degraded and hideous drudges. At times, however, they were consulted by the council, and in certain contingencies could nominate a chief. The line of descent was always reckoned through them. The children were never punished, and were allowed to grow up like animals, though Garnier tells us of many of his Senecas who were extremely watchful over the morality of their offspring.

Their cruelty, which was fiendish in the extreme, was made worse by an affectation of tenderness for their victim, even while they were burning and gashing his limbs, or making him writhe in agony at the stake. It is not generally adverted to, that they were atrocious cannibals. De Lamberville informs us that 600 captives were killed and eaten in a single expedition against the Illinois. In de Denonville's attack on the Senecas the Ottawas are credited with digging up the dead and devouring them. Even little children would be plucked from the mother's breast and boiled and eaten. Radisson gives us some details which the priests do not dare to describe. The head and heart of the victim was the portion of the chief, the carcass was tossed to the crowd.

They had a very vague idea of a Supreme Deity. Their chief object of worship was Agreskoué, the God of War, who is often confounded or synonymous with the Sun. General Clark has no hesitation in describing this as " liter-

INTRODUCTION.

ally *devil worship;* that is they believed first in a good spirit, who favored them with all that was desirable; was the author and preserver of their lives, &c. Besides, there was another character who was in all things antagonistic, whom they called the devil, as they understood it, meaning a sorcerer, bad, wicked, cunning, who demanded sacrifice, and to whom prisoners were sacrificed. Governor Colden uses the word "Satanas" to describe the people who believed in this particular character; and Megapolensis, Van der Donck and others make it simply *devil,* and *devil worship.* When Jogues learned of the character of this worship every fibre of his being revolted. He could not and did not submit to the requirements demanded, and was willing to abide the consequences. In the belief of the younger Mohawks, his actions in prostrating himself before the cross, in baptizing persons and infants, and in short, all his movements, were interpreted as the acts of a sorcerer, antagonistic to their great god *Aireskoué."*

No more valuable testimony than this could be had as to the reason why Jogues was put to death, and why the other missionaries encountered such opposition. Their adoration of the Great Spirit, as now practised, and which is sometimes adduced as proof of their intelligence, was taught to them as late as 1669, by Father Pierron, and was subsequently adopted, even by pagan Indians. They had nothing corresponding to a priesthood, and each brave had his *oki* or *manitou,* which he adopted after a protracted period of fasting and seclusion. Animate or inanimate beings might be *okis,* and even men could be regarded as such. Father Jogues had that distinction. Some symbol of this personal divinity was always carefully kept, and absolute trust was put in it. It was spoken to as if it were gifted with intelligence. What rites were practiced at the secret meetings of the False Faces or Masks only the initiated knew.

All these horrible propensities were, of course, more unrestrained than ever when the Europeans introduced their

INTRODUCTION.

firewater. The scenes that occurred when men, women and children were wild with liquor, the missionaries do not attempt to describe in detail. So, also, they are very reserved in speaking of the dances, incantations, and the orgies of the dream-feasts, and the like. In a word, the Indian was quite the reverse of the "noble savage," such as the novelists describe him. Though intelligent, he was commonly a furious and degraded creature, sodden with every kind of vice. Of the Iroquois, especially, Parkman says: "No race ever offered greater difficulties to those laboring for its improvement."

Nevertheless, the impression made by the missionaries on them was very great and lasting. Many of them were led to the practice of Christian morality. They were taught to pray; to practice virtue, to receive the sacraments. We even hear of sodalities among them, and not a few attained to extraordinary sanctity. Constant wars, however, prevented a wider spiritual conquest; and when the wars were over there were no Iroquois. They were either dead or driven to the Far West.

AUTHORITIES.

The Jesuit Relations; Rochemonteix, S.J., *Les Jesuites et la Nouvelle France;* Charlevoix, S.J., *La Nouvelle France; Documentary History of the State of New York;* Morgan, *The League of the Iroquois;* Winsor, *Narrative and Critical History of America;* Shea, *Colonial Times;* Parkman, *The Jesuits in North America;* Martin, *Chaumonot, Jogues;* Lindsay, *Notre Dame de Lorette et La Nouvelle France;* Chauchetière, *La Vie de la B. Catherine Tegakoüita;* Cholenec, *Vita Catherinæ Tegakwitæ,* M.S.; Harris, *History of the Early Missons in Western Canada;* Beach, *Indian Miscellanies;* Beauchamp, *Bulletin of N. Y. State Museum;* Hawley, *Early Chapters of Cayuga History;* Innes, *New Amsterdam and Its People;* Donohoe's *The Jesuits and the Iroquois;* Walworth, *The Lily of the Mohawk.*

ISAAC JOGUES.

THE first priest to enter New York arrived drenched in his own blood. He had been taken captive by the Iroquois on the banks of the St. Lawrence, and was going to be burned to death at Ossernenon, on the Mohawk, the place now known as Auriesville, forty miles west of Albany. He was Isaac Jogues, then about thirty-six years of age.

With Protestant historians Jogues is an especial favorite; Parkman, among others, being very emphatic in his praise. Catholics, of course, admire him, and it is said that Gilmary Shea's manuscript of the *Life of Jogues* was stained with the author's tears. Jogues' gentle, almost shrinking, but nevertheless heroic nature is in striking contrast with the bold, aggressive and martial character of his friend and associate, Brébeuf. Perhaps that is why he appeals so strongly to ordinary people.

He was born at Orleans, January 10, 1607. The cathedral of the city is dedicated to the Holy Cross, which may explain Jogues' repeated description of himself as a "citizen of the Holy Cross." He was baptized, however, in the Church of St. Hilary; a patron he was often sorely in need of. They gave him in baptism the curious name of Isaac, for it was the fashion among the French Catholics of those days to imitate their Protestant neighbors in adopting names from the Old Testament. Thus Isaac, and Samuel, and Joshua, and David, and even Shadrach appear frequently on the registers of those days. There is such a Calvinistic ring about it, however, that one Canadian historian will have it that Champlain was not originally a Catholic because his name was Samuel. But the inference is not correct.

The family of Jogues still resides at Orleans. For some time after the departure of their great representative for Canada they were known as Jogues de Guédreville, but that

1

name is now no longer used, and they are called de Dreuzy. It will be of interest to Americans to know that the present Vicomtesse de Dreuzy is a German-American, born in New York. Her father was also a native of the city, while her mother was from Bogota. The maiden name of the Vicomtesse is de Lüttgen.

Another coincidence is that their house faces the church of N. D. de Recouvrance. This was the title given by Champlain to the church he erected in Quebec after " recovering " Canada. Under the sanctuary of N. D. de Re-couvrance in Orleans, repose the remains of the family of Jogues de Guédreville, some of whom were eminent in their native city.

The courtesy of the distinguished Curator of the Musée Historique d'Orléans puts at our disposal the family crest whose peculiar quarterings it will be hard for our democracy to interpret. It consists of two stags' heads *regardants avec cols arrachés,* with a silver lake below on which a water fowl is floating, while in the centre rises a rock from which gushes a fountain. The Jogues de Guédreville were of noble blood.

Jogues' first schooling was at Rouen, but at seventeen he entered the Jesuit novitiate at Paris. Shea says it was at Rouen, and Rouvier in his *Apôtre Esclave* agrees with him, while Rochemonteix pronounces for Paris. Perhaps he was in both. They all concur, however, in giving him the famous Louis Lalemant, the author of the well-known *Conférences Spirituelles,* as novice master. Lalemant had two brothers in Canada, Charles and Jerome; and later on, their nephew Gabriel died at the stake, side by side with Brébeuf.

Perhaps this intimate connection with the missions in America was the reason why, when the young novice was asked what he was seeking by entering the Society and replied: " Ethiopia and martyrdom," Lalemant said: " Not so, my child. You will die in Canada." It turned out to

2

ORLEANS.

be true, but there is no need of regarding the utterance as a prophecy.

When his studies and teaching were over, he embarked for Quebec, and after two stormy months on the ocean he set foot on the shores of the New World, October 2, 1636. He was then twenty-nine years of age. On the vessel with him was Champlain's successor, the great Montmagny, whom the Indians called Onontio, which is a translation of his name, and means Big Mountain, a title given to all subsequent rulers of Quebec. Onondaga is a word from the same root.

Fortunately we have the first letter that Jogues sent home. It was to his " Honored Mother," as he called her, in the dignified fashion of those days, and was written immediately after his first Mass in America. He had been looking at the vast river, the like of which he had never seen before. He had already met the painted red men at whose hands he might at any moment expect death; and the far West to which he was to go was still a mystery for him, but he told his " Honored Mother: I do not know what it is to enter heaven, but this I know—that it is difficult to experience in this world a joy more excessive and more overflowing than I felt on setting foot in the New World, and celebrating my first Mass on the day of the Visitation. I felt as if it were Christmas Day for me, and that I was to be born again to a new life and a life in God."

A glimpse of the future was afforded him two or three weeks later when he was standing on the bank of the St. Lawrence, near the stockade which in course of time has grown into the city of Three Rivers. Down the stream was coming a flotilla of canoes, in the first of which stood Father Daniel, barefooted and bareheaded, his cassock in rags, and his breviary suspended by a string around his neck, and though haggard and extenuated by hunger and fatigue, plying his paddle as vigorously as any redskin. Thirteen years after that, Daniel fell pierced with arrows

3

and was then flung into the blazing ruins of his little chapel. But the light-hearted hero cared little what fate was in store for him as he sprang ashore on that October morning to embrace the new soldier who was going to the battle-field to fight for God.

Daniel was to remain in Quebec for a short time, but the Hurons would not return to their home without a priest. So Jogues took his place in the canoe and set out for Lake Huron. A glance at the map will show what that means, but a detailed description by Bressani, who made the same journey ten years later, will help us to better appreciate its hardships.

"The distance," he says, "is more than 900 miles over dangerous rivers and great lakes whose storms are like those of the ocean, especially on one, which is 1,200 miles in circumference. The greatest danger, however, is on the rivers. I say 'rivers' because there are several, and we can only follow the St. Lawrence for 400 miles. After that we have to make our way over other lakes and streams which we reach by skirting rapids and precipices until we finally arrive at the great Lake Huron, which is known as the 'Fresh Water Sea.'

"On our journey we meet with about sixty cascades, some of them falling from a great height. To get around them we have to carry our boats and provisions and luggage, or at times drag our canoes through the rapids for four, eight, or ten miles; a labor which is attended with great peril, for often the water is up to our waists or necks, and is very cold, and if we are caught in the current we are in danger of being swept away and lost. But it is commonly to be preferred to the portage, which means making our way in our bare feet through dense forests, or through pools and marshes, where we have to wade, helping ourselves perhaps by a fallen tree which may serve as a bridge, but is often as dangerous and disagreeable as the water and mud. Swarms of insects follow us, and there is also constant danger of dying from starvation. For on these journeys, the provisions, which are nothing but corn, have to be carried for going and returning; and to lighten the load a portion is often concealed in the woods to be used when going back, but these stores are frequently discovered by other Indians, or dug up by the bears or rotted by the rain and moisture. In any of these events we have nothing to do but to fast, and paddle away until by hunting or fishing we obtain some relief. If the journey is made late in the year, there is a likelihood of finding the rivers and lakes frozen, and then there is danger of dying of hunger and cold; or if we escape that, we may have to spend six months in the woods, hunting to live rather than journeying to reach the desired country. Arriving there, other difficulties await us." He says nothing of the lurking Iroquois all along the route from whom a horrible death could be expected at any moment.

Such was Jogues' first experience of missionary life. Living on Indian corn and water; sleeping on rocks and in the woods, paddling day after day against a rapid current, dragging heavy burdens over the long portages, a part of the time with a sick Indian boy on his shoulders, were not things he had been brought up to, but he survived it all and with a light heart staggered through the triple stockade of the Indian town of Ihonatiria, and fell into the arms of Brébeuf and his companions, whose delight was greater as his coming was unexpected.

His cheerful appearance was only assumed. In a few days he was down with a fever which the others caught from him, and the bark cabin became a hospital, but with only mats for beds, and a decoction of roots for their whole supply of drugs. Moreover, the cold of November was upon them. Le Mercier writes: "We had a hen which gave us an egg, but not every day. We used to watch for the egg and then debate as to who should *refuse it.*" Jogues' condition became alarming. He was bleeding profusely from the nostrils and the blood could not be staunched. It may go against modern practice, but the *Relations* tell us "hence we decided to bleed him. The great question was where to find a surgeon. *We were all so skilful in this trade that the patient did not know who should open the vein for him, and every one of us was waiting for the benediction of the Father Superior to take the lance and do the work.*" Ordinary people would like to have better medical assurance than a benediction. So Father Jogues, whose whole surgical experience consisted in "having bled a savage very successfully on the way up," took the lance and did it himself, furnishing thus a fair sample of the cool courage he had at command. The *Relations* very naïvely say in referring to the "savage who was bled successfully" that what was wanting in skill was supplied by charity.

When the missionaries recovered, a pestilence broke out among the people, and hundreds of them died. The medicine men tried to conjure it away, and when the wild and indecent orgies which they ordered were ineffectual, they blamed the pestilence and their own failure on the missionaries and clamored for their death.

It was on this occasion that, fully expecting to be murdered, the little band of priests assembled at Ossossané. Brébeuf had come over from Ihonatiria, and, together, they boldly walked into the wigwam where the sachems were deliberating about when and how to kill them. Brébeuf remonstrated, and pleaded, and explained, but he was listened to in gloomy silence, until at last, amid muttered threats of vengeance, the victims withdrew to Ragueneau's hut, and under the light of a torch wrote a letter of farewell to their friends at Quebec. They were about to be put to death, they said, and their only sorrow was that they had not been able to suffer more for the Faith. Jogues was not actually present at this meeting. He was unable to leave his little mission. But his name was appended to the document, for he expected to be put to death like the rest. The letter was given to a faithful Indian, who brought it to its destination. For one reason or another the savages did not carry out their threat, but every moment was filled with terror. "The missionaries," says Parkman, "were like men who trod on the lava-crust of a volcano palpitating with the throes of a coming eruption, while the molten death beneath their feet gleamed white hot from a thousand crevices." Finally the plague ceased, but out of fickleness or hatred for the place, Ihonatiria was abandoned by the Indians, and the Fathers established the mission of Ste. Marie, which became the centre of all their work for many years and the one for which they always manifested the greatest attachment. Parkman regrets the Jesuits wrote so little about it.

If you take the train at Toronto and travel north through the forests, which are still dense enough to attract the hunter but which the lumbermen are rapidly clearing, you arrive at Lake Simcoe, from the northern end of which flows the little River Wye into Georgian Bay, which is the eastern portion of Lake Huron. On that river was built the new mission. It was fortified, because it was intended to be a place of refuge for fugitive Indians, a storehouse for provisions, and a home where the missionaries could come from the woods and lakes to restore their courage by meditation and prayer.

A branch of the Grand Trunk which runs north to Midland and Penetanguishene brings you within a few hundred feet of that once famous establishment. You can still trace the lines of the walls which are laid in hydraulic cement, and are said to be a puzzle to engineers, for there is no cement in the neighborhood, and it could not have been brought a thousand miles from Quebec. At the four corners are bastions, and around it is a moat now filled with rubbish, but when it was in use, affording easy access for boats from the river and lake.

Father Martin, the famous Rector of St. Mary's College

7

of Montreal, who has done more than anyone else to revive the memory of those old heroes of the seventeenth century and who inspired Gilmary Shea to carry on the work, visited Ste. Marie in 1859. He was accredited by the Canadian Government to make the investigations.

"Without difficulty," he says, "we found the ruins of Fort Ste. Marie. Its walls, in good masonry, rose a metre above the ground. It was in the form of a long parallelogram with bastions at the angles, and in spite of some peculiarities of which at the present day it is difficult to understand the reason, one recognizes in the construction an acquaintance with military engineering carried out with great care. The curtains on the west and north are complete, but there are no traces of them on the south and east. Probably solid palisades which were subsequently destroyed by fire were placed there. There was no attack to be feared on that side; on those two sides also there is a deep ditch which protects the enclosure. The south one extends to the river and so formed a shelter for the canoes. It widens out into basins at three places. Along this ditch on the south is a vast field protected on the side facing the country by a redan whose earth parapet is still distinguishable. In that field were the wigwams of the visiting Indians, the hospital, and guest-house. At the side of the southeast bastion was a square construction with a very thick wall, doubtless intended as the basis of a future observation tower. We opened a trench on the inside angle of the northeast bastion, and at the depth of 60 c. found portions of a burned plank, large nails, pieces of copper and the bones of beavers. The interior constructions were all in wood, which explains how nothing is left except a chimney in ruins."

Of course the missionaries were not cooped up in the fort. The soil around was carefully cultivated and produced an abundant harvest. There was such an amount of maize in 1649 that the Superior thought they had a supply that would last for three years. They kept fowl and swine and cattle, and the wonder is how the animals were transported to that distant place. It was a god-send for the poor, starving Indians, and at times three or four thousand of them were within the walls of Ste. Marie. No doubt, while being fed and cared for, they wondered at the unexplainable charity that prompted it all. But it was not only in famine times that they were harbored. On every alternate Saturday they came in crowds from the farthest villages, and during Saturday, Sunday and a part of Monday they were bounteously feasted and of course instructed and made to feel the influence of the solemn religious rites performed in the great church which, for the Indians, was a marvel of beauty, but as Ragueneau deprecatingly wrote, " very poor for the rest of us." Nothing is now left of all this but the stones of the foundation, which for historical if not for religious motives ought to be made a public monument.

To this central mission the Fathers all came for their conferences and annual retreats, and possibly it might be of interest to quote the well-known passage of Parkman, even if it is colored somewhat by his poetry and lack of spiritual appreciation. It is found in his *Jesuits in North America*.

" Hither," he says, " while the Fathers are gathered from their scattered stations at one of their periodical meetings, let us, too, repair and join them. We enter at the eastern gate of the fortification, midway in the wall between its northern and southern bastions, and pass to the hall, where at a rude table, spread with ruder fare, all the household are assembled—laborers, domestics, soldiers, priests.

" It was a scene that might recall a remote half feudal, half patriarchal age, when under the smoky rafters of his antique hall some warlike thane sat, with kinsmen and dependents, ranged down the long board, each in his degree. Here doubtless Ragueneau, the Father Superior, held the place of honor; and for chieftains, scarred with Danish battle-axes, was seen a band of thoughtful men clad in

9

threadbare garb of black, their brows swarthy from exposure, yet marked with the lines of intellect and a fixed enthusiasm of purpose. Here was Bressani, scarred with firebrand and knife; Chabanel, once a professor of rhetoric in France, now a missionary bound by a self-imposed vow to a life from which his nature recoiled; the fanatical Chaumonot, whose character savored of his peasant birth—for the grossest fungus of superstition that ever grew under the shadow of Rome was not too much for his omnivorous credulity, and mysteries and miracles were his daily food; yet, such as his faith was, he was ready to die for it. Garnier, beardless like a woman, was of a far finer nature. His religion was of the affections and the sentiments; and his imagination, warmed with the ardor of his faith, shaped the ideal form of his worship into visible realities. Brébeuf sat conspicuous among his brethren, portly and tall, his short moustache and beard grizzled—for he was fifty-six years old. If he seemed impassive it was because one overmastering principle had merged and absorbed all the impulses of his nature and all the faculties of his mind. The enthusiasm which with many is fitful was with him the current of his life—solemn and deep as the tide of destiny. The Divine Trinity, the Virgin, the Saints, Heaven and Hell, Angels and Fiends—to him these alone were real, all else were naught. Gabriel Lalemant, nephew of Jerome Lalemant, Superior at Quebec, was Brébeuf's colleague at the mission of St. Ignace. His slender frame and delicate features gave him an appearance of youth, though he had reached middle life; and, as in the case of Garnier, the fervor of his mind sustained him through exertions of which he seemed physically incapable.

"Of the rest of that company little has come down to us but the bare record of their missionary toils; and we may ask in vain what youthful enthusiasm, what broken hope or faded dream, turned the current of their lives, and sent them from the heart of civilization to the savage outpost

10

of the world. No element was wanting in them for the achievement of such a success as that to which they aspired —neither the transcendental zeal, nor a matchless discipline, nor a practical sagacity very seldom surpassed in the pursuits where men strive for wealth and place, and if they were destined to disappointment, *it was the result of external causes,* against which no power of theirs could have insured them."

Barring the malignant characterization of Chaumonot, which is like a shot from an ambush, as well as the nonsense about disappointed hopes and faded dreams, the picture is vivid enough to be quoted. We regret that the figure of Jogues does not appear in that "half-feudal, half-patriarchal group"; especially as it was his "practical sagacity very seldom surpassed in the pursuits where men strive for wealth and place" that prompted his superiors to appoint him to superintend the construction of those very works which Parkman so much admires.

That he was the chief builder of Ste. Marie dispels the impression about his being little else than a religious enthusiast eagerly seeking death. On the contrary he was the most practical of all the missionaries. Whatever he undertook was scrutinized carefully in all its bearings; its difficulties were weighed; its dangers estimated; but " once the word ' go ' was given," wrote his Superior, " then neither man nor devil could stop him."

His first apostolic work away from the post was among the Petun or Tobacco nation; a name which indicates the occupation of that tribe. With him was Garnier, who some years later was to die under the blow of a tomahawk while he was crawling on the ground after being riddled with bullets to absolve a dying Huron brave. Garnier and Jogues had been consecrated priests together at the same altar in France a few years before.

Holy as they were, their efforts failed. Abandoned by their guides, they had to make their beds in the snow; were driven out of the wigwams in the dead of night; and were followed by excited Indians with threats and imprecations from village to village. They did nothing at all but baptize one poor old squaw. But possibly her prayers were powerful with God, for the next year Garnier returned and established a prosperous mission among his hard-hearted Petuns.

Meantime a number of Ojibways or Chippewas had come down from Lake Superior to take part in the great decennial feast of the dead with their friends the Hurons. Astonished at what they saw, they asked for a mission in their country, and Jogues and Raymbault were assigned to the work. They stepped into their little bark canoe on September 17, 1641, and paddled for weeks along the eastern shore of Georgian Bay, and then across the upper reaches of Lake Huron and finally arrived after many dangers and hardships at the place which is now a great centre of commerce, Sault Ste. Marie. The missionaries gave it that name.

You say to the dwellers in those regions: " That must have been a journey of two or three hundred miles," and they smile at your simplicity and answer: " More like a thousand because of the way a canoe has to travel. A shell like that can never make a cut across the open."

They reached their destination, and it is a distinction worth noting that they were the first white men to stand on the shores of Lake Superior; for though Nicolet had been in those parts before them, yet he had gone down through the Straits of Mackinac and explored Lake Michigan, while they kept on to the north and west.

At the Sault they met 2,000 Indians, whom Jogues addressed in their own language, assuring them that after reporting to his Superior he would establish a mission there. " Then," he added, " after instructing you we shall go thither," and he erected a cross which faced the country of the Sioux, who were settled about the headwaters of the Mississippi. That was thirty years before Marquette started from the same place to find the great river, which

ISAAC JOGUES.

Jogues would certainly have attempted had he been spared. In fact, as we see in Le Jeune's *Relation* of 1636, all the missionaries were eager to make the attempt. But Jogues never returned to Lake Superior. He was captured by the enemy and killed on the far-off Mohawk. But it is more than likely that by securing the good will of the savages of those parts Jogues made it possible for the great Marquette to be a missionary without being a martyr.

It is very pleasant to meet in *Picturesque America* a description of this scene: "Two hundred and thirty-two years ago," says the writer, "the first white man stood on the shores of Lake Superior. Before him was assembled a crowd of Indians—two thousand Ojibways and other Algonquins—listening with curiosity to the strange tidings he brought, and in some instances allowing the mystic drops to be poured on their foreheads; for like all the first explorers of the lake-country, this man was a missionary. Only religious zeal could brave the wilderness and its savages, cold and hunger, torture and death, for no hope of earthly reward, for no gold mines, for no fountain of youth, but simply for the salvation of souls. And whatever posterity may think of the utility of their work, it must at least admire the courage and devotion of these Fathers, who, almost without exception, laid down their lives for the cause. What can a man do more? Five years later came the turn of this first white man of Lake Superior, murdered by the Indians in the forests near the Mohawk River."

They paddled back the way they came, to announce the good news and to prepare for the great enterprise, but Raymbault was in a dying condition from hunger and exposure, and someone had to go with him to Quebec where he could be cared for. Incidentally also the mission had to lay in supplies; for nothing had come from below for three entire years. Who would attempt the perilous voyage? Jogues maintained that he could be most easily spared, though no one shared that view with him, but he succeeded in persuading his Superiors and set out to carry his dying friend over the intervening thousand miles, at every foot of which there was a menace of death from dangerous cataracts or wild beasts or prowling Iroquois. They reached Quebec in safety though with much suffering, and there Raymbault soon breathed his last. He was the first Jesuit to die in Canada. He was buried by the side of Champlain; but the exact spot where the priest and the soldier were laid the people of Quebec cannot tell you to-day.

Jogues was successful in obtaining supplies, and he set out on his return journey with his canoes well packed with provisions. With him were about forty persons; one a famous Huron chief who was thought to bear a charmed life, so often had he escaped injury in battle; another a former sorcerer who had become a Christian and was now as pious as he had formerly been wicked. René Goupil and William Couture, two *donnés* or laymen who for religious motives had devoted themselves to the help of the missionaries, also made part of the convoy; and finally Theresa, an Indian girl, who had been educated by the Ursulines of Quebec, and who was now unwillingly leaving her beloved nuns, and returning to her country to assist by her piety and knowledge in spreading the faith. She is to disappear in the forests only to be found again just before Jogues' martyrdom.

Knowing the dangers that confronted them, the Governor offered the convoy a detachment of soldiers, but the Indians, who never appreciate danger until the enemy appears, indignantly refused all help. They were able to take care of themselves. But they were only a day's journey beyond Three Rivers, which they had left on August 1, 1642, when a suspicious trail revealed itself. The great chief said haughtily: " If it is the trail of friends there is no fear; if it is an enemy's we are strong enough to conquer "; but a war-whoop and a volley of musketry soon told another story. They were ambushed by almost twice their number. There

14

were seventy Mohawks in all, and significantly enough they were led by a Huron apostate. An Indian in the canoe with Father Jogues was hit by a bullet, and regardless of danger the priest hurried to his assistance, but when he rose from where he had been kneeling he found the greater number of his Hurons in flight, and those who had held their ground already in the hands of the enemy. What would he do? He was as fleet of foot as any Indian and could have escaped if he wished. But before his eyes he saw his beloved Goupil and some of his Huron Christians bound hand and foot, and the thought of deserting them never entered his mind. To the amazement of the Indians he strode out from his concealment and stood beside them. It is worth noting that the one who made the most splendid fight in this encounter was René Goupil. When nearly every one had fled he remained almost alone facing the whole host of enemies and fighting fiercely. The fact is worth remembering, for there is such stress laid on his piety and gentleness that we are prone to fancy him as timid and shrinking and somewhat feminine in his disposition, and not the heroic fighter that this occasion showed him to be. Jogues describes him as " a man of remarkable intrepidity."

The deep affection with which the priest was regarded by the rest of the company revealed itself as the battle was ending. Couture was well out of reach when he discovered that the Father was not with him. He deliberately turned back, though he had to fight his way through a crowd of Iroquois who almost cut him to pieces in his effort to reach the side of Jogues. The " invulnerable " Huron chief, who had taken to flight, came back of his own accord also, though he knew it meant torture and a horrible death.

It was while embracing and consoling Couture, who was brought in covered with blood, that Father Jogues was felled to the earth by the sticks and clubs of the Iroquois. He awoke to consciousness only to find two savages gnawing his fingers off with their teeth. As the battle was now

15

over, the captives were flung into canoes, and the party hurried up the stream to where the Sorel flows into the St. Lawrence, but not before they had cut a record of their exploit on the trees of the forest. The exact spot where the battle was fought has been forgotten.

Nothing more disastrous could have happened to the missions than this capture of Jogues. " Had we received those supplies," wrote Father Le Mercier, " we could have held out indefinitely." But of course Jogues was not responsible. He knew too well the needs of his brethren and the advantage of having soldiers as protectors on a journey like the one on which he had started, and he had seen too many an example of the foolish self-reliance of the Hurons. But the " invulnerable " chief had decided, and now the ruin of all the missions of the Northwest was only a matter of time.

Their course lay up the Richelieu to Lake Champlain and Lake George and over to the Mohawk. As they hurried along they were beaten with sticks and clubs; their wounds were torn open by the long nails of the Indians; they were refused food and drink, and at night were picketed to the earth to prevent their escape.

The traveller on Lake Champlain to-day is shown an island which the State has set aside as a government reservation. It is marked Jogues Island. It is thought to have been the scene of the occurrences which Jogues describes at this stage of his journey. A number of braves on the warpath had halted there awaiting the raiders, and their thirst for blood had to be satiated by the usual savage pastime of the gauntlet. " We were made to go up the slope from the shore between two lines of savages armed with clubs and sticks and knives," writes Jogues. " I was the last, and blows were showered on me. I fell on the ground and I thought my end had come, but they lifted me up all streaming with blood and carried me more dead than alive to the platform." The usual tortures of gashing and

16

stabbing and beating and burning and distending followed. More of the martyr's fingers were gnawed or burned off, and at one time he was on the point of consecrating that island of Lake Champlain by a horrible death at the stake. The torture was drawing to an end. A huge savage stood above him with a knife to slash the nose from his face, which was the usual prelude for death by fire. Jogues looked at him calmly, and to the surprise of all the executioner strode away. Again the effort was made with the same result. Some unseen power averted death at that time. His martyrdom was to be more protracted.

From there they resumed their journey, stopping, however, to repeat the sport whenever a new band was met with. It took them till the tenth of August to reach the southern end of Lake George; and then for four days the wretched captives dragged themselves along the trail which passes by what is now Saratoga, bleeding and famished, supporting their miserable life by the fruit or berries they could pluck from the trees or the roots they could dig up in the woods. They were loaded meantime with heavy packs, and beaten when they faltered or fell on the road. On the eve of the Assumption, 1642, they arrived on the north bank of the Mohawk, opposite the village of Ossernenon, a little above where the Schoharie Creek flows into the river.

A conch-shell, an instrument usually reserved for religious rites, announced their coming, and men and women and children swarmed down to the river bank to give the victims a savage welcome. It was the gauntlet again, and the miserable line moved up the steep ascent; Jogues, as usual, coming last. " I saw René in front of me," he afterwards wrote, " fall, horribly mangled and covered with blood; not a spot of white was visible as he was dragged to the place of torture." But while grieving for his friend and forgetting his own pitiable state, he himself was struck by a huge ball of iron in the middle of the back, and fell gasping on the pathway; but he struggled to his feet and

2   17

followed the procession to the platform, where the usual horrors of such performances were carried out in all their details, till darkness brought them to an end. But even then their sufferings were not over, for they were pinioned to the earth and given over to the boys of the camp, who amused themselves the greater part of the night by sticking knives and prongs into the victims, and heaping coals and hot ashes upon their naked bodies to see them writhe in agony. Jogues narrates that René's breast was a pitiable sight after this torture. He does not allude to his own condition, except to say that he was more fortunate in being able to throw off the burning coals.

One incident occurred, on this first day at Ossernenon, which is worthy of special notice, as illustrating the wonderful self-control of the great martyr. A captive Indian woman, a Christian, and chosen no doubt for that reason, was compelled, under menace of death, to saw off with a jagged shell the thumb of the priest. She complied, though horror-stricken; and when it fell on the ground, Jogues picked it up, and, as he himself humbly says, " I presented it to Thee, O my God! in remembrance of the sacrifices which for the last seven years I had offered on the altars of Thy Church and as an atonement for the want of love and reverence of which I have been guilty in touching Thy Sacred Body." " Throw it down," whispered Couture, at his side, " or they will make you eat it." He cast it aside, and possibly some prowling dog of the camp devoured it. It would be hard to find a parallel for such an act in the annals of the martyrs.

The next day these tortures were repeated, and then the adjoining villages of Andagarron and Tionnontoguen had to be regaled in similar fashion, until the ferocity of the savages was sated.

By this time the other captives were either killed or sent elsewhere among the tribes; Jogues and Goupil alone remained. It had been decided first to burn them at the

18

ISAAC JOGUES.

stake, but other counsels prevailed, and they were brought back first to Andagarron and then to Ossernenon. On the 7th of September the news of their capture had reached Fort Orange, and the Commandant Arendt van Corlear in person, accompanied by Jean Labatie and Jacob Jansen, came to arrange for their ransom. But the news had arrived that the war party which had tortured Jogues on Lake Champlain had been badly beaten at the fort which Montmagny had hastily thrown up at the mouth of the Richelieu after the capture of Jogues. Furious with rage on that account, they would not give up the prisoners. Once again there was question of the stake.

Soon afterwards, Goupil was killed for making the sign of the cross on the head of a child. It occurred when the lonely captives were returning to the village reciting their beads. A savage stole up behind them and buried his toma-hawk in the skull of Goupil, who fell on his face uttering the Holy Name. Jogues seized him in his arms, gave him the last absolution, and then waited his own turn, but the victim was torn from his embrace and two more blows by the murderer ended the work. " Thus," says Jogues, " on the 29th of September, this angel of innocence and martyr of Jesus Christ was immolated in his thirty-fifth year, for Him who had given His life for his ransom. He had con-secrated his heart and his soul to God, and his work and his life to the welfare of the poor Indians."

The next day he went to search for the corpse but was prevented. On the following morning, however, in spite of threats to kill him, he set out with an Algonquin and discovered the remains in the stream at the foot of the hill. The body had been given to the boys of the village, who had stripped it and dragged it there for sport. It was al-ready partially eaten by the dogs. All that he could do at the time was to hide it deeper in the stream, intending to return later to give it burial. Two days passed and he was unable to carry out his purpose. When he sought it again,

19

it was gone. His description of this search reads like a threnody: "I went to the spot where I had laid the remains. I climbed the hill at the foot of which the torrent runs. I descended it. I went through the woods on the other side; my search was useless. In spite of the depth of the water, which came up to my waist, for it had rained all night, and in spite of the cold, I sounded with my feet and my staff to see whether the current had not carried the corpse further off. I asked every Indian I saw whether he knew what had become of it. Oh! what sighs I uttered and what tears I shed to mingle with the waters of the torrent, while I chanted to Thee, O my God! the psalms of Holy Church in the Office of the Dead." After the thaw he found some bones, and the skull which had been crushed in several places. "I reverently kissed the hallowed remains and hid them in the earth that I may one day, if such be the will of God, enrich with them a Christian and holy ground. He deserves the name of martyr not only because he has been murdered by the enemies of God and His Church while laboring in ardent charity for his neighbor, but more than all because he was killed for being at prayer and notably for making the sign of the cross."

The exact place which holds the remains of the martyr, whom this other martyr canonized, has never been discovered. Perhaps it will be God's will, as Father Jogues prayed, to reveal it in time. It is somewhere in the Ravine at Auriesville.

Then followed his awful captivity for more than a year, a partial catalogue of whose horrors he has left us in the account which his Superiors commanded him to write. Parkman has studied it carefully and pronounces it a living martyrdom. He was employed in the filthiest and most degrading work of the camp, and was held in greater contempt than the most despicable squaw. Heavy burdens were placed on his bruised and livid shoulders, and he was made to tramp fifty and sixty and a hundred miles after his savage masters, who delighted to exhibit him wherever they went. His naked feet left bloody tracks upon the ice or flints of the road; his flesh was rotting with disease; his wounds were gangrened; he was often beaten to the earth by the fists or clubs of crazy and drunken Indians; and more than once saw the tomahawk above his head and heard his death sentence pronounced. The wretched deer-skin they permitted him to have was swarming with vermin; he was often in a condition of semi-starvation as he crouched in a corner of the filthy wigwam and saw the savages gorging themselves with meat, which had been first offered to the demons and which he therefore refused to eat, though his savage masters raged against this implied contempt of their gods. According to General Clark that was the determining cause of his death. But over and above all this bodily agony, his sensitive and holy soul was made to undergo a greater agony by the sight of their shameless moral turpitude and the awful spectacle thrust upon him as they devoured their captives.

Meanwhile he was baptizing what dying children he could discover, and comforting the Huron captives who were brought into camp, sometimes even at the risk of his life rushing into the flames to baptize them as they were burning at the stake.

The wonder of it all is how human endurance could be equal to such a strain. Indeed only the help of supernatural grace can explain how he did not die or lose his mind. That God gave him such assistance there is no doubt, for we find in the record he has left that he spent hour after hour kneeling in prayer in the deep snow of the forest, protected from the wintry blast of the storm only by a few pine branches. The Indians dreaded the cross which he used to cut in the trunks of trees, and took his prayers for incantations, often threatening to kill him when he was so engaged. We learn also that he was at times favored with heavenly visions during that long martyrdom. He heard the songs of angels above the roar of the tempest, and saw the palisaded town transformed into a celestial city, and beheld the Divine Master as a King in royal robes. Besides these heavenly consolations, he had a human comforter also, a poor old squaw in whose cabin he lived and whom he called his "Aunt." She would try in her rude way to heal his wounds; would weep over them when she could not succeed; and invariably warned him of any danger that she happened to hear of. We do not know if he converted the poor old creature. We cannot help thinking that he did.

There is another touching incident of rewarded affection that occurred during his journeys. He stumbled into a miserable cabin where he found a dying Indian. " Do you not know me? " said the sufferer. " It was I who cut you down when you were suspended by ropes at Ossernenon and were just about to die." God rewarded the poor wretch and he received baptism before he expired. No doubt also a poor squaw whom he saved from a furious torrent, plunging in to save her and her babe while the Indians looked on apathetically, must have done her best to repay him.

Month after month dragged on, and repeated efforts were made to purchase him from the Mohawks. Even the Sokokis of distant Maine, who had been well treated by the French, came to intercede for him. In fact he tells us himself that he might have escaped, but could not find it in his heart to do so while there were any Christian captives to whom he might be of service. His baptisms that year, he informs us, amounted to seventy altogether, all, of course, of persons at the point of death. It is New York's first baptismal record. Unfortunately we have only the number, not the names.

Finally, after about thirteen months, his release became imperative. On June 30, 1643, he had secured a scrap of paper, and with full knowledge of the danger he was exposing himself to, sent a letter to Montmagny informing him that the Mohawks were about to attack Fort Richelieu. An Indian had asked for it, hoping to profit by it in one way or other. The savages found themselves forestalled and attributed their failure to Jogues.

It is this action which serves as the foundation of the charge that he was really not put to death for the faith, but in punishment for this " treachery."

To this the answer is plain. In the first place, he was not put to death then. Consequently the feelings of the Indians, at that time, can be eliminated as the motive of an execution which took place three years later, unless those same feelings persisted, wholly or in part; which was not the case. Secondly, it may be safely asserted, that even if he had been put to death then, he would have been a martyr of charity. To deliberately accept death in order to save one's brethren from being wantonly massacred by implacable savages led by an apostate Christian, is heroic virtue fully worthy of canonization. Let a prisoner in the hands of a civilized enemy do something like that to save his countrymen and he will be immortalized as the nation's hero. Thirdly, anyone acquainted with the code of Indian ethics knows that once wampum belts are exchanged, all causes of complaint, past and present, are obliterated. That was their recognized purpose. They were treaties of peace, and an Indian accepting them would not remember the death of his own brother. We have notable examples of this in Indian history. It was even adopted by the whites themselves. Thus Kondiaronk, " The Rat," was made a captain of French troops, and was buried with unusual honors after having deliberately caused the most bloody massacre in all Canadian history. We have another instance in the case of Ouraouhara, the Iroquois, who after having been sent to the galleys in France was trusted by Denonville as his special envoy. Hence, after the presents were exchanged later on at Three Rivers, and Jogues was chosen as the ambassador of France, all past offences, real or imaginary, were not only condoned but forgotten, and had no influence whatever on subsequent negotiations. Moreover, he was killed not by the Mohawks as such—and they were the ones who had suffered harm—but by a few fanatics of the Bear family, in spite of the protest of the nation; and for no other reason than that he was a sorcerer who was making the *okis* and *manitous* of the Mohawks powerless. To die for that is to die for the faith.

The Dutch were aware of his impending death, and a positive order came from Governor Kieft of Manhattan to the commandant at Fort Orange to secure his release at all risks. Consequently, when, a short time afterwards, Jogues arrived at the Fort with his captors, the commandant insisted that he should escape, promising that if he once got on board the vessel which was lying in the river he would be landed safely in France.

To his amazement Jogues refused. He could not desert his post. He had written in that sense to his Superior in Quebec. The worthy and perhaps wrathy Dutchman remonstrated that it was throwing away his life uselessly. The Mohawks would not talk to him any longer about religious matters, nor would they let him approach the Huron or other captives; and finally, he was made to understand that his death was not to be deferred, but was to take place as soon as he got back to Ossernenon. He listened to all this and then spent all night in prayer considering what course was most in conformity with the glory of God and the good of souls. In the morning he presented himself to the commandant. He would escape and return again when peace was restored.

It was arranged that during the night he should steal out of the place where he had to sleep among the Iroquois. A small boat would be waiting on the shore, and he could paddle to the ship whose sailors had sworn to defend him. All seemed easy except the first step. The structure where the Indians passed the night with their prisoner was a

24

wooden building about 100 feet long, one end of which was used as the house of a settler who had married a squaw; the rest being occupied by the Mohawks. Going out at nightfall to explore the ground, the poor captive was nearly devoured by dogs, and hastily retreated to the cabin. The charitable Dutchman bandaged his wounds in a rough fashion, but the Indians, suspicious that something was going on, securely barred the door and lay down to sleep alongside of him. Hour after hour passed, and he heard the cock crow announcing the morning. All hope was gone, when suddenly a door opened at the other end, and a white man appeared. Making signs to him to quiet the dogs, Jogues stealthily picked his way over the prostrate forms of the savages—he would have been tomahawked if he awakened them—and succeeded in getting into the open. It is characteristic of the man that before he began this race for life, he tucked somewhere in his miserable rags a wooden cross he had made and two little books of devotion which he had found. There was a fence to be cleared which he clambered over, and then running as fast as his mangled legs would allow, made for the river, reaching it in an exhausted state; but alas! the boat was high and dry in the mud. He cried out to the vessel in the stream, but no one heard him. The sailors were asleep. At last by superhuman efforts he got the boat into the water, and soon after climbed up the ship's side, a free man. He was more than welcome, but his happiness was brief. Furious at the escape of their prisoner, the Mohawks threatened to burn the settlement, but the commandant laughed at them. He knew perfectly well they would not dare to risk a war with the Dutch while they were fighting with the French. Nevertheless, for reasons hard to understand, Father Jogues was compelled to come ashore in the night, though the faithful sailors were loud in their condemnation of the act, and was hidden in one of the houses while the Indians were parleyed with, and finally induced to relinquish their claim on him by the payment of 300 livres. But his whereabouts was kept secret for fear of his being tomahawked, and for six weeks he lay in a garret within a few feet of the Indians, who entered the house at pleasure. Often the slightest movement or a moan would have betrayed him. The ship, meantime, had departed, and the unhappy prisoner was subjected to the most brutal treatment by the boor into whose charge he had been given. Had it not been for the kindness of the famous minister, Dominie Megapolensis, he would have died of ill-treatment and starvation.

The Dominie was a conspicuous character among the Dutch of Governor Kieft's time. He was more than kind in this instance, and an affectionate intimacy sprung up between him and Father Jogues; the priest laboring strenuously for his conversion, and the Dominie showing him every consideration. In fact he was so outspoken in praise of Jogues that he had to answer a charge before the Classis of Manhattan of being a Jesuit. His reply may be found in the New York State papers, indignantly repelling the accusation.

At last another vessel was ready to sail, and Father Jogues was conducted on board by the chief men of the colony and he and the Dominie came down together to Manhattan Island. The crew were jubilant. They all loved and admired Jogues and " half-way down," he says, " they celebrated my release by stopping at an island which they called by my name, and gave evidence of their pleasure by the discharge of cannon and the uncorking of bottles." We have no more indication than that of what the island was which was " half-way down the Hudson," and which was christened in such a cordial fashion.

Where is this island that is described as " half-way down the Hudson "? There is no other piece of land that fits in with this geographical indication except that which is now known as Esopus Island. Thither the Jesuit novices from West Park used to go on holidays, and had no doubt that

ISAAC JOGUES.

they stood on the holy ground where Father Jogues had been—265 years before. It lies in the centre of the river, and is within the corporate limits of Ulster County. It is about half a mile long, and probably one hundred feet at its greatest width. It is composed mostly of trap and sandstone rock. On the south end there is a cleft forming a landing-place on a sandy beach where it is safe for boats to ride, while on the northern end of the island there is a formation shaped like a mackerel's tail, giving the island the appearance of a huge fish lying on top of the water. Legend says that the island in early days was known from its peculiar formation as Fish Island. The sides rise precipitously from the water, forming a battlement on both sides, and there is no place where a boat could land. The surface is covered with stunted oaks. Near the north end is a smooth greensward, around which the great stones standing on edge form battlements and give the place the appearance of a fort.

More than likely this was the island to which the good-natured Dutchmen gave Father Jogues' name. But in course of time other stories began to cluster about it. Captain Kidd is said to have hidden his treasures there, and on the eastern edge, in a green and level place, stands a stunted pine known far and wide as Captain Kidd's tree. All sorts of gruesome stories have been invented about how the bold buccaneer buried his millions of doubloons somewhere on the island and left them to the care of the Prince of Darkness. Captain Kidd and Father Jogues are very positive opposites.

After six days they reached New York, where the Governor gave him a most honorable reception, seated him at table beside the Dominie, provided for his wants and furnished him with suitable clothing to replace the ragged and half-savage costume in which he was attired. Naturally the presence of a priest and a Jesuit on Manhattan Island, especially with all the marks of his terrible sufferings upon

27

him, caused a profound sensation among the colonists. They crowded around him to ask about his captivity, and it is narrated that, on one occasion, a young man fell at his feet and, kissing the mangled hands of the priest, exclaimed: "Martyr of Jesus Christ! Martyr of Jesus Christ!" "Are you a Catholic?" asked Jogues. "No, I am a Lutheran, but I recognize you as one who has suffered for the Master."

There were two Catholics in New York at that time— one the Portuguese wife of the Ensign, who, singularly enough, had a picture of St. Aloysius in her room; the other was an Irishman who had come up from Maryland. He gave Father Jogues intelligence about the Jesuits there and profited by the occasion to perform his religious duties.

The official documents of the State of New York have embodied Jogues' lengthy account of the colony as he saw it during the month he remained with his Dutch friends. He happened to be there just when a war was going on with the neighboring Indians, eighty of whom had been killed in one encounter and sixteen hundred in another; but he merely mentions it without going into details. About the material condition of the colony he is more explicit. "Manhattan," he says, "is seven leagues in circuit, and on it is a fort to serve as a commencement of a town to be built there and to be called New Amsterdam." His practiced eye takes in the defects of the construction, and no doubt he compared it with the one he himself had built on Lake Huron. "It is at the point of the island. It has four regular bastions, mounted with several pieces of artillery. All these bastions and the curtains were in 1643 only mounds; most of them had already crumbled away so that it was possible to enter the fort on all sides. There were no ditches. The garrison for that and another fort further up consisted of sixty soldiers. They were beginning to face the gates and bastions with stone. Within the fort there was a pretty large church, the house of the Governor, quite

28

neatly built of brick, and also storehouses and barracks."
The Governor told him that there were people on the
island speaking eighteen different languages. " No religion
is publicly exercised but the Calvinist, and orders are to
admit none but Calvinists; but this is not observed. There
are in the colony besides Calvinists, Catholics, Puritans,
Lutherans, Anabaptists who are called *Mnistes,* etc." He
describes the character of the river, the ships in the harbor;
the exposed position of many of the settlers, the method of
colonization, the climate, etc.; and then reverts to what he
had seen further up the river at Fort Orange. " The settlement of the Renselaers is a little fort built of logs with four
or five pieces of cannon and as many swivels. The colony
is composed of about 100 persons in 25 or thirty houses
which are built along the river. They are merely of boards,
and thatched roofs, and with no mason-work except the
chimneys."

Finally the wretched little vessel which the Governor
was hurrying to get ready to bring the news to the home
government about the Indian aggressions weighed anchor
in the river. It was a lugger of only fifty tons burthen, and
left the harbor of Manhattan on the 5th of November, so
that in mid-winter, with thin and wretched clothing and
with nowhere to rest his aching limbs but the deck on a
coil of rope, or in the offensive hold, the poor sufferer was
tossed on the waves of the Atlantic until the end of December, 1643, when after frightful sufferings the vessel
entered the harbor of Falmouth in Cornwall hotly pursued
by some of Cromwell's ships, for the rebellion was then in
progress against Charles I.

Left alone on the ship, he was robbed at the pistol's point
of most of his poor belongings by marauders who boarded
the vessel. Later on, a compassionate Frenchman whom
he met on shore obtained a free passage for him across the
Channel on a collier—a favor grudgingly accorded. On
Christmas morning, 1643, when the bells were ringing for

Mass, he was flung on the coast of his native country some-where in Brittany. The exact place cannot be identified from the indications which he has left. Some poor peasants saw the ragged and emaciated creature standing on the beach and fancied he was an Irish refugee escaping from the Cromwellians. Finding to their astonishment that he was a Frenchman and a priest, they gave him some decent wearing apparel and went with him to the church, where for the first time since his capture at Three Rivers he was able to go to confession and communion. The maimed condition of his hands precluded his saying Mass.

It took him eight days after that to reach the College of Rennes, helped on his journey by some charitable soul who took pity on him. He arrived there early in the morning of the Epiphany and asked the porter to inform the Rector that he had news from Canada. Hearing the magic word " Canada," the Rector, though about to say Mass, laid aside his vestments and hurried to the door. " Do you come from Canada ? " he asked the dilapidated and ragged man before him. " I do," was the answer. " Do you know Father Jogues ? " " Very well, indeed." " Is he alive or dead ? " " He is alive." " Where is he ? " " I am he," was the reply.

The amazement and joy of the household may be imagined as they crowded around him to embrace him, to kiss his mangled hands and kneel for his blessing. They led him to the chapel and intoned the *Te Deum* for the dead who had come back to them.

The news of the missionary's return rapidly spread throughout France. Everyone was speaking of him; and the Queen Regent Anne of Austria, the mother of Louis XIV, intimated her desire to see him, but was compelled to express her wish more than once before Father Jogues could be induced to be the subject of such a public distinction. Who were present at the famous audience? We have no details about it, but we know that Condé and Turrenne were

ANNE OF AUSTRIA, QUEEN REGENT OF FRANCE.

then in their young manhood; that St. Vincent de Paul was chief almoner of the Queen, and that possibly they with many other of the most famous personages of the realm—for the interest in him was universal—may have been near the throne when, humbled and abashed, with his hands concealed in the folds of his cloak, he entered the royal presence. He replied very slowly and reluctantly to the various inquiries about his adventures, and when at last he was compelled to show his mutilated hands, and tell of the hideous way in which the fingers had been eaten or burned off, the Queen, descending from her throne, took his hands in hers and with tears streaming down her cheeks, devoutly kissed the mutilated members and exclaimed: "People write romances for us—but was there ever a romance like this? and it is all true."

Public exhibitions of this kind, however, were like Iroquois torture for Father Jogues. He became exceedingly sensitive about it, and those who called to see him were warned by the Superiors not to refer to his sufferings. He even refused to visit his own people. Apparently he did not see his "Honored Mother," though perhaps she was dead then. But what grieved him most was that, on account of the condition of his hands, he was forever debarred from saying Mass. His friends did not leave him long in that distress, but sent a petition to the Holy Father to remove the canonical impediment. The answer quickly came: "*Indignum esset martyrem Christi, Christi non bibere sanguinem.*" "It would be wrong to prevent the martyr of Christ from drinking the blood of Christ." It is noteworthy that this quasi-canonization was pronounced by Urban VIII, the very Pope who has laid down such stringent laws on the canonization of saints.

What his feelings were when this privilege came we do not know. He has left us a record about his first Mass in Canada. With regard to this first Mass on his return to France he is silent.

PIONEER PRIESTS OF NORTH AMERICA.

Naturally one should fancy that this battered warrior would now rest on the laurels which he had won. On the contrary he was on board the first vessel that left France for America. He had plenty to do on the voyage. The sea was tempestuous, but a worse storm arose among the sailors. They were in mutiny, and had it not been for Jogues' ascendancy over them, the captain might have been thrown overboard. The ship was thought to be unseaworthy, and the men insisted on turning back. Influenced by the persuasive words of their holy passenger, they abandoned their purpose, and reached Quebec in June, 1644.

Maisonneuve was just then making his splendid fight behind the stockades of Montreal, and thither Jogues was sent, to keep up the courage of the defenders and help the sick and dying. Finally the Indians asked for a parley, and a conference was called at Three Rivers, for July 12, to arrange the terms of peace.

Among the Indians and wearing their dress was William Couture, the *donné* who had been captured with Father Jogues two years before. He had been adopted by the tribe and was now coming as its envoy. He never returned to his Indian life, but settled down in Canada, married, and lived to the age of ninety.

The Council assembled under a great tent in the courtyard of the fort. In the most prominent place sat Montmagny; before him in the centre were the Iroquois deputies, while back of them stood the Algonquins, Montagnais, and Attikameges, the Hurons and French being on either side. The chief orator was Kiotsaeton, who appeared covered with wampum belts, and very proud of his official position. His speech was a notable one, and those who wish to study Indian eloquence may find it in detail in the *Relations,* with comments by Father Vimont, who calls attention especially to the wonderful pantomime of this American Demosthenes. When he came to the fifteenth belt he walked up to Montmagny and presented it, saying that it was to wipe out the

ISAAC JOGUES.

memory of the ill-treatment of Father Jogues. "We wished," he said, with splendid mendacity, not knowing that Jogues was listening to him, "to bring him back to you. We do not know what has become of him. Perhaps he has been swallowed up by the waves, or fallen a victim to some cruel enemy. But the Mohawks did not put him to death." Jogues merely whispered to his neighbor that the stake had been prepared all the same. Apparently he did not let himself be known, and when the treaty was made and the games and banquets began, he had already gone back to his work. He had seen too much of Indian revelry to be tempted to stay. It was decided in the Council to send an ambassador to the Mohawks to obtain the assent of the tribe to the concessions made by the deputies. All eyes turned on Jogues. He alone knew the language, and in due time he received a letter from his Superior assigning him the task. The common of mortals will be thankful to him when they read in his letter that he confessed to a shudder when he learned of the appointment. Of course his official character as ambassador would protect him. But he was also a priest and the Iroquois knew it. In fact, the Christian Algonquins came to him to express their fear about his going, and advised him not to speak of the Faith in his first interview. "There is nothing," they said, "more repulsive at first than this doctrine, which seems to uproot all that men hold dear, and as your long robe preaches as much as your lips, it will be prudent to travel in a shorter habit." This is the first example of the "clerical garb" difficulty in New York. It is at the same time a very valuable testimony as to why Jogues was put to death. When he appeared as a layman and an ambassador he was treated with honor, as we shall see; when he went immediately afterwards with his cassock and cross he was tomahawked, and he unwittingly precipitated the disaster by not adhering strictly to the advice of the Algonquins. He brought with him the famous box with its religious articles,

33

and the Iroquois saw that his office of ambassador had not done away with his priestly character. They found out also that while at Ossernenon on this visit he had secretly baptized some dying children and had heard the confessions of the captive Hurons. Evidently he had some other purpose besides that of making peace.

It took some time before the embassy started; for there was much squabbling between the French and Iroquois as to whether the Algonquins were included in the treaty, and for a moment there was imminent danger of all the negotiations coming to naught. In fact it was almost two years after the conference, namely, on May 16, 1646, that Father Jogues, accompanied by one of Canada's conspicuous colonists, Jean Bourdon, left Three Rivers with their Indian guides. They reached Lake Andarocté, or what is now Lake George. Jogues had been there three years before, but he could not then see its beauty, as he lay bleeding to death in the bottom of an Indian canoe. But now, when he beheld it in all the splendor with which summer had clothed the woods in which it was embedded, and gazed around at the countless garden-like islands reflected on its surface, he gave it a name; one suggested by the day on which he found himself crossing the beautiful expanse. It happened to be the eve of Corpus Christi, and he therefore called it the Lake of the Blessed Sacrament. It kept that name for almost a century until a Protestant Irishman, Sir William Johnson, to gain favor with the English king, changed it to Lake George. It is most unlikely that it will ever recover the historically appropriate designation given to it by the holy missionary, or even that Gilmary Shea's suggestion of changing Lake George to Lake Jogues will ever be carried out.

The travellers did not take the trail by Saratoga, but swerved over towards the Hudson, to what is now Beaver Dam, then a fishing settlement of the Mohawks. There Father Jogues had the happiness of meeting the Indian girl

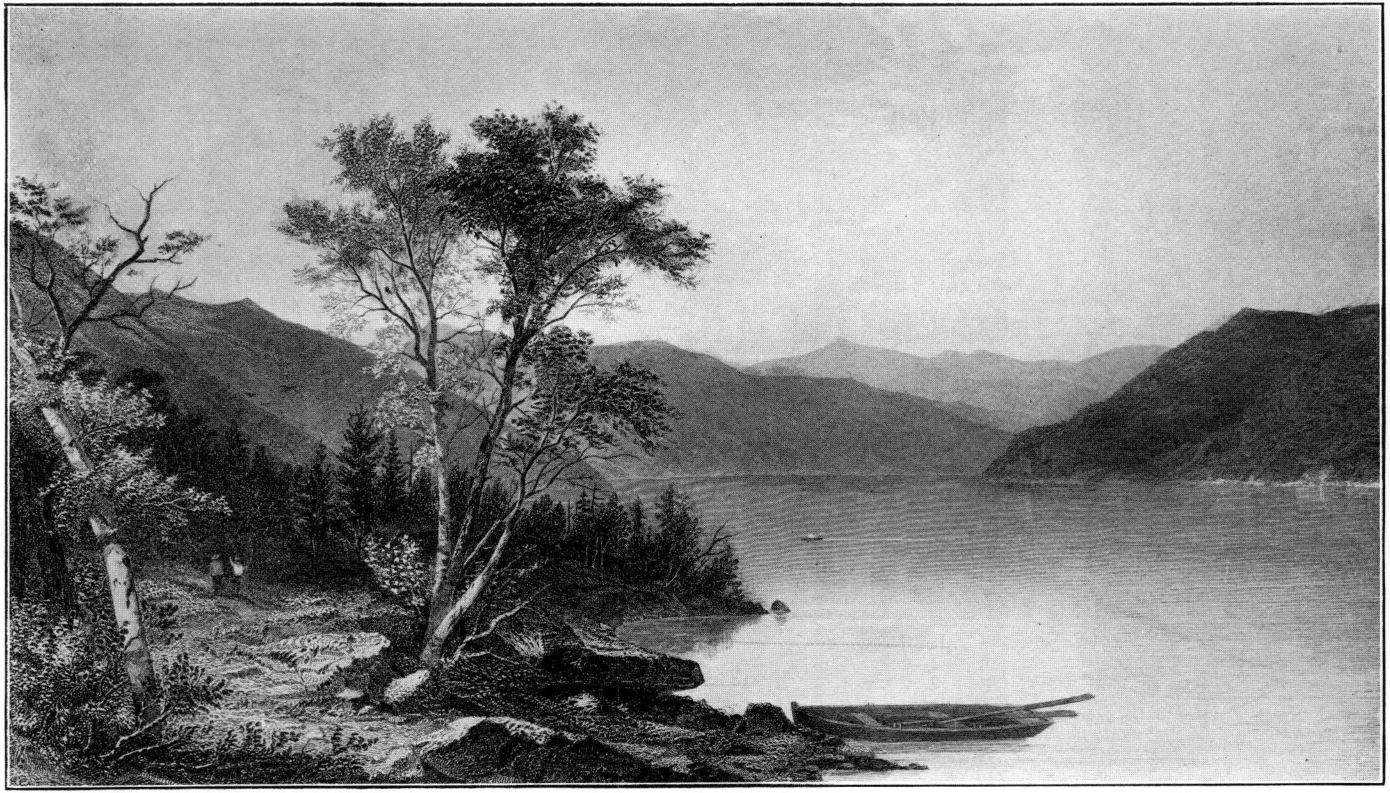

LAKE OF THE BLESSED SACRAMENT.

ISAAC JOGUES.

Theresa, who had been captured at the same time as himself on the St. Lawrence. She had remained as good and pious in her savage surroundings as she had been in the nunnery at Quebec. She had been protected by an uncle for some time until she married a warrior of the tribe. Her delight at meeting Father Jogues may be imagined, and he made haste to tell her that his first care would be to purchase her freedom. The freedom indeed was granted, but its execution was never carried out; and we meet her again years afterward in the Onondaga country, where Father Le Moyne saw her and told his friends in Quebec of the wonderful holiness of her life. She never reached her own country.

The party then proceeded down the Hudson, and passed through Fort Orange, or Albany, a familiar place for Jogues, who was glad to see and thank his old friends, and reimburse them for the money they had expended on his ransom. On June 5 he reached Ossernenon after a three weeks' journey from the St. Lawrence. His arrival was the occasion of surprise and delight for his former captors. The council was held on the 10th. He was the principal orator, and assured his ancient enemies " that the council fires lighted at Three Rivers would never be extinguished." " Here," he said, " are 5,000 beads of wampum, to break the fetters of the young Frenchmen you hold as captives, and 5,000 more for Theresa, that both may be set free." All the arrangements made at Three Rivers were acquiesced in, and the treaty formally concluded. The Wolf clan was particularly attentive to him and made him a special present, saying: " You shall always have among us a mat to rest upon and a fire to warm you," a manifestation of friendship which shows that the tribe as such did not remember the incident of Fort Richelieu.

There were several Onondagas present, and Jogues made an earnest and successful effort to win their favor. He offered them presents, which they accepted, and he induced

35

them to promise at the same time to receive missionaries for their tribes. They of their own accord indicated the safest way to travel, viz., not through the Mohawk country but by the St. Lawrence. It was probably this acceptance of the belts that enabled Le Moyne and his associates later on to announce the gospel among the Onondagas.

On June 16 the ambassadors left Ossernenon, going by trail to the Lake of the Blessed Sacrament, and reaching Quebec on July 3. Bourdon received valuable land grants as his reward for making the treaty. Jogues received the reward of death, for he asked immediately to return as missionary to the Mohawks. The request was long and seriously considered, for the bloodthirsty and unreliable character of the Mohawks was a matter of common knowledge. At last, on September 27, he left Quebec for the Iroquois territory, his Superiors giving it then the name of " The Mission of Martyrs "; for said they, " It is credible if the enterprise succeed for the salvation of this people, it will not produce fruit before they be sprinkled with the blood of martyrs." Evidently Father Jogues was convinced of it, for on bidding farewell to a friend he wrote the memorable words: " Ibo sed non redibo "—" I go but I shall not return." The utterance is remarkable inasmuch as it did not mean that he was going to remain indefinitely, for his instructions were merely " to winter " there. He did not even purpose to say Mass during this visit, for he brought no vestments with him.

Was his fate revealed to him? Did he foresee what was to happen? The Venerable Marie de l'Incarnation declared that in her opinion his words were a veritable prophecy. Ordinary people will read that meaning into it also.

With him were some Huron guides and a *jeune garçon* named Lalande—a *donné* like Goupil, who wanted to die for the faith. Before they reached Ossernenon the news came that the Mohawks had dug up the hatchet. Jogues' box had started the war.

ISAAC JOGUES.

Indeed he had been apprehensive of such a calamity on his previous visit, for he had shown its contents to the Mohawks before he left, so as to allay their suspicions which he perceived were aroused even then. He saw, too late, that he had made a mistake in trusting to his own judgment and not following the advice of his Algonquin friends; for the box was a declaration to the Iroquois that he was still a priest, and hence when the pestilence broke out, and the crops withered, the savage inference was rapid; viz., the evil came from the mysterious box. They hastened to get rid of it, and threw it in the river. But that very mistake, fatal as it was, serves to establish beyond any doubt that their wrath was aroused against him, not because he was a white man, or a Frenchman, or a friend of the Hurons, or because he had revealed their plans to Montmagny, but solely and absolutely because his *Manitou* had wrought them harm. That "manitou" was Christianity as they conceived it. In their eyes he was displacing their ancestral gods, and in the wilds of America they did precisely what the old Romans did when they strove to crush out the Christian "superstition;" nothing more nor less.

As soon as his guides were apprised of what had happened they took to flight. But he kept on his way, though he might have easily saved himself by returning to Quebec. By his side walked the faithful Lalande. Two days more would have brought them to Ossernenon when the Iroquois met them. Approaching them was the sorcerer Ondessonk in his priest's garb. He was no longer an ambassador but a priest, bent on teaching them the religion which they not only hated but which had brought disaster on their nation, and they fell upon him, stripped him of his garments, slashed him with their knives, and led him, mangled and bleeding, to the very place where he had been so honored when in another capacity he stood there that summer.

The old Jesuit associates of Jogues call attention to a very remarkable and almost startling parallel between this

37

scene in the forests of the Mohawk and another memorable one in the streets of Jerusalem. Surrounded by his enemies, Christ asked: "Why do you wish to kill me?" and they answered: "Because you have a devil." To which He replied: "I have not a devil; but I honor My Father, and you dishonor Him."

Father Jogues could scarcely have been reflecting upon the import of the words that rose to his own lips when the Indian knives were slashing his body, but he uttered almost the same words as those of our Saviour. "Let us see," said one of the savages as he cut off a strip of the victim's flesh, "if this white flesh is the flesh of a *Manitou*." "No," he replied, "I am a man like you all. Why do you put me to death? I have come to your country to teach you the way to heaven, and you treat me like a wild beast." It was merely a difference of place. For the Iroquois Jogues had a *Manitou;* for the Pharisees Christ had a devil; and for that they put Him to death. The servant was indeed very like his Master.

A council was held at Tionnontoguen to decide what was to be done, and it is noteworthy that the famous Kiotsaeton, who had spoken so eloquently and so mendaciously in the peace conference at Three Rivers, was the priest's chief defender. Both the Wolf and the Tortoise family were against putting the victim to death, as were most of the Bears, and the official verdict arrived at was to spare his life. But one faction of the Bears clamored for his blood, and were determined to have it in spite of the reasoning and pleading of the rest of the tribe.

It is comforting to see, in the gloom and confusion of this last act of the tragedy, the sympathetic figure of the kind old squaw, Father Jogues' "Aunt," going around overwhelmed with grief, and begging pathetically with tears in her eyes for her "nephew's" life. "Kill me if you kill him," she repeatedly said to his murderers. Can there be any doubt that the "aunt" is now with her "nephew"?

ISAAC JOGUES, S.J.

ISAAC JOGUES.

But she and the others failed. The Bears were bent on vengeance, and on the 18th of October they invited Jogues to a feast. It was a sort of a Judas kiss. To refuse was to be killed immediately as outraging hospitality, and so the poor sufferer, who was found crouching in a cabin nursing his bleeding wounds, rose up and followed the savage. Behind the door stood an Indian with a tomahawk in his hand, and as Jogues stooped down to enter, the axe descended with a crash into his skull. His long and bloody battle was ended. They cut off the head and fixed it on a stake of the palisade, and then flung the mangled body into the Mohawk. That stream ought to be sacred for Catholics.

"So died," says Ingram Kip, the Protestant bishop of California, "one of that glorious band that had shown greater devotion in the cause of Christianity than has ever been seen since the time of the Apostles; men whose lives and sufferings reveal a story more touching and pathetic than anything in the records of our country, and whose names should ever be kept in grateful remembrance; stern, high-wrought men who might have stood high in court or camp, and who could contrast their desolate state in the lowly wigwam with the refinement and affluence that waited on them in their earlier years, but who had given up home and love of kindred and the golden ties of relationship for God and man. *Ibo sed non redibo* said Isaac Jogues as he went for the last time into the valley of the Mohawk. He fell beneath the blow of the infuriated savage and his body was thrown to feed the vultures, whose shrieks as they flapped their wings above him was his only requiem." The Fathers in Quebec thought he needed no requiem. A *Te Deum* would be better. His companion was killed on the following morning.

Rumors of the tragedy gradually reached Quebec, but all doubt was dispelled by an official letter of Governor Kieft, of Manhattan, dated November, 1646, to Montmagny: "I sent the minister of Fort Orange to find out the cause of

39

the murder, and he could get no other answer than that the Father had left a devil among some articles confided to their keeping which had caused all their corn or maize to be eaten by worms." This letter of Governor Kieft is extremely precious, as there could be no more convincing testimony than that of a Protestant minister and a Protestant governor reporting officially on the cause of the crime. They put it beyond question that it was not a matter of politics, or race hatred, or of thoughtless savage fury. It was hatred of what the Indians conceived to be Christianity, and as in greater persecutions, their pretext was that its teachings brought disaster upon the country.

Independently of the nature of his death, the holiness of this wonderful missionary was of the most extraordinary kind. What he said of Goupil may be applied to him. " He was an angel of purity." His obedience was heroic and never faltered under any trial; the extent of his mortification is evident from his sufferings, which were not only accepted but sought; his sprit of prayer was uninterrupted, and of that higher kind to which visions are vouchsafed; his patience was without bounds, his charity most tender even to the fiercest of his persecutors. " The only sin I can remember during my captivity," he told his spiritual guide, " was that I sometimes looked upon the approach of death with complacency "; an admission which will give ordinary saints a shiver.

Was his death a martyrdom? To be certain about that we must await the decision of the Church, but most people who read of his sufferings will agree with the Lutheran on Manhattan Island who went down on his knees and saluted him as a martyr; with the Queen of France who wept over his wounds, and with the Sovereign Pontiff himself who almost canonized him before his death. All of the Protestant historians, some of them ministers and bishops, give him that title; Catholic writers have no doubt about it; the Venerable Marie de l'Incarnation, who is so revered in

40

ISAAC JOGUES.

Canada for her sanctity, reiterates it incessantly; the Fathers of Canada, some of whom were subsequently martyrs themselves, had no hesitation in privately invoking his intercession; and the Plenary Councils of Baltimore and Quebec have asked for his canonization. Immediately after his death a tribunal was established to officially inaugurate the process, and the original documents containing the testimony given on that occasion have fortunately come down to us. In our own days the process has been resumed and the taking of testimony about the virtues and death of Jogues and the other martyrs of the Canadian missions was continued for more than a year. To conclude, it is abundantly clear that more than for any of the other missionaries, the cause of Jogues' death is freed from any possibility of its having been associated with political or race feeling. It was simply out of hatred of the cross, of dislike of his doctrinal teachings, and detestation of the Christian morality which he inculcated.

None of his relics have been found. His clothing, his breviary and missal were given to the Dutch, but all traces of them have been lost. As to the place where the martyrdom occurred there can be no reasonable doubt that it is at what is known as Auriesville, on the south bank of the Mohawk just above the Schoharie.

JOSEPH BRESSANI.

IN the war with the French and Hurons the old Iroquois
showed themselves not only fierce fighters, but marvelous military tacticians. They were not numerous, but
they swept every enemy before them. Their aim was to
destroy the French and Hurons simultaneously. For that
purpose they proposed, besides fighting, to get the best of
the French by cutting off the supplies from the Northwest,
and diverting them to the Mohawk Valley, a business conflict which still endures with their civilized successors. In
that they succeeded so well that at times there was not a
peltry sold at Quebec, while the burghers at New Amsterdam were growing rich, not precisely by putting their feet
in the scales, but by getting all the fur they wanted. On
the other hand, the Hurons were being crushed by indis-
criminate slaughter or by absorption into the Iroquois Confederacy.

To carry out their plans the Iroquois had established an
uninterrupted line of posts from what is now Ottawa to
Three Rivers, each one admirably chosen for discovering
the enemy before he could get near enough to be dangerous.
Those who know the old "castles" at Auriesville and
Sprakers have always appreciated their wisdom in this
respect.

They had divided their fighting men into ten sections.
Two were assigned to the most western post, which, being
so exposed, on account of its remoteness, needed most defenders. It was the present Ottawa, and was then called
"The portage of the Chaudières." The third section was
stationed at the foot of the Long Sault; the fourth above
Montreal; the fifth on the island itself; the sixth on the
Rivière des Prairies; the seventh on Lac St. Pierre; the
eighth not far from Fort Richelieu on the Sorel; the ninth

GOVERNOR DE MONTMAGNY.

(ONONTIO.)

JOSEPH BRESSANI.

near Three Rivers; while the tenth formed a sort of flying squadron to carry devastation wherever the opportunity presented itself.

This line of strategic positions was so uninterrupted that one does not so much admire the heroism that would endeavor to break through it, as wonder how any attempt could ever be made at it. It looked like going straight to death. And yet it was done, time and time again. Of course, there was many a failure. Father Jogues was one of those who dared it, but paid for his ill-success by captivity and torture.

In 1643 the condition of the Hurons and of the missionaries in the then Far West was deplorable. Lalemant writes: "The desolation is extreme. War, with its usual ravages, filled up the whole summer. Almost every day poor women are found murdered in the fields; the villages are in continual alarm, and every attempt made to repel the invaders is met with defeat and the loss of hundreds dragged into captivity. Often we have no other messengers of these dreadful tidings but unhappy wretches who have escaped from the flames, and whose half-burned bodies and mangled hands give us better proof than their words of the misfortunes which overwhelmed them. Added to these horrors is that of famine almost everywhere for a hundred leagues around. Grain is rare, and the people are living on roots often dug up in fields red with blood. The missionaries were about to cease saying Mass, for there was no wine or bread."

This was at the end of March, 1644. In April the Superior, Father Vimont, commissioned Father Bressani to carry "some letters and packages" to his brethren on Lake Huron. They had received nothing for three years.

Who was Bressani? As his name denotes, he was not a Frenchman. He was born in Rome, and entered the Society August 15, 1526. He was then only fourteen years old, but he must have been a gifted lad, for he finished his philosophy in the Roman College when he was eighteen. He then made three years of teaching; took three of theology in Rome and a fourth year at Clermont in France. He made his tertianship in Paris, and after teaching rhetoric, philosophy and mathematics, was thought of as the future preacher for great cities, but he set out for Canada in 1642, not, however, before some holy soul had foretold all the tortures he was going to suffer. That did not deter him, however. Quite the contrary. It made him extremely happy. He was only thirty-two when the savages were mangling and burning his body.

His acceptance of the dangerous mission was altogether voluntary. There were only two other men who could be thought of to attempt it just then. One was Jogues, who had not yet returned to Canada after his escape from the Mohawks. The other was Davost, who was completely exhausted by his ten years' work, and died soon after on the ocean when returning to France to recuperate.

Bressani was then at Three Rivers looking after the Algonquins. Previous to that he had been Parish Priest at Quebec, "preaching to the French with remarkable results." Aware of the difficulties in which the Superior found himself, he offered to make the journey with the party that had been chosen. A young Frenchman was to go with him; the others were Hurons, two of whom had just escaped from captivity among the Iroquois. Altogether there were eight men who got into their three canoes at Quebec in the latter part of April, 1644, and started for the Northwest.

All went well till they passed the entrance of Lake St. Pierre. It was Jogues' unlucky spot. Bressani's canoe had been damaged, and the next night there was a fall of snow which delayed them still more. Both events were fatal. It is said also that one of the Indians shot at a wild goose. Bressani said it was an eagle. It must have been a goose. It revealed their whereabouts to the enemy.

JOSEPH BRESSANI.

On the next day, when doubling a point, they found themselves suddenly surrounded by hostile canoes. There was a feeble attempt to escape. In the fight one Huron was killed, and the rest surrendered. They were then about twenty-three miles above Three Rivers and seven or eight from Fort Richelieu. The booty was divided. Most of the provisions were devoured, and what remained was packed away for transportation. But part of the feast was the dead Huron—a Christian. They cut him in pieces and, putting the arms, legs and heart in a pot, boiled and ate them. Thus refreshed they proceeded down the Richelieu to Ossernenon.

Bressani's capture was particularly agreeable to the Iroquois. Maisonneuve had just then killed a great Iroquois chief in a desperate sally outside of the palisades of Montreal. Deserted by his men, the chevalier found himself throttled by a huge Iroquois. With his free hand he reached behind the Indian's head and with the butt end of a pistol brained him and escaped to the fort. The priest would be made to pay for that death.

On the way down the Richelieu he heard his captors discussing a plan. They did not know he understood them, and they talked freely. They proposed to descend upon Sillery and carry off the nuns. As soon as he could, he wrote a warning to his friends on a piece of birch bark and fastened it to the trunk of a tree. One week afterwards it was in the hands of Montmagny. Some friendly Indians had found it and carried it to Quebec.

Like Jogues, Bressani has left us an account of what he underwent. The narrative is a model of good writing for its literary purity and simplicity. It was published in Italy during his lifetime, and was dedicated to Cardinal de Lugo. Though the reader may be shocked by some of its pages, his sympathy and pity cannot fail to be touched. Not only are physical sufferings described, but the interior struggles are revealed, as well as the lofty sentiments which sustained

45

him in his trials, all with the most unaffected candor. It is
marvelous how he could have succeeded in writing it at all.
He had but one finger remaining on his right hand. Some
of his narrative was written with ink which he had made
from gunpower and water. His desk was the ground in
a wigwam. In some respects it is more heartrending than
the story of Jogues, and it is additionally interesting in
that they both suffered in the same place. The complete
account may be found in the *Relations* and in Bressani's
letters. We give a few excerpts.

"I will not narrate," he writes, "all that I had to suffer
on the journey from Fort Richelieu to Ossernenon. It will
suffice to say that we had to carry our baggage in the
woods by untrodden roads, full of stones and thorns and
holes, and covered with snow and water; for the snow had
not yet altogether melted. We had no shoes, and had to
wait sometimes till three or four in the afternoon, and
sometimes the whole day, before they gave us anything to
eat. At night I had to hunt for wood and water and to
cook for the savages when they had any provisions. When
I did not do my work well or did not understand what they
told me I was cruelly beaten.

"On the fourth day, which was the 15th of May, we
found ourselves about three in afternoon, without having
yet eaten anything, on the banks of a river where 400
savages were fishing (probably the upper Hudson). They
came to meet us about 600 feet from their wigwams. They
stripped us naked, and made me march at the head of the
procession. The young braves formed a hedge on the
right and left, all armed with sticks except the first, who
brandished a knife. When I attempted to advance he stood
in front of me and, seizing my left hand, he split it with
his knife between the ring and little finger with such force
and violence that I thought he had opened my entire hand
to the wrist. Then the others began to beat me with their
clubs, and did not stop till we reached the platform, where

46

they were to torture us. We had to mount a pile of rough bark, nine or ten palms high, so as to give the crowd a chance to see and revile us. I was all covered with blood, which was dripping from every part of my body, and the cold wind congealed it on the skin. A chief, seeing me shivering, gave me the thin soutane which they had taken from me, but it was then in rags. It was enough to cover, but not to warm me.

"They kept us some time there, but left us when they were done with us to the discretion or the indiscretion of the boys and children, who stuck sharp-pointed instruments into my flesh, struck me, tore out my hair, and beard, and so on. . . . At night the chiefs went around to the cabins and called out to the young men, ' Come and caress our prisoners.' Immediately they rushed to where we were. They tore off the shreds of the garment I wore, and in this condition of nudity some stabbed me with sharp sticks; others burned me with torches or stones heated in the fire; others made use of hot ashes or firebrands. They made me walk around the fire on the burning cinders, under which they had placed sharp-pointed sticks. Then they slowly burned off a nail and a finger, taking a quarter of an hour to do it. I have only one complete finger now, and they tore out the nail of that one with their teeth. One night they would tear out a nail; the following day the first joint; and the next day a second. I had to sing during the torture, and they kept it up till one or two in the morning. Then they left me staked to the ground and with nothing to cover me. When I had anything to lie on it was only a piece of skin only half long enough. Frequently I had nothing to cover me, for they had torn up the soutane which they had given me.

"We left that place on May 26, and after many days' traveling reached their first village, Ossernenon (Auriesville). There our reception was like the first, only more cruel, for besides beating me with their fists and clubs on the most sensitive parts of the body, they split my left hand between the index and middle finger, and they kept on showering blows on me till I fell half dead. I could not rise, and they continued to beat me on the breast and head. I should have certainly died under their blows if a chief had not dragged me away and placed me on a platform as before. There they cut off my left thumb and split the index finger. That night a savage made me enter his cabin, and there we were tortured with greater cruelty and ferocity than ever. They dislocated all my toes and drove a firebrand into my foot. I scarcely know what they did not try to do.

"After having satisfied their cruelty, they sent us to a village nine or ten miles further on (Tionnontoguen, where Jogues and Goupil had been tortured). Besides the torture I have already spoken of they hanged me head downward, sometimes with ropes and sometimes with chains which the Dutch had given them. During the night I was stretched out on the bare earth, picketed, as is their custom, by the hands and feet and neck. During six or seven nights the means they took to make me suffer are such that it is not permitted me to describe.

"After this treatment I became so offensive that everyone kept away from me, or if they did not, it was only to add to my torments. I was covered with insects and vermin, and could not rid myself of them or keep them off. Worms began to drop from my wounds. I was a burden to myself, and were I alone to be considered I would have counted death a gain. I longed for it, and expected it, but not without a feeling of horror of dying by fire. Death did not come and I was given to an old squaw to replace an uncle whom the Hurons had formerly killed. Instead of letting me be burned, as all desired and decided, she bought me for some wampum beads."

One incident occurred while he was there which is especially worth recording. "I baptized no one except a

48

JOSEPH BRESSANI.

Huron," he says. "He was about to be burned, and I
was urged to go to see him. I went with repugnance, as
they told me he could not understand me. I passed through
the crowd; they formed in line for me, and allowed me to
approach the man, who was already quite disfigured by the
tortures. He was lying on the bare ground, without being
able to rest his head in any place. Seeing a stone near
him, I pushed it with my foot as far as his head, that he
might use it as a pillow." (Poor Bressani could not use
his hands.) "Then looking at me, and either by some wisp
of beard which I had left, or by some other sign, judging
that I was a stranger, he said to the person who had him
in custody: 'Is not this the European whom you hold
captive?' And the other having answered him 'Yes,' looking at me the second time with a somewhat pitiful glance,
'Sit down,' he said to me, 'my brother, near to me, for I
desire to speak to thee.' I did so, not without horror at
the stench which emanated from that half-roasted body,
and asked him what he desired, rejoicing to understand him
a little, because he spoke Huron, and hoping through this
opportunity to be able to instruct him for baptism, but, to
my utmost consolation, he anticipated me. 'What do I
ask?' he said; 'I ask nothing else than baptism. Make
haste; the time is short.' I began to question him and found
him perfectly instructed, having been received among the
Catechumens in the country of the Hurons. I baptized
him then with great satisfaction both to him and myself;
but although I had done so with some artifice—having used
a little water which I had brought him to drink—the Iroquois, nevertheless, perceived it. They drove me from the
cabin and began to torment him as before, and the following morning they finished roasting him alive." The poor
Indian was then skinned and dismembered and beheaded,
the head being placed before Bressani to gaze at. It will
be interesting for New Yorkers to learn that this account

is dated " New Amsterdam, August 31, 1644." He wrote it after he was ransomed.

From his writings we obtain very valuable information as to the reasons which prompted the Indians to perpetrate these cruelties.

" The Iroquois hate us," he said, " not because we are Europeans, for they do not hate the Dutch, but because we identify ourselves with our Huron Christians, whom the Iroquois are determined to destroy. If we were not willing to throw in our lot with our converts and undergo the same bodily sufferings as they, we should not be believed when we would talk to them about the soul. To be hunted as they are is part of our ministry. Thus the first origin of this enmity is the Faith, which binds us, even at the peril of life, to friendship with those we convert, and indirectly to enmity with the Iroquois. Added to this is the hatred which the Iroquois bear to the Holy Faith, which they consider and describe as magic. It is that which prompted them recently to prolong for eight days the torments which they commonly despatch in one day when they put to death Joseph Onabré, a Christian Indian, who publicly boasted of his Christianity. But they particularly hate the sign of the cross, which they have been taught by the Dutch is a real superstition. It was on this account they killed the good René Goupil, a companion of Father Jogues." (This was written before Father Jogues' death.) " For the same reason they took away from me the boy whom I had taught to make the sign of the cross, as well as to say his prayers. He was horribly tortured and killed before my eyes."

It is needless to remark that the testimony of one who was almost a martyr himself is invaluable in obtaining a correct appreciation of the mental attitude of the Indians with regard to the missionaries whom they put to death.

Very precious also is his study of the condition of the soul in the midst of these trials. Replying to his Superior's inquiry, he says : " I should have difficulty in answering

50

JOSEPH BRESSANI.

if I did not know that it is honorable to reveal and confess the works of God. Though I was always within two inches of death, my mind was, nevertheless, constantly free, so that I could do everything with proper reflection. The body was extremely feeble—scarcely could I open my lips to say one *Pater Noster*—but inwardly I discoursed with the same freedom and facility that I use at present. Again, in proportion as the dangers and pains increased, my mental condition changed, and I had continually less horror of death and fire. I had not the first impulse of resentment against my tormentors. On the contrary, I pitied them. I was consoled in my desolations, but do not imagine I did not feel the torments. I felt them keenly, but I had such strength to suffer them that I was astonished at myself, or, rather, at the grace. I account this favor greater than deliverance from pain.

"I did not lack, however, some interior distress, but not at the time of torments, which I feared more before experiencing them than when I actually suffered them, and often I was more terrified on seeing them practised on others than while undergoing them in my own person. Other troubles which I underwent were temptations against faith; which, I think, must be common enough at the hour of death. I judge so, because of my own personal experience and because the desolation that comes upon the soul when all human consolation is lost is naturally an excellent opportunity for the evil spirit to suggest doubts of divine truth. But the goodness of God, who leads man down to hell and leads him back again, did not abandon me. By suggesting to myself the thoughts that I would have put before another person in similar circumstances I recovered my peace of mind."

While we are compelled to admire this searching analysis of the condition of his soul, we are almost amused to hear him relate that " one evening, while they were burning the ring finger of my right hand for the last time, instead of singing, as they commanded me, I intoned the *Miserere* with so awful a voice that I made them afraid, and all listened to me with attention. Even the one who was burning me remitted a little of the severity with which he had begun, but he did not therefore forbear, fearing that they would scoff at him. Nevertheless, I thought then that I should die, so cruel was the pain.

"Often," he says, "when unbound in the morning—and I never had realized when considering the passion of Our Lord what a torment it was to be tightly bound—I found I had been dreaming that I had been suddenly healed, and on awakening I looked to see if it were true. This thought, though only in a dream, gave me such strength and vigor that after one or two hours' rest, I was as full of strength to suffer as on the first day when I began to be tortured."

We have given only a hurried sketch of his sufferings at Ossernenon, but there are many things in the complete narrative which reveal an extraordinary spirituality in this great champion of the Faith. He tells us how he swooned away at the indecencies committed before his eyes; how he would awake in the night and reflect on how awful purgatory must be; how when the worms were falling from his wounds, he thought of Job; how he felt no resentment against his persecutors; how he turned to the *Consolatrix Afflictorum* when they were preparing to burn him; how when he was lying in agony in the cabin of the squaw, he considered that no one can live without crosses, though his "present suffering was like sugar in comparison with the past."

The squaw soon grew tired of him. He was clearly a losing speculation. He was no use to her, and was only encumbering the cabin, for he was so loathsome that no one would enter it; so she sold him to the Dutch for two or three hundred francs. It was "fine profit for a belt of wampum," her original investment. The Dutch eagerly

JOSEPH BRESSANI.

bought him and nursed him back to something like health, and then carried him down the river to New York as they had done with Jogues. He had been for five months at Auriesville, and remained about a month in Manhattan. Finally a vessel was ready and he started on his wearisome journey over the Atlantic, having with him the following safe-conduct of the sympathetic Governor Kieft, who was rude to others, but always sympathetic and kind to Catholic priests:

" Francis Joseph Bressani, of the Society of Jesus, captured in Canada, some time since, by the Iroquois savages, commonly called Maquas, tortured a long time by them, and on the point of being burned, was happily, after many difficulties, saved from them by us, by a ransom and set free. Now that with our consent he sets out for Holland to return to France, Christian charity exacts from all those to whom he may present himself to receive him with kindness. Consequently we entreat all Governors, Commandants, or their lieutenants, to afford him help on his arrival or departure, promising in like emergency to do them similar service.

" Given at the Fort of New Amsterdam in New Belgium, Sept. 20, in the year of salvation 1644."

Harsh words are said about Kieft, but the Jesuits have every reason to regard him with a feeling almost of affection.

We have no description of how New York appeared to Bressani while he was waiting to be carried over the sea, but from a letter from the Isle of Rhé, and dated November 16, 1644, we learn that after he left Manhattan his journey was far from a pleasant one. He thanks God for being delivered " not only from the hands of the Iroquois, but also from the fury of the sea, on which we had experienced horrible tempests; one, among others, lasted twenty-four hours, and brought us to the pass of resolving to cut the masts of the ship. We were chased by Turkish corsairs

53

for whole days, and I made the entire voyage with Hugue-
nots, to whom the name of 'papist' or 'Jesuit' was, of
course, displeasing. I had no other bed than a bare box,
whereon I could not stretch out at full length. The victuals
and the water itself failed us, and yet, except for sea-sickness,
to which I am subject, *I was always very well*. After fifty-
five days of wearisome navigation I arrived in sailor's
dress at the Isle of Rhé in better health than I have thus
far had in the eighteen years and over, in which I have
been in the Society. I was obliged to ask alms, but with
such satisfaction that could scarcely be imagined."

We do not know if Bressani was ever brought to the
French Court as Jogues was, but it is very likely. He had,
however, a greater consolation. He saw Pope Innocent X,
who kissed his mangled hands and gave him permission
to say Mass: "You were mutilated for preaching the
Gospel; you should not be deprived of the honor of saying
Mass."

Like Jogues, he came back to America and immediately
plunged into the sacrifices and danger of the missions. He
returned in time to be present at the famous conference at
Three Rivers, where he met Jogues. What a spectacle it
must have been for those two battle-scarred warriors to
find themselves among their old enemies now anxious to
make peace! Jogues seems to have kept out of sight, but
Bressani went around among his friends and asked for
presents, which he distributed to the astonished Mohawks.

After that he started for the upper missions. "He did
not know the language," says Ragueneau, "but his mutilated hands spoke for him." We have in his own writing
a description of some of his work.

"I would advise those who come to convert these barbarians," he says, "to be armed with a patience of bronze.
On my last journey in these great forests we were in
twenty-three different places inside of six months. These
stations were sometimes on very high mountains, some-

POPE INNOCENT X.

times in deep valleys, or, again, in the level country, which, for the most part, is covered with pines, cedars and firs. We crossed many torrents, rivers and lakes. This is the way we lodged. We made a great ditch in the snow, in which we planted thirty or forty poles which we got in the woods, and which served to support the pieces of bark which formed the cabin. The door was an old skin, and the floor some pine branches. We could not stand upright, not so much because the cabin was low as because of the smoke which compelled us always to lie down. If you attempt to go out, the cold, the snow and the danger of fainting compel you to return as soon as possible and remain in your narrow prison, which has four very appreciable inconveniences—the cold, the heat, the smoke and the dogs. As for the cold, your head almost touches the snow, unless some little branch of pine protects you. The winds come in everywhere, especially through a large opening at the top, which serves as chimney and window, through which at night I beheld the stars and moon just as well as I should have seen them in the open country. The cold, however, did not treat me as badly as the fire, which was extinguished at night, when it was most necessary, but which by day roasted us. Nor could I defend myself from it because of the scantiness of the space. I could not stretch myself without putting my feet in the fire, and to stay continually cramped with the feet crossed is a posture which fatigues. This inconvenience is not so great for the savages, who squat down like apes, being accustomed to it from childhood. But a torment greater than the heat is the smoke, which continually draws tears from the eyes. We are often constrained to put our mouths to the ground in order to breathe. It was, so to speak, necessary to eat the earth in order not to drink the smoke. I have thus passed many hours, especially during the intense cold and while it was snowing. Even the savage feels it, for the smoke enters through the mouth, through the eyes and through the nostrils. Oh, what a bitter beverage! Oh, what an evil smell! I thought I should lose my eyes. They were inflamed like fire, and they distilled like an alembic. I could not see except confusedly, like the blind man of the Gospel who saw men like trees walking. I said the psalms of the Office as best I could, by memory, reserving the lessons for a time when the pain should give me a little respite. They appeared to me written with letters of fire or scarlet, and I was often compelled to close the book, no longer seeing in it aught else than a blur. Do not say to me, ' You should have gone out to take a little air.' The air at those times was so cold that the trees, which have a harder skin than we and harder bodies, could not resist it, splitting with a sound like that of a musket. I went out, nevertheless, but the cold and snow constrained me to return. I know not whether I ought to complain of the fourth discomfort: the dogs. These poor animals, not being able to resist the cold, came to bestow themselves now on my shoulders, now on my feet. While giving me a little warmth they robbed me of my sleep. They were large and numerous and dying of hunger, and would wander over the cabin, sometimes passing over our faces with such vehemence that, tired of scolding them, I would cover my face, and let them scour about at pleasure. If we threw a bone to them, when we had any, they would in their fight for it upset everything. Often they would first taste the contents of our bark dishes, according to the ancient permission they have from these barbarians. At first, not being able to accustom myself to food without salt, I contented myself with a little smoked eel. I had used it for mending my robe, but *hunger compelled me to unstitch it and eat it*. I would sometimes go into the woods and gnaw the tenderest part of the trees and the softer bark. I saw many Indians who had eaten only once in five days. They looked like skeletons. I was sick for about ten days, but could not get anyone to give me even a drink of water.

JOSEPH BRESSANI.

To add to my misery, I was in the company of a noted sorcerer, who showed his hatred of me in every way, and taught me the filthiest expressions without my knowing it. I could write a whole book if I were to narrate the blasphemies he uttered against God. I was obliged to be silent for entire days not to exasperate him."

Bressani remained in the upper Huron district for three years and saw the Iroquois rapidly closing in on the missions. All communication with Montreal was completely cut off. The situation grew desperate. It meant ultimate starvation, and an attempt had to be made to break through the lines. Bressani led the forlorn hope, and started out with 120 Hurons. No soldier ever attempted a more hazardous enterprise.

The journey was made with more than usual precaution. Watch was carefully kept each night, for at every step they were dogged by the pursuing Iroquois. At length they reached Montreal and were now approaching Three Rivers. In order to indulge their usual vanity by painting themselves properly and arranging their feathers for a triumphal entry, they got out of their canoes and began their preparations. The first section was more expeditious than the others, and when fully tricked out, started off for the fort. Hardly were they separated from the main body when down upon the laggards came the Iroquois, who saw in this division their last chance to inflict a blow. The battle began. The party ahead immediately retraced its steps; the garrison sallied from the fort to take part in the mêlée, but to the amazement of the French, the whole body of fighting Indians, Huron and Iroquois, disappeared in the forest. Among them was Bressani, who was eager to be in the thick of the fight to attend to the wounded. Angrily the soldiers returned to the stockade. They were obeying orders but abandoning their friends. They could hear the distant fusillade and the war-whoops of the combatants, but could know nothing of the issue of the battle, till at last they saw a Huron canoe pursued by two others which belonged to the Iroquois coming down the stream. They rushed out to protect the fugitive, but it was Bressani, holding aloft the banner of the cross, and hastening to announce the defeat of the Iroquois. The victors arrived soon after, and entered the stockade with great pomp, making their prisoners kneel down before the cross of the village to do it reverence. The victory was celebrated in the usual gruesome way. A Huron renegade who had been captured among the Iroquois was burned to death; the missionaries not being able to prevent the execution.

While his Indians were selling their peltries, Bressani hurried to Quebec to see what help he could get for the perishing Northwest. There he met the last detachment of missionaries who ever went up to the Lakes. Among them was Gabriel Lalemant, who was the next year to be burned to death at the side of Brébeuf.

On August 6, 1648, Bressani and the new missionaries started from Three Rivers in sixty canoes. There were twenty-six Frenchmen in the expedition, among whom were twelve soldiers. St. Mary's was reached in safety, but calamities immediately began to multiply. Daniel and Garnier and Brébeuf and Lalemant were murdered, and Bressani saw the ravages of the famine and witnessed the terrible slaughter that ensued when the Iroquois invaded the country. He was one of the sad company on the raft when St. Mary's was burned and the missionaries and their neophytes rowed away to St. Joseph's. The situation was every day becoming more alarming, and the wonderful Bressani was again chosen to face death in an effort to reach Quebec to ask for help. He started in September, 1649. That was seven months after the death of Brébeuf. Strange to say, he reached the city in safety, but begged in vain for assistance to defend the missions; and six days afterwards started back again on his way to the Huron country, but got no farther than Montreal.

JOSEPH BRESSANI.

His heart must have been heavy when he was sent as preacher to Quebec, but when the news came of the proposed removal of all the Hurons to the new settlement at Isle d'Orleans, up the river he sped with a flotilla of twenty-three canoes to gather in the fleeing Hurons. Twenty leagues above Montreal his party landed to pass the night. Near where they pitched their camp ten Iroquois lay in ambush. It was not long before the Hurons were buried in slumber, but in the dead of night Bressani, who could not sleep, heard the stealthy tread of the enemy coming with tomahawk in hand to massacre the sleeping foe. His cry, " To arms " startled the Hurons. A bloody fight ensued. Six Iroquois were killed, two made prisoners and the two others escaped. Six of the Hurons also were slain, and a number wounded. The victory was won, but Bressani was found streaming with blood. Three arrows had struck him in the head, and they cared for him as best they could in the forest.

This adventure was bad enough, but a little farther on they nearly came into collision with another great body of Indians whom they mistook for foes. Fortunately they discovered in time that it was Father Ragueneau with his 400 starving fugitives coming down the river; and so bloodshed was happily averted. Together they sailed down the stream, and the whole miserable convoy reached Quebec in safety, July 28, 1650. It was the end of the Huron missions.

It comes almost as a surprise to find this battered and mangled hero in the midst of his apostolic duties at Quebec and elsewhere, busying himself in making scientific observations to answer the queries of some of his friends in Europe. Thus he discusses the ebb and flow of tides; whether the beginning of the movement comes from the middle of the sea or from the shores of Europe to those of America. " After diligent examination with the aid of excellent seamen I have found that it takes place in neither one way

59

nor the other." Then follows a detailed account of what he has observed. Another problem is the permanency of the supply of water in the great lakes; and the third, the result of his studies about the declination of the needle. " I have been able to make these latter observations in the four voyages I have made to these parts."

On November 2, 1650, a year and a half after the death of his friends, Lalemant and Brébeuf, he bade farewell to America, weeping bitterly. It was affection for him that sent him home. His health was shattered, and, besides, all the posts of danger, which were his particular predilection, were for the moment inaccessible. He returned to his native land and became a preacher in all of its great cities. His natural eloquence, his admitted sanctity, the story of his suffering, and also the marks of his martyrdom which he bore on his deeply scarred features and fingerless hands made it easy for him to sway men's hearts. He died at Florence, September 9, 1672.

JOSEPH PONCET.

IN the summer of 1638, two Jesuit priests, quite unlike each other in almost every respect, left Rome together on their way to the Canadian missions. One was Joseph Marie Chaumonot, the son of a Burgundian peasant, the other the aristocratic Joseph Antoine Poncet de la Rivière, a Parisian by birth, who, after a brilliant career as a student in his native city, entered the Society when he was a lad of nineteen. He was instructor at the college of Clermont from 1631 to 1634, and made his theological studies successively at Clermont, Rome, and Rouen. The two missionaries left France in 1639.

On the vessel with them, sharing in the discomforts and dangers of the long voyage, was the famous Mme. de la Peltrie. She was on her way to establish the Ursulines at Quebec, and with her was another woman who occupies a very conspicuous place in early Canadian history: Marie de l'Incarnation, whom Charlevoix calls the " Theresa of New France."

The story of Mme. de la Peltrie is one instance among many of the romantic character which religious enthusiasm assumed in those days. She was young and beautiful and a widow, with an ample fortune; and her aged father very properly was desirous of seeing her marry again. She had no children. Without refusing her father's request, she evaded it in a very singular fashion. She asked a rich widower named de Bernières, who was then Treasurer of France, to marry her or to pretend to do so, leaving her to the prosecution of the projects which she entertained for helping foreign missions.

De Bernières at that time was engaged in the very extraordinary work—to give it no other name—of directing the spiritual progress of a certain number of ecclesiastics

61

who had withdrawn into solitude for meditation and the practice of austerity. Among them was the future bishop of Quebec, Laval, who was at that time about to be sent as a bishop to Tonquin, and also Palloux, who actually went to that country. This strange community, under the direction of a layman who was living in the world, was visited about that time by the famous Jesuit missionary, Alexander de Rhodès, who was endeavoring to have a hierarchy established in Tonquin, which he had just opened to Christianity. There was question of sending de Laval there, but Palloux was the only one appointed.

De Bernières assented to the strange proposal of the young widow. He either married her or let it be understood that he did. But they lived apart; he directing the finances of both of their estates into religious channels. Canada, however, for a long time did not share in these benefactions until after a chance reading by Mme. de la Peltrie of the *Relations,* which had just been published. Impressed very much by the conditions there described, she heard, or thought she heard, a voice while she was kneeling in prayer, enjoining upon her to devote her energies and her resources to the foundation and support of a house of education in the new colony. Just then Father Poncet arrived in Paris on his way to the missions, and without knowing Marie de l'Incarnation, who was a nun at Tours, though doubtless he had heard of her, wrote to say that she was to devote herself to evangelical work in the New World. Amazed at the letter advising her to do what she had been long thinking of, though no one but her confessor was aware of it, her astonishment increased when Mme. de la Peltrie and de Bernières arrived at the convent at Tours inviting her to undertake the journey to Canada.

There is no reason to seek for anything supernatural in all this, as things would so adjust themselves in the ordinary course of events. Mme. de la Peltrie, hearing of Poncet's arrival in Paris, on his way to the missions, would naturally

MME. DE LA PELTRIE.

JOSEPH PONCET.

consult him about the kind of women he would suggest for the new foundation. Marie de l'Incarnation was attracting attention in France at the time, and so Poncet thought of her, though it is hard to see what his opinion was worth, as he had never been in Canada. There was, perhaps, too much flutter about the whole scheme to be reassuring, but it all turned out for the best and soon Marie de l'Incarnation and her nuns, with their protectress and Fathers Poncet and Chaumonot, were cooped up in their little vessel on the broad Atlantic, on their way to America.

Charlevoix gives a very graphic description of their landing at Sillery, August, 1639. He tells us that " the day when they arrived was a holiday for the whole city; all labor ceased and the shops were closed. The Governor received these heroines at the river-side at the head of his troops, who were under arms, and with the sound of cannon. After the first compliments he led them, amid the acclamations of the people, to the church, where the *Te Deum* was chanted in thanksgiving. These pious women on their side, in the first transport of joy, kissed the earth for which they had so long sighed, which they promised themselves to water with their sweat, and did not even despair of dyeing with their blood. The French mingled with Indians, pagans with Christians, and continued for several days to make the city resound with their cries of joy."

Poncet was not left at Quebec to direct the holy woman, Marie de l'Incarnation, whom he had thus guided to America, but was sent immediately to the Huron mission. He arrived there just after Brébeuf and his companions had invited the Indians to the famous banquet of death where all the missionaries, among whom was Poncet's cousin, Garnier, expected to be massacred. Poncet himself does not seem to have done anything particularly worthy of mention beyond founding an Algonquin mission in 1645 on the Island of St. Mary's, but we find his name on the list of the great men whom Parkman has glorified. " In all the

voluminous accounts of that barbarous period," he says,
" not a single line permits us to suspect that a single one of
that loyal and brave little band of Jesuits ever faltered:
the indomitable Brébeuf, the gentle Garnier, the courageous
Jogues, the enthusiastic Chaumonot, Lalemant, Le Mercier,
Chastelain, Daniel, Pijart, Ragueneau, du Perron, *Poncet*
or Le Moyne. All bore themselves with a tranquil intrepidity which confounded the Indians and won their respect." To have been named in such company is glory
enough for any man.

Shortly after this he returned to Quebec, and was engaged
chiefly in ministering to the needs of the people of the city.
Misfortunes were multiplying in the upper missions, until
they were finally destroyed. Proud of their victory the
furious Iroquois were carrying their depredations to the
walls of Quebec. The whole colony was in consternation,
and one day when Poncet was out giving the alarm to the
colonists at Cape Rouge and helping them to gather in their
harvest, the savages swooped down on the little settlement
and took him prisoner. With him was a Frenchman named
Mathurin Franchetot. On August 20, 1653, they found
themselves dragging their weary feet down to the very
place where Jogues had been martyred seven years before.

Poncet was very popular in Quebec. Marie de l'Incarnation calls him *" le doux et sympathique Poncet."* At the
news of his capture 300 men seized their arms and started
off in pursuit, while public prayers were offered in the city
for his safety. Hurrying off in the direction of Three
Rivers the party struck the trail, and on their way saw on
the trunk of a tree a picture of two heads under which were
Poncet's and Franchetot's signatures. A little later they
found a book in which the Father had written: " Six
Hurons, naturalized as Iroquois, and four Mohawks are
carrying us off, but as yet have done us no harm." He
could not say as much a few days later.

In an account which he was subsequently ordered to

write, he tells us: " The savage who had captured me at Cape Rouge tore my reliquary from my neck and put it on his own. One day when he was running in the woods the reliquary flew open, all the relics were lost, and nothing remained but a small piece of paper on which I had written in my own blood, when I was still in the country of the Hurons, the names of our Fathers martyred in America, and a short prayer in which I asked Our Lord for a violent death in His service, and the grace to shed all my blood for the same cause. Having thus secured the paper, I saw constantly before my eyes the sentence of my death written in my blood, so that I could not revoke it. Nevertheless I had a feeling that those great souls and stout hearts who preceded me in the conflict had merited actual martyrdom because of their great virtues, and that I, who had only the shadow and faint likeness thereof, would be crucified only in appearance."

On the second day he was lame and scarcely able to proceed on account of his crippled limbs, hunger, and exhaustion. While crossing the Mohawk he heard his companion's confession. It was fortunate, for poor Franchetot was burned at the stake a day or so afterwards. They were now at Ossernenon, and were subjected to the usual torture of beating and stretching and burning. An Indian with one eye seems to have been an especial object of terror to Poncet. At the end of the first day when he was all mangled and bruised, an old squaw took a fancy to one of his fingers, and to humor her, the ogre with the single eye called up a little child and ordered him to cut off the finger. The order was promptly obeyed, and the same childish hand applied a live coal to the stump to staunch the blood. " I sung the Vexilla," says Poncet, " while it was being done, but as the blood did not cease to flow, they wrapped the wound some time after in a leaf of Indian corn, and that was all the dressing applied till my life had been granted to me. At night they left us to the mercy of the mob; some struck my wounded finger, put hot calumets or coals upon it, and the like. During two nights we were suspended in the air and bound so tight that we suffered excruciating pain. One night they applied firebrands to our flesh, making us sing and dance meantime. Sunday arrived, and it was spent in council to determine what should be done with us. Both of us expected to be killed, but it was decided to put only Franchetot to death, while I was given to an old squaw in place of a brother she had lost. As soon as I entered the cabin I was made to sit down on a sort of a table near a fire, and she and her two daughters began to chant the song of the dead. The departed was supposed to live again in me. These poor creatures did what they could for me, poulticing my hands and covering them with filthy rags worse than any dish-cloth. They also gave me a greasy shirt, all with much kindness and affection."

Suddenly, on September 11, messengers were seen coming in great haste to the village. They ordered Poncet's release. What had happened? The rescue party which had set out for Quebec arrived at Three Rivers, and to their surprise found it invested by the Iroquois. The Indians were caught in a trap: three hundred men in their rear and the fort in front. They made a brief struggle and surrendered. They were all going to be massacred, or made to believe so, unless they despatched their swiftest runners after the captors of Poncet and brought him safely back to Quebec. The offer was accepted. They not only arrived in time to save his life, but brought such wonderful stories about the esteem in which he was held by the white men that he was " treated with as much consideration as he had before met with indignity." Nothing was too good for him, and he was brought down to the Dutch at Fort Orange.

Here he met some white people whose history is of unusual interest. One was a *dame écossaise*. Who this Scotch woman was, unfortunately Poncet does not tell us. Perhaps he did so in his original manuscript, which reached

JOSEPH PONCET.

Quebec only in a tattered condition, but at all events her name has not come down to us. It would be of interest to know, for she had journeyed from Quebec in search of a little French boy who had been captured by the Indians. He was the son of the farmer of the Jesuits at Beaupré. That is all we know of this kind-hearted woman who had incurred such dangers for the little lad who never came back. Was she a Catholic? We do not know. That she was Scotch would not suggest the contrary, for Abraham Martin, who gave his name to the Plains of Abraham, was usually called *l'écossais*.

He also met there a " Waloon merchant " from Brussels who lavished kindness upon him. His name, however, we are left in ignorance of. But the most romantic figure that appeared on that occasion stepped out of the throng of Indians and addressed the missionary in excellent French. This was the famous Radisson, who afterwards not only was conspicuous in Canadian history but became of international importance, and is so to-day. Hence it may be of interest to interrupt the story of Poncet for a moment to say a word of this remarkable man.

Pierre Esprit Radisson was born at St. Malo, in France, and arrived in Canada in 1651. The next year he was captured by the Mohawks and adopted by the tribe. He has left an elaborate account of his travels, and if we are to take him literally, he was about as bad as the savages. However, when he says " we killed the old man and left the helpless old woman to starve," and the like, he is merely chronicling what the Indians did. At all events, he was out on a warlike expedition with his brothers the Mohawks against the Dutch. Apparently, after a short fight an agreement had been reached, and Radisson found himself at Fort Orange with his " family," the Iroquois. After a few days he and the Indians departed, but evidently the grace of God was working in the poor fellow's heart. He made his escape and presented himself at Fort Orange to ask for protection. The whole troop of Indians followed him, mourning his loss rather than angry at his flight, for they appear to have been very much attached to him. But the Dutch refused to give him up and kept him in concealment. Meantime the fugitive paid frequent visits to Father Poncet, or *Noncet,* as the papers of the Prince Society call him, and straightened out the affairs of his soul. He was probably very badly in need of it. Finally, after three weeks the Dutch got him down to New York and sent him to Europe, but he came back to America and married a wife in Three Rivers in 1656.

About that time Father Ragueneau was setting out for the mission at Onondaga, and our brave Radisson went with him. He remained there until the mission broke up, and has left a minute description of the flight, which may be referred to later when we come to the story of Father Ragueneau's adventures.

Here a new character enters. There was a certain Médard Chouart, who had come to Canada as early as 1641 when he was only fifteen years of age. We find him with the missionaries on Lake Huron in the capacity of a *donné,* but in 1646 he married and developed into a fur trader, and having met with considerable success and acquired a grant of land, he assumed the title of Sieur des Groselliers, a name destined to be associated with Radisson in important events of the colony.

In the *Relations* of 1655-56 we are told that on August 6, 1654, " two young Frenchmen, full of courage, having received permission from Monsieur le Gouverneur to embark with some of the people who had come down to our French settlements, began a journey of more than 500 leagues, under the guidance of these Argonauts, not in great galleons or long-oared barges, but in little gondolas of bark. They fully expected to return in the spring, but these people did not conduct them home until towards the end of August, 1656. Their arrival caused the country unusual joy, for they were accompanied by 500 canoes laden with goods which the French came to this end of the world to procure." It is surmised that these two young Frenchmen were des Groselliers and Radisson. The latter, as we have said, then went up to the Onondagas with Father Ragueneau, while his companion is credited, after the collapse of the first New York mission, with being one of the seven Frenchmen who accompanied Father Ménard on his terrible journey out to the swamps of Wisconsin, where the missionary perished.

Meantime des Groselliers had become a widower, and married Radisson's sister, and the two traders were from that out inseparable. In 1662 they started for Hudson Bay, and coming back to Quebec, told the authorities that it was folly to travel to the far West in quest of furs. There was an inexhaustible supply at their very doors. They were not listened to, and in disgust they left the colony, went down by the way of Boston and took ship for England. There they interested Prince Rupert, the hero of Naseby, in the project, and in June, 1668, they left the Thames in the good ship "Nonsuch," in command of Captain Zachary Gillam, and in September reached Hudson Bay. The territory was called Prince Rupert's Land, a name which it still retains, the English flag was hoisted, and the Hudson Bay Company started operations.

In our own day a dispute has arisen about the rights of American fishermen in Hudson Bay, and in the interesting correspondence on the subject there frequently appears the name of "the picturesque Radisson," as he is called; not, of course, by the diplomats, but by the press. This is the escaped Indian captive whom Father Poncet shrived behind the stockade at Fort Orange away back in 1653.

Poncet grumbles a bit at the Dutch Commander at Albany, who gave him nothing to eat and allowed him to sleep on the ground, "though I had a letter from the Governor of Quebec"; but an Indian brought him to the house of the Waloon merchant, where he was hospitably treated.

PIONEER PRIESTS OF NORTH AMERICA.

The day had come for his departure. He was dressed up like a Dutchman. "My hosts urged me to take some food for my journey, but I contented myself with some peaches from a Brussels merchant," which would suggest that he was not a practical missionary. The good old Scotchwoman, he says, also helped to pack some fish in his wallet, and "when I departed I had to promise them all to come back and see them next summer, so much kindness and affection did they manifest to me."

One article of apparel which he left behind became very famous in the course of time. It was an old, tattered cassock. Years afterwards, an Onondaga squaw, woman-like, had a dream that she ought to have a black dress. Learning that there was a cassock at Fort Orange, she tramped all the way from Onondaga and purchased the rag from the thrifty Dutchmen, who made her pay a good round sum for it. She furnished the money and no doubt paraded around in state in the soutane at the great Indian festivals.

Ordinarily the road to Canada was by Lake Champlain, but Poncet did not go that way. "Leaving the Dutch settlement," he says, "I was conducted to the village of the man who had captured me. Upon going to visit him he returned me my breviary. I remained two days in the cabin where I had been adopted; and then I went with 'my sister,' who had given me my life, to the largest of the Iroquois villages for the purpose of attending the councils and assemblies in which the question of peace was to be discussed. This conclusion was reached in the village where the first Frenchman, the good René Goupil, companion to Father Isaac Jogues, had been killed by the Iroquois."

This remark does not imply that Jogues was not killed there also. But Poncet was always finding coincidences. He is merely laying emphasis on the fact that Goupil was the *first* killed, and that the suggestion of peace was made "on the very day of St. Michael, and I had always expected that this festival would not pass without some important

70

occurrence." The holy man seems to have been a trifle sentimental in his piety.

"Three days after, I was told that the chief who had escorted me to the Dutch settlement would be my conductor to the country of the French—not by water, because of the storms which ordinarily prevail at this season upon Lake Champlain, but by another route which was very fatiguing to me, as it meant a journey on foot through those great forests for seven or eight days, and I had neither strength nor legs for such an undertaking." But the Indian, he says, "was very patient with me," and so Poncet dragged himself along this trail, which led up the Mohawk as far as the present Herkimer, and then north, following the West Canada Creek, and finally reaching Ogdensburg on the St. Lawrence. They descended the river in boats to Montreal. He notes that he was very much alarmed as they shot the Lachine Rapids.

"On the 3d of October I left behind me the last village of the Iroquois. On a little hill, a short distance from the village, I met the captains and old men of the country, who were waiting for me with presents which they sent in ratification of the peace. They made their last harangue to me, urging me to bind our new alliance firmly. All those whom we met bestowed some endearment on me according to their custom, and begged me to use my influence in concluding a satisfactory peace with the French."

Before they reached the end of their journey runners overtook them to say that the Iroquois hostages at the fort had been put in irons. For a time the guides hesitated about going on; but on the assurance of Poncet that he would be responsible for their lives they resumed their tramp. It was found out afterwards that the man who had been put in irons was not an Iroquois but a drunken Algonquin. "At last we landed safely on the 24th of October," he says, "nine weeks having been passed in honor of St. Michael and all the holy angels since the beginning of my captivity.

71

"Finally, on the 5th of November, we set foot on the shore at Quebec; on the 6th our Iroquois made their presents in the cause of peace, which were responded to with other presents, and thus upon Sunday evening, eighty-one days after my capture—that is to say, just nine times nine days—the great affair of peace was brought to a close." This mathematical piety of Poncet is peculiar, especially in connection with such undoubted heroism. Thwaites has ascribed to him the chief credit of bringing about a reconciliation with the Indians.

Those eighty-one days constitute the whole of Poncet's enforced stay in New York. Possibly he regretted not having stayed longer, for he subsequently found himself the storm-centre of an ecclesiastical war in Quebec.

When the question of establishing a bishopric in Quebec was mooted, one of the most distinguished Sulpitians of the time, the famous Abbé Queylus, was thought rightly or wrongly to be aspiring to the honor; though why he should do so is hard to conjecture, for the colonists were just then seriously thinking of going back to France in a body, so aggressive had the terrible Iroquois become. The names of the Jesuits, Ragueneau, Le Jeune, and Lalemant, had also been suggested for the place, but the General set his embargo on any such honor. Finally, after much discussion, it all ended in the disappointment of Queylus and the nomination of M. Legauffre, who, however, died before he was able to come to his see. This episcopal controversy unfortunately gave rise to another trouble. The question came up about the source of the ecclesiastical faculties of the priests of Canada. Rome had bestowed them on the Jesuits, but the Bishop of Rouen maintained that they should come from him, as the vessels sailing for America usually weighed anchor in that port, which of course was an absurd contention. To settle the matter, however, and to be provided with a double authorization, Father Vimont was sent to France to secure episcopal faculties in addition

72

VEN. MARIE DE L'INCARNATION.

to those given by the Pope. They were granted, and over and above that the Superior, Father De Quen, was made the Bishop's Vicar-General. Things went smoothly for a while until the irrepressible de Queylus arrived a second time in the colony, armed with the authority of Vicar-General also. De Quen had received no notification of the revocation of his own powers, and very unwisely did not dispute the claims of Queylus, who forthwith proceeded to dispose of things as he chose, while de Quen remained quiet. Having taken a fancy to Father Poncet, de Queylus appointed him Parish Priest of Quebec. As Poncet did something displeasing to his religious Superior, he was transferred, and that aroused the wrath of Queylus, although he had previously agreed that the Jesuit Superior might exercise that power. To remove all cause of trouble Poncet was therefore ordered to the Onondaga mission. He obeyed like a good religious, but passed through Montreal on his way, and there met de Queylus, who usually resided in that place. The Vicar-General became angry and not only forbade him to proceed on his journey, but brought him back to Quebec. The storm of course grew worse after this clash of jurisdiction. It all ended in Poncet's being sent back to Europe, and we find him installed as French Penitentiary at Loretto, where he and Chaumonot had knelt as pilgrims years before on their way out to America. But he still had to see many men and cities, and in 1665 he was sent to Martinique.

We do not know what he did there, though possibly the forthcoming work by Rochemonteix will afford us some information. Unfortunately he found himself in an atmosphere of litigiousness as bad as the one from which he had escaped. The Jesuits had been there since 1640, and at the time of Poncet's arrival they numbered about fourteen priests and some lay brothers. In 1655, the Paris Nuncio reports that " in Martinique alone there were from 15,000 to 20,000 souls with some Jesuit Fathers." An official summary of conditions about that time reports that in St. Christopher, Guadaloupe, and Martinique the greater number of missionaries who live in those islands are Jesuits, and they render the greatest service to God." As usual, there were the stock accusations, which in this case were concocted by an anonymous Scotchman whose charges were improved upon by a certain Urbano Cerri about the Jesuit opposition to any ecclesiastical government or hierarchy. Dissension also raged throughout all the Antilles between the Dominicans, Augustinians, Carmelites, etc., about their relative jurisdictions. Even the good Dominican Sisters in Martinique kept up a long wail about the refusal of the Jesuits to be their spiritual directors.

The most prominent Jesuit there was Father Grillet, and we meet him in association with the famous de la Barre, who afterwards figured so disastrously in Canadian history in his attempt to subdue the Iroquois. De la Barre very warmly commends Father Grillet to the English Lord Willoughby, who in his letter says: "As to Father Grillet, he merited much more of civility than I was capable to show him; and doubtless it is his goodness if he doth not complain." But though Grillet was so acceptable to the French and English, he did not find favor with the Dutch, for they were angry at him for some reason or another and carried him off as a prisoner to Holland.

It was in these turbulent surroundings that Poncet spent the last ten years of his life. What were his occupations there we do not know. He gave up the ghost on June 18, 1675, no doubt glad that his weary journey was ended.

SIMON LE MOYNE.

IN 1651, two years after the death of Brébeuf, the colonists of Canada were seriously thinking of giving up their fight with the Indians and of returning to France. Their Huron Allies had been annihilated; the efforts of the missionaries to establish a permanent settlement near the great lakes had failed, and the conquering Iroquois of New York were threatening the very citadel of Quebec. A little later they defiantly carried off prisoners from the Isle d'Orleans; they were beleaguering Three Rivers for months; and Montreal would have succumbed but for the amazing courage of its little garrison. The situation was saved by the return from France of Maisonneuve.

Maisonneuve was one of the many splendid picturesque cavaliers who figure in Canadian history. He had accepted the post of Commandant, mostly, if not altogether, for religious motives, and his life there reads like a chapter from the history of the knights of olden times who engraved the cross on their armor, and battled for the cause of Christianity. Very properly his statue adorns the Montreal of to-day and recalls the exalted heroism of his long fight with the red men that made the city a possibility by the victory he won.

All he could get in France was one hundred soldiers, whom he paid for himself. But that was enough to turn the tide of battle and make the Indians come to terms, which shows how easily the French could have held their grasp on their American possessions if the home government had been gifted with better sense. Possibly the Indians thought this corporal's guard was a promise of more to come, and deemed it prudent to make peace, though Thwaites thinks that Father Poncet, who was then a prisoner among the Mohawks, had something to do with this change of heart.

75

But that is doubtful. The Indians had decided to stop fighting for other reasons; though Poncet, on his way back, was paid every honor, and was earnestly solicited to lend his aid in securing peace. But no matter from whom the offer came, Governor De Lauson was only too ready to accept a parley, and so in November, 1653, it was agreed to let the grass grow on the warpath.

When the treaty was made, a delegate had to be sent to the Indians. A Jesuit would, of course, be the most available representative, not because the Order systematically trained its members to be politicians, as Douglas, in his " Quebec in the Seventeenth Century," assures his readers, but because they knew the Indian languages and ways, and it did not matter much whether they were killed or not. General Clark, who has made such a profound study of Indian customs, used to think that some of the Fathers rather invited that method of happy despatch, which would prove that they were not politicians.

Looking around for the proper man, the choice naturally fell upon Father Chaumonot, who knew the Iroquois dialects, and was a *persona grata* to the savages. But he could not leave his Hurons on the Isle d'Orleans, so Father Simon Le Moyne was chosen in his stead.

Le Moyne was then about fifty years of age. He had entered the Society at Rouen, in France, when he was a boy of eighteen, and had been in Canada ever since 1638, working chiefly in the various Huron missions. It is worth noting that while he was a professor at Clermont, in his native country, he was an active member of a " League of Prayer for the Canadian Missions."

On his arrival in America he was immediately sent up to Lake Huron and was there associated with Brébeuf, Daniel, Lalemant, Jogues, and the rest of those splendid heroes and martyrs; from which we can measure his spiritual stature. The Indians gave him the name of *Wane*, probably the result of an Indian effort to pronounce the name *Moyne*. Having no *m* in their language, they compromised on half the sound. In English we should write it phonetically *Won*. Fifteen years later, when he came down to the Iroquois of New York, they called him by Father Jogues' old title of *Ondessonk*.

Le Moyne's first experience of Indian methods was not a pleasant one. It occurred on the way up to the Huron country. The details of it are found in a letter from Father Du Perron to Father Le Mercier (*Relations,* 1638).

" I left Three Rivers on the 4th of September and reached the Huron country on St. Michael's Day (29th) at twelve o'clock at night. The journey is one of 300 leagues by water, through many long and dangerous rapids, some two or three leagues in length; consequently, none but savages can undertake the journey. The Huron captain showed me every courtesy along the way, which was not the case with Father Lalemant and Father Le Moyne, who departed before I did. The former was almost strangled by one of the Algonquins, who tried several times to put a bowstring around his neck to kill him, in revenge for the death of one of his children who had been bled by one of our men and had died."

Evidently Le Moyne did not find favor with the Indians, for he and another Frenchman were thrown out of the canoe, and left to shift for themselves in the forests. They nearly died of starvation, but fortunately Du Perron, who was following his party, found them two weeks later and induced the Indians, by bribing them with a blanket, to take in the two castaways. Du Perron's own position was not by any means safe, for, like Lalemant, he also narrowly escaped strangulation. Le Moyne witnessed both these attempts.

The journey was hard enough to satisfy all his expectations.

" Our food," says Du Perron, " was only a little Indian corn, crushed between two stones, and boiled in water; our lodging *sub dio*. Nevertheless, I was always very well,. thank God."

We have a characteristic letter from Le Moyne himself,. describing his feelings after being thrown out of the boat. An extract will suffice. " I do not know whether it is my sins that close to me the gate of the country I have so greatly desired, but, at all events, here I am, stripped and forsaken, on a point of sand, beyond the little nation of the Algonquins, with no other house than the great world. Only three days ago the canoe that carried our little baggage upset in the water, and our packages were carried away by the current. We fished up one of them with a great deal of trouble, but the other was lost, so that we have nothing whatever with us. God be blessed for all."

After many mishaps he reached Lake Huron, and a letter to his friend, the Curé of Beauvais, in France, describes his feelings. It is addressed to " Monsieur and dearest Cousin," and exclaims: " Marvellous if this scrap of paper should reach you after shooting so many rapids and encountering, as it must, so many dangers. Is it not because my spirit has opened the way for it, not once, but, again and again, a thousand times? " He would have cried " marvellous! " with still more emphasis, if he had been able to foresee that after 250 years, a Protestant publishing house in America would rejoice at the discovery of this " scrap of paper " and not only put its words in print, but photograph it just as he wrote it, so that we may see the exact handwriting of the lonely missionary in his little hut far out on Lake Huron, which he describes as " *Notre Residence de la Conception.*" The letter is worth quoting.

" Oh, if you could see me here, in this end of the world, blessing the water, singing at the aspersion, and saying holy Mass for the *Parishioners* of this district—for after eight or nine months we count in this barbarous region two or three Churches or Gatherings of Neophytes. But what a consolation it is to a sympathetic heart to see here every day in our cabins how our good Jesus is adored by a people to whom He is as yet only partially known. I say every day, for, although they do not come to hear the Mass, except at the solemn feasts and on Sundays, yet they come to our bark chapel every morning and often every evening to say their prayers. Do you know how? We have translated into their language the sign of the cross, a suitable Act of Contrition, of 12 or 13 lines, the *Pater,* the *Ave,* and several prayers of that sort, which these faithful Neophytes—most of them adults and aged men—recite after me on all sides, with great feeling. God from the beginning must indeed have made good their defects of understanding, since they themselves so discreetly feign not to notice our blunders in the pronunciation of their language. Until such time as you have the satisfaction of reading our *Relation* of this year, I send to my Brother the Jesuit what will serve to whet rather than satiate your curiosity. I hope that my mother will show it to you. I recommend her and myself to you in your Holy Sacrifices and prayers, for I am from the other world, to you cordially the same as ever, that is,

" Sir, and dearest Cousin,

" Your very humble and obliged servant and cousin,

" SIMON LE MOYNE,

" Of the Society of Jesus."

The letter to " my brother the Jesuit " has not come down to us. Possibly the beloved mother, who was to show it to the Curé, would not give it up. From the portrait of Le Moyne's brother, who was handsome, we may guess what the great missionary looked like. Unfortunately, we have no portrait of the greater of the two.

All this was in 1639, when everything looked rose-colored to the enthusiastic young missionary. The next ten years was a period of privation, suffering, danger and destruction, such as no mission on the globe at that time was called to undergo. It ended in the awful deaths of Brébeuf, Lale-

mant, Garnier, Chabanel and others; the massacre of the
Huron Christians and the utter annihilation of the tribes,
who could have easily crushed the Iroquois, if they had not
lost their courage; but they fled like hares in all directions
and were either slaughtered or absorbed into the Neuters,
Petuns and other tribes.

Where was Le Moyne during that time? The *Relations*
merely say that he and others followed the fugitives through
the woods and over the mountains, doing all that was possible to bring help in the universal ruin.

The French found him, however, when he was needed
for the dangerous mission to the Iroquois. " In accepting
it," says Douglas, " he took his life in his hands." Shea
tells us: " He left it in the hands of the Almighty,"—which
was better.

He started from Quebec on July 2. "At Montreal," according to the *Relations,* " a young man of stout heart and
long a resident here, very piously joined him." Le Moyne
kept a careful diary of this remarkable journey, a few quota-
tions from which reveal the light-heartedness of this wonderful old Frenchman, going right into what might be, at
any moment, a terrible death. It was written in a canoe, or
in the forests, and almost every line of it bubbles over with
what seems almost like merriment, while displaying at the
same time the most splendid and unflinching heroism.

" On the 17th day of July, St. Alexis' Day, we set out
from home *with that great saint of many travels* toward a
land unknown to us.

" The 19th—The river continues to increase in width,
and forms a lake, pleasant to the sight, and eight or ten
leagues in length. In the evening a swarm of troublesome
mosquitoes gave us warning of rain, which drenched us all
night long. *It is a pleasure, sweet and innocent beyond conception,* to have under these conditions no shelter but the
trees, planted by nature since the creation of the world.

" The 20th—We see nothing but islands of the most
80

beautiful apearance in the world, intercepting here and there the course of this very peaceful river.

"The 21st—The islands continue. It rains all night, and the bare rocks serve us as bed, mattress, and everything else. *He who has God with him rests calmly everywhere.*

"On the 22d we reach the rapids, and the same day see a herd of wild cows proceeding in a very calm and leisurely manner. In the night we wait patiently, while the swarm of mosquitoes attack us—a task often more difficult than facing death itself.

"On the 25th we arrive at the mouth of Lake St. Ignace, where eels abound in prodigious numbers.

"On the 26th a high wind forces us to land. A cabin is soon made; bark is stripped from the neighboring trees, and thrown over poles planted in the ground on either side, and made to meet in the form of an arbor, and there you have your house complete. Ambition gains no entrance to this palace, and it is every whit as acceptable to us as if its roof were of gold.

"On the 28th—Nothing but thunder and lightning and a deluge of rain, forcing us to seek the shelter of our canoe, which, turned bottom upward over our head, serves as a house.

"On the 29th and 30th of July the windstorm continues and checks our progress at the mouth of a great lake, called Ontario, etc."

He was now in Iroquois territory, but his diary does not indicate that to reach it he went up as far as the Oswego River. For, on St. Ignatius' Day, we find him "penetrating pathless wastes, crossing long islands, and shouldering the baggage and provisions and canoe. *This road seems long to a poor man who is thoroughly fatigued.*"

"He apparently followed an overland route," says Thwaites, "from Lake Ontario to Onondaga village, probably from the mouth of the Salmon River southward."

On August 1st the first Indian he meets is a Huron captive, whom he had instructed and baptized some years before. The joy of both can be imagined. The next day there was a tramp of fifteen leagues through the woods. On the 3d he came to a river " a hundred or a hundred and twenty paces in width." On that day "*I baptized some little skeletons,* who, perhaps, were only waiting for the drop of the precious blood of Jesus Christ." He found many sick people, and " I was regarded as a great medicine man, although I had as my sole remedy only a bit of sugar to give to those feeble creatures."

On the 5th he arrived at the chief village of Onondaga. " The roads are full of people, going and coming, who are out to greet me. One calls me brother; another, uncle; another, cousin. *I never had so many kinsfolk before.* At a quarter of a league from the village I began a harangue, which brought me into high favor. I called by name all the captains, families, and persons of importance." (Bressani, who had been a captive among the Iroquois, had coached him in this knowledge of genealogy.) " I spoke slowly and in the tone of a captain. I told them that peace was attending my course; that I was dispelling war in the more distant nations, and that joy was accompanying me. Two captains made a harangue upon my entrance, with a joy and light on their countenances I had never seen in savages. That night I caused the chiefs to assemble, in order to give them two presents. The purpose of the first was to *wipe their faces,* so that they might look on me with favor; the second was to *remove any gall,* etc."

These extraordinary results were, of course, metaphorical and moral, for the children of nature are nothing, if not poetic. Later on we find him applying a poultice of porcelain to an Indian who was stabbed in the neck, and the victim admitted he was soothed.

The 10th of August arrived, Le Moyne in the interim seeing many of the Christian Hurons who were captives there. " The chiefs assembled," the journal continues,

82

SIMON LE MOYNE.

" and I opened the proceedings with a public prayer which I offered on my knees, and in a loud voice, *using the Huron tongue throughout*. I appealed to the great Master of Heaven and Earth that He might inspire us to act for His glory and our own good. I cursed all the demons of hell, since they are spirits of discord, and I prayed the guardian angels of the entire country to speak to the hearts of my hearers when my words should strike their ears. I astonished them greatly when they heard me name them all by nations, bands, and families, and each person individually, who was of some little consequence—*all by the help of my written list,* which was to them a thing full both of charm and novelty. I told them I had nineteen words to lay before them."

These " nineteen words " were so many discourses which accompanied the bestowing of belts, each of which bound the Iroquois to one or another act. " With the nineteenth present, I wiped away the tears of the young warriors for the death of their great captain." Then follow, in the diary, résumés of the Indian discourses. After this the convention came to an end.

Le Moyne tells us that on this occasion he strutted around like an actor, gesticulating extravagantly, imitating the manner of their great orators, each time winning great grunts of applause from the attendant chiefs, and keeping up his flood of eloquence for over two hours. The amusing part of it is that it was all in Huron, of which the Iroquois had only a general knowledge. It was the parent stock. The impressive manner which he assumed—he was a past master in mimicry—no doubt overwhelmed them, and possibly whispered interpretations were being given at the same time to let them know what he was saying.

That first council was held on Indian Hill over against the present Pompey, and Le Moyne's eyes were the first to rest upon that scene of enchanting beauty, with its great hills covered by dense forests, with the deep valleys between, and the gleam of Lake Onondaga on the sky-line beyond. The smoke of Syracuse is not far from there now.

It is doubtful if the Huron captives, as is sometimes supposed, were corralled in any special place in those valleys; for Le Moyne met them even in the distant fishing villages when he entered the country.

On the 12th he happened upon a treasure which must have made his heart thrill with delight. " I recovered from the hands of one of these barbarians the New Testament of Father de Brébeuf, whom they cruelly put to death five years before, and another little book of devotion that had been used by Father Garnier, whom these very people killed four years ago. These two Fathers were at their missions when that blessed death overtook them as a reward for the labors of many years which they spent in holy service in these regions. As for myself, who had been a witness to the sanctity of their lives and the glory of their deaths, I shall all my life attach greater value to these two little books, their beloved relics, than if I had found a mine of gold or silver."

On the 13th he convoked the council again, and " in the name of the Superior-General of all the Missions of our Society in these regions," he says, " I began by planting the first stake for a new cabin. This corresponds to our French custom of laying the foundation stone of a new building." The exact place where this precious stake was driven is hard to determine.

" On the 15th I give my Farewell Feast. On the 16th we arrived at the entrance to a little lake in a great basin that is half dried up; I taste the water from a spring of which these people dare not drink, as they say there is an evil spirit in it which renders it foul. Upon tasting it, I find it to be a spring of salt water, and indeed we made some salt from it, as natural as that which comes from the sea, and are carrying a sample of it to Quebec. The lake is rich in salmon trout and other fish." Later on he told the Dutch

SIMON LE MOYNE.

at Albany of these salt springs, but old Dominie Megapolensis wrote to the burghers of New Amsterdam that it was "a Jesuit lie." The lie is there yet and productive of vast revenues in the world of business.

The route which he took on his return may be roughly indicated as follows: Starting a little S. E. of what is now Manlius, he followed the trail leading to the Senecas as far as the Onondaga River. Then descending to Onondaga Lake, he stopped near one of the salt springs, north of the present Syracuse. Continuing down this lake and stream, he reached the Seneca, which is called there the Oswego. Three leagues below the mouth of the Onondaga, he passed its junction with the Oneida. The fishing village where he halted was probably near the present village of Phœnix. Still descending the Oswego, he apparently followed it to where it empties into Lake Ontario, and coasting its eastern shores, he went to "the place assigned for our residence and for a French settlement." It may have been either the mouth of Salmon River or Sackett's Harbor—both good landing points of strategic importance.

The painstaking editor of the new *Relations* makes these suggestions.

On the 19th he is on his way down the river. "On the 20th we arrive at the great Lake Ontario." The journey homeward is of course quicker, for they are going with the stream and over the rapids.

"On the 6th our Sault St. Louis frightens my men. They put me ashore, four leagues above the settlement of Montreal, and God gives me strength to reach that place *before noon* and to celebrate Holy Mass, *of which I had been deprived during my entire journey.* We arrived at Quebec only on the eleventh day of the month of September of this year 1654."

Just before reaching Montreal an incident occurred of which Le Moyne made no report. He probably suppressed it to avert a panic, for it looked like treachery on the part

85

of the Indians and as if their plea for peace had been only a trick and part of a plot for a general massacre. It was found out afterwards from the Iroquois themselves, and Charveloix gives us an account of it.

Le Moyne was in a canoe with two Onondagas. The Hurons and Algonquins followed. As they approached Montreal they were surprised to see themselves surrounded by several canoes full of Mohawks, who poured a volley upon them from their muskets. The Hurons and Algonquins were all killed as well as one of the Onondagas. Father Le Moyne was taken and bound as a prisoner of war, and the Onondaga was told to return home, but he protested that he could not abandon the missionary, who had been confided to him by the sachems of his canton, and he menaced the Mohawks with all the wrath of the upper Iroquois. At first they laughed at his threat, but when they saw he would not flinch they unbound their prisoner and put him in the hands of his faithful conductor, who led him to Montreal. The chief who was at the head of these Mohawks was known as the Flemish Bastard; the same savage who was concerned later on in the murder of Father Garreau.

Quite undisturbed by this unpleasant occurrence, which he understood merely indicated the state of the Mohawk and not of the Onondaga mind on the question of peace, he proceeded to the authorities of Quebec to assure them that the upper Iroquois were peacefully disposed, and that a mission could be attempted at Onondaga. In consequence, Dablon and Chaumonot were sent down to begin the work of evangelizing Western New York.

This was the end of Le Moyne's first diplomatic mission among the Iroquois. He would return again soon.

The results of his embassy to the Onondagas were eminently satisfactory, but its very success gave rise to difficulties in another quarter. The Mohawks were indignant that the upper Iroquois should have received this mark of confidence from the French, and they demanded that an envoy should be sent to them also.

The request was, however, looked upon with suspicion. They were the Indians who had murdered Father Jogues eight years before, and possibly this was only a trick to capture another distinguished victim. They were the fiercest and most treacherous of all the Iroquois and not at all as easily managed as their kinsmen, the Onondagas. However, they could not be set aside lightly, and something had to be done to keep them in humor. Le Moyne was, therefore, asked to again " put his life in the hands of Almighty God." He did not hesitate, but went down to do his best, and after a dangerous journey found himself in the very town which had been sanctified by the blood of his friend, Isaac Jogues.

He does not seem to have kept a diary of this expedition, or at least it has not come down to us. All that we have is the succinct notice left by Father De Quen in the *Relations* of 1656, and is as follows:

" It was necessary to send a Father to the Agnieronnon Iroquois, and the lot *fortunately* falling on Father Le Moyne, he left Montreal on the 17th of August, with twelve Iroquois and two Frenchmen. The route is one of precipices, lakes, rivers, etc. . . . They were wrecked in an impetuous torrent, which carried them into a bay, where they found the gentlest calm in the world. Some days after, hunger overtook them, and they were sometimes forced to lie down at night with no refreshment but boiled water *mixed with earth and clay*. Wild fruits lost their bitterness and seemed delicious, hunger serving excellently to sweeten them." What this route was, we have no means of knowing.

" He reached the village of Agniée (Auriesville) on September 17, and was received with extraordinary cordiality." The usual presents were given and received. The finest of them, we are told, represented a sun, and was composed of

6,000 porcelain beads " to let the Sun illumine them in the darkest night "; but, add the *Relations,* " these nations are composed only of tricksters, and yet we must trust ourselves to their fickleness and surrender ourselves to their cruelty. Father Isaac Jogues was killed by those traitors while they were showing him most love."

It is curious that we have no description by Le Moyne of the sacred place where his beloved friend was martyred. Did he search for some relic? There can scarcely be any doubt that he did. We saw what delight he manifested in Onondaga when he recovered the little books belonging to Brébeuf. Jogues was his devoted friend also, and it is more than likely that he sought for the body of Goupil and some mementoes of Jogues, and that when he returned to Quebec he had some relics with him. For a man who so carefully noted the physical peculiarities of the places in which he happened to be, we would imagine also that he would have described in detail the village of Ossernenon, with which Jogues' letters had made all the Fathers familiar. Perhaps he did, but the valuable document was probably lost when the Society was suppressed. A few years afterward Father Raffeix, who came with Tracy in the famous raid, wrote in detail about the kind of dwellings that the Iroquois made for themselves at Ossernenon; their storehouses of grain, their reservoirs of water, etc. There are illustrations of them to be found in the *Relations.*

It is interesting to read that after reaching Ossernenon, Le Moyne went down to see the Dutch at Manhattan. " He was received with great demonstrations of affection." The old minister, Dominie Megapolensis, Jogues' friend, was there, and made much of Le Moyne. The welcome was all the more notable because the Dutch were having fierce encounters with the neighboring savages. Le Moyne tells us that " some Indians living near *Manhathe,* the chief town of New Belgium, in a quarrel with a Dutchman had come to blows and had fared badly, leaving two or three of their

PETER STUYVESANT.

men dead on the spot. To revenge this grievance, the Indians rallied to the number of about two hundred and set fire to a score of small farms scattered here and there, slaughtering those who resisted and carrying the rest, men, women and children, about a hundred and fifty in all, into captivity."

It must have required courage and skill to get into Manhattan while this was going on, for the fight was still raging when Le Moyne was there. He says: "We do not know how it terminated."

Governor Kieft, who had rescued Jogues, was no longer in America. He had been called back to Holland, and when Le Moyne arrived, old Peter Stuyvesant was stumping around the Stadt Huys on his "silver leg." The burghers were not then in their historic good humor, for testy Peter was a hard master. Apart from his autocratic manner in dealing with his Dutch compatriots, he was busy persecuting Baptists and Quakers and Lutherans; so that it is doubtful if Le Moyne dared to walk down in his cassock to the Fort to present himself to the doughty Peter. But the New York Dutch were always partial to the Jesuits; and, besides, Le Moyne was an official of the Governor of Quebec and, of course, had to be treated civilly. As we have seen, he describes their treatment of him as affectionate. How far this affection showed itself we do not know, but doubtless he enjoyed the Governor's hospitality just as Druillettes a few years before had been welcomed by the Puritan notables of Boston; but of this we have no detailed information, nor of what he did in *Manhathe*. He had, however, much to see and deplore.

New Amsterdam had just then received the charter as a *city;* but, beyond the charter, it had little else to boast of. It had still the motley population which Jogues had seen a few years before, when no less than eighteen different languages and dialects were heard in the streets. "An ominous feature," says President Roosevelt in his "New

York," " was the abundance of negro slaves and brutal-looking black savages, brought by slave traders and pirates from the gold coasts of Africa, with a-plenty also of low, shiftless and criminal whites. There was considerable display of riches among the well-to-do, but grimy poverty prevailed among the poor." On an etching of the town as it was in those days we can make out the Church of St. Nicholas, with the Governor's house near it, both towering above the walls of the fort. There are some well-built houses of brick or wood, but also a great number of miserable huts to shelter the larger part of the population. The inevitable windmill is at one end of the town, and the equally unavoidable tavern at the other, while midway we see the impressive West India Company's storehouses, with their characteristic Dutch gables ending in steps at the roof. A huge gallows looms ominously on the shore, and the figure of a malefactor is seen swinging from it. Pirates abounded in those days, and usually ended their career in the air. Some stragglers roam along the beach, and near by are two or three small craft. That is all New York was when Le Moyne saw it. Eleven years afterward the English were to come into possession, and then such as he would no longer be free to ramble at will.

After finishing his work at Manhattan, Le Moyne returned to Ossernenon, where he narrowly escaped death at the hands of a drunken or crazy Indian. The savage stood above him with a tomahawk to cleave his skull, when a quick-witted squaw ran up and exclaimed: " Kill my dog instead." Whereupon the madman grew calm and, striking off the poor animal's head with a single blow, carried it around in triumph as Le Moyne's. The incident was not reassuring, and a day or so later a Huron Christian was killed on suspicion of having revealed some of the Iroquois plans to the missionary. Other things happened, which showed that his life was hanging by a hair, and although

90

the winter was far advanced, he determined to set out for Montreal.

The journey was a hard one. Fearing the Algonquins, his party abandoned their canoes and baggage and took to the woods. It was a pathless pine forest, full of marshes of stagnant and half-frozen water. The sky was overcast, and they lost their way. Night came on, and they halted. They slept in the swamps on the roots of trees and some moss. The cold was severe, for it was November, and they were in the North Woods. The following day found them up to their knees in a bog the most of the time. Tramping on, they came to a deep and swift river—which we cannot identify—and they had to build a raft to cross it, laboring all the while without a morsel to eat. On the third day they climbed the trees to reconnoitre. There was no indication of where they were, but toward evening they came to a stream which they recognized. The discovery gave them courage, although they were then almost dying of hunger. Finally, after the fourth day of despair and weariness and starvation, they reached the St. Lawrence and saw Montreal on the other side. They had no means of crossing that wide expanse, but by means of a fire which they lighted and by discharging their muskets they attracted the notice of their friends, and a canoe was sent to take them over to the place they had left three months before.

Le Moyne had promised the Mohawks to give them missionaries, so that they might stand on the same plane as the Onondagas, and preparations were immediately begun for that purpose. Meantime, however, the news came that not only had their rivals been favored with missionaries, but that a colony of Frenchmen had also been established on Lake Onondaga. That was another affront to them, or, perhaps, they saw in it a scheme to divert all the trade in furs down the St. Lawrence, instead of through the Mohawk country to the Hudson. They were furious in con-

91

sequence and demanded similar treatment, or else there would be war.

Again Le Moyne had to go down to pacify them. After his narrow escape from being treacherously slain, it required no small determination to comply with the request. But he did not hesitate. We have no details about this second visit, but as the fifty Frenchmen who were sent to Onondaga had exhausted all the available resources the French could command at the time, and a similar favor could not be granted to the Mohawks, it is clear that Le Moyne must have had a difficult task to keep the savages in good humor, while he played his dilatory tactics with them, and at the same time tried not to betray the exhausted and helpless condition of the colony. Had the Indians suspected the defenceless state of Quebec, they would have soon made an end of it. He eventually returned to Quebec, very likely following the same route on which he had a few months before undergone so many hardships and dangers.

Evidently he had not succeeded in calming the Mohawks, for he had to go back a third time to Ossernenon, and this last expedition came near putting an end to his career. Outwardly he was treated with the greatest consideration, but it was all pretense, for he discovered from a friendly Indian that, at a general convention of the Mohawks, it was resolved to kill every Frenchman they could lay hands on. The Dutch at Fort Orange and Manhattan heard of it and began to make arrangements to send him back to Quebec by sea, and apparently he went down to consult the Governor about the plan. For one reason or another, possibly because the Indians had discovered that their designs had leaked out, or they had been warned by the French Governor not to harm the envoy, the escape by sea, which would have irritated the Mohawks all the more, was deemed unwise or unnecessary, and the Mohawks themselves conducted him in safety to the St. Lawrence.

Suddenly, however, all hopes of humoring the Iroquois by

AS SEEN BY LE MOYNE.

diplomacy came to an end. The settlement of the fifty Frenchmen on Lake Onondaga had collapsed. Discovering a plot to massacre them, they had all decamped in the night and, after much suffering, made their way to Montreal. Furious at the revelation of their treachery, the Onondagas again dug up the hatchet, and the Mohawks, having no longer any hopes of a trading-post among them, joined their friends, and for two years the St. Lawrence witnessed many a bloody fray. The villages of the tribes in alliance with the French were given over to the flames, white and red men were massacred, and Montreal was besieged by the angry Iroquois.

One day in July, while the storm was at its height, a number of Iroquois canoes were seen coming down the river toward Montreal. The garrison rushed to the stockade and watched them as they approached the shore. In front was a flag of truce. The savage warriors in paint and feathers stepped out as if assured of a friendly reception. The gate was thrown open and, followed by four French captives, the Iroquois advanced into the town. The spokesman was a redoubtable Cayuga chief, named Saonchiowaga, whom, years after, Father de Carheil converted. Solemnly he broke the bonds of the French prisoners, and promised the liberation of others still in the Onondaga country. Then he began his address, offering his presents meanwhile. Coming to the fifth present, he said: " This is to bring the Frenchman back to us. We still keep his mat; his house is still standing at Ganentaa. His fire is still lighted; and his fields have been tilled and await his return for his hand to gather the harvest." Then, altering his tone and raising aloft the last belt, he exclaimed: " A black gown must come to us; otherwise there will be no peace. On his coming depends the life of twenty Frenchmen at Onondaga," and he placed in the Governor's hand a leaf of a book, on the margin of which the twenty unfortunate captives had written their names.

Was it a trick to lure other Frenchmen to their death? Opinion was divided. Le Moyne offered to go to test the sincerity of the offer, and so for the fifth time he started for the country of the Iroquois. " It was the happiest day of my life," he wrote, and on July 21, 1661, he left Montreal for Onondaga.

The day after their departure from Montreal they were attacked by some Mohawks, but a battle was averted. " Three days afterward," writes Le Moyne, " when we had crossed the rapids, twenty-four Oneidas, having discovered us, advanced upon us in the night. They charged on us, weapons in hand, and carried manacles with them to make us prisoners. Some of them pressed around me, brandishing their hatchets and knives as if they were about to kill me. I was released by some presents which the Onondagas gave. At Lake Ontario we met more Oneidas on the warpath, and later on a detachment of forty on their way to Montreal to avenge the insult against their chief Otreonate, who had been imprisoned there." Such was his entry into Onondaga. It was enough to appal a stouter heart, but he kept on nevertheless.

The prospects were brighter when he approached Onondaga. Six miles from the town he was received in the usual way, with shouts of joy and offering of presents. It was very likely all pretense, but, making the best of the situation, he assumed his air of bravado, which, he knew, impressed the Indians, and on the 12th of August was solemnly received by the chiefs of the Onondaga, Cayuga and Seneca tribes. He delivered his presents, concluded the peace and then began to preach the doctrines of Christianity. The famous Garagontié had fitted up his own cabin as a chapel. " It was rude indeed," writes Le Moyne, " but Our Lord, who deigns to veil Himself under the forms of bread and wine, will not disdain to dwell beneath a roof of bark, and the woods of our forest are not less precious in His eyes than the cedars of Lebanon,—since where He is, there is paradise."

Garagontié, whose name means " the sun that advances," was the Indian to whom this renewal of friendly relations was due. He stands pre-eminent in those bloody days as an example of what grace can effect, though its workings in his case were extraordinarily slow. It is possible that he was not a chief or even a sachem, though Lafitau and Charlevoix maintain that he was, confounding him, it is suggested, with his brother, yet he exerted a marvelous power over the Onondagas. Strange to say, he never came near the chapel, though intimate with Chaumonot and Dablon, who had been there three years before. But he was the steadfast friend of the Christians, both red and white, especially after the flight of the colonists. He rescued or ransomed them from the other cantons, and at one time had twenty-four of them, whom he assembled night and morning for prayer at the sound of the bell. It was at his instance that the Cayuga chief went to Montreal to negotiate peace, and he himself started on the same errand as soon as Le Moyne arrived. Again and again he returned to Quebec, struggling hopelessly against the restlessness or the treachery of his people, and constantly entreating the French for missionaries. Yet all this time he was not baptized, although for sixteen years he had been constantly concerned with the planting of the Church in his country. Suddenly, in 1670, at a council in Quebec, which had been convened on account of an outbreak between the Senecas and Ottawas, he exclaimed: " As to the faith which Onontio wishes to see everywhere diffused, I publicly profess it; I renounce polygamy, superstition, dreams, and every kind of sin." Bishop Laval happened to be present. He questioned the chief; found him sufficiently instructed, and resolved to baptize and confirm him. The ceremony took place in the Cathedral, the Governor standing as his god-father, and the daughter of the Intendant as his god-mother.

The church was crowded with Indians from every tribe on the St. Lawrence. The Governor de Courcelles gave him his own name of Daniel, and every honor that could be conferred was bestowed on the distinguished convert. This wonderful Indian continued till the end to be the friend and adviser of the missionaries. He died in 1676 in the arms of Father de Lamberville.

Le Moyne had often sore need of his protection, for it is certain that the chiefs had given orders to kill the priest. There were twenty French captives among the Iroquois at the time, and from them it was learned later how badly Le Moyne was treated. On one occasion, for instance, a number of Onondagas threw themselves upon him, stripped him naked, dragged him through the streets, hooting and yelling, made him mount the scaffold, and then lighted fires around him and prepared to burn him to death. For one reason or another, however, they did not carry out their purpose. Later on an Indian induced the chiefs to come and set fire to the chapel. On another occasion he was bound to a stake, and his legs were so frightfully burned with torches that it took six months to heal the wounds. Then an Indian broke into his chapel and assaulted him, in an attempt to rob him of his cassock, which he was bidden in a dream to procure. Another dreamer made an attempt to tear down the cross from the altar. Le Moyne saw him and leaped in front of him to prevent the act. He was just about to receive a tomahawk on his skull when someone seized the uplifted arm of the savage and prevented the murder. Indeed, conditions became so desperate there that he had to take refuge among the Cayugas, who were milder than the other Iroquois. They received him with cheers, and he repaid their affection by healing many of their sick. He remained a month with them until the return of Garagontié from Montreal enabled him to resume his work among the Onondagas.

What kind of work was he doing? Nothing with the

braves, of course. They were always on the war-path, and would not listen to him when they happened to be at home, but an epidemic of smallpox was raging, and great numbers of the little children were baptized and sent to heaven. There were captives there also from the various tribes, many of whom were Christians, and the missionary instructed them and steadied them in their faith. The Christian Huron women were especially remarkable for the devices they used to visit the priest, traveling long distances and enduring great hardships to receive the sacraments. The French captives also needed his ministrations. Their lot was most miserable, but, according to the testimony of Le Moyne, nearly all led lives of most exalted virtue in the midst of the horrors they saw around them.

In the *Relations* of 1660 several letters of these unfortunate men are given. Some of them were written on birchbark or scraps of powder paper. One was from a mere lad, François Hertel by name, whose family was conspicuous in Canadian history. He himself afterward became famous. He was held captive by the Mohawks, and Le Moyne describes him as of "comely appearance and delicate, and the sole delight of his mother." Writing to Le Moyne, he says:

"Reverend Father: On the very day you departed from Three Rivers, I was captured, toward three o'clock in the afternoon, by four of the lower Iroquois. The reason why, to my misfortune, I did not make them kill me, was that I feared I was not well enough prepared to die. If you should come hither and if I should have the happiness to confess, I believe I could go back with you. I pray you to take pity on my mother in her great affliction. You know the love she bears me. From a Frenchman captured at Three Rivers, I have learned that she is well and takes comfort in the thought that I shall be near you."

Later on he adds: "Dear Father, I pray you bless the hand that writes to you, which has had one finger burnt in a calumet as a reparation to the majesty of God, whom I

7   97

have offended. The other hand has a thumb cut off, but do not tell my poor mother. Will you come to see me before winter? I have had the consolation of finding one of your breviaries here, and it serves me in my prayers."

He writes also to his " very dear and honored mother," and tells her: " I know my capture must have greatly afflicted you. I ask your forgiveness for having disobeyed you. My sins have brought me to my present condition. Your prayers and M. de St. Quentin's and my sister's have restored me to life."

" Your poor FANCHON."

Letters from other captives tell of the sufferings to which they were subjected; how they were made to dance around a fire, into which they were kicked by the savages as one would kick a ball, etc. " I must give you tidings of Pierre Recontre," says another; " he died like a saint. I saw him while he was being tortured, and he never said aught but these words: ' My God, take pity on me,' which he repeated until he ceased to breathe.

" Did you know Louis Guimont who was captured this summer? He was beaten to death with clubs and iron rods, but yet he did nothing but pray to God, so that the Iroquois cut away his upper and lower lips entirely. What a horrible sight! And still he ceased not to pray, which so irritated the savages that they tore his heart throbbing with life out of his breast and threw it in his face. We are a pitiful sight to behold! We are glad to eat the scraps left by the dogs. Father Le Moyne is said to be at Onondaga negotiating peace, but he will not succeed. Nor will the Dutch help us any more, as it costs too much. They tell the Iroquois to cut off our arms and legs and kill us where they find us, so as no longer to be burdened with us."

Le Moyne at this time was doing all he could to arrange for the ransom of these unhappy captives. It was a sore trial when he succeeded at first in obtaining the freedom of only nine who set out with Garagontié, but even they came near never reaching Montreal. On their way they met a band of Onondagas, with French scalps at their belts, while the chief wore the cassock of a priest, the Abbé Le Maitre, a Sulpitian, whom he had murdered near Montreal. The Senecas in the party conveying the captives refused to proceed. "How can we present ourselves to the French," they said to the Onondagas, "after what you have done? Garagontié forced them, however, to continue their journey; but they were again discouraged by meeting a band of Oneidas on the war-path, but Garagontié induced them to turn their arms against some other enemies, and so he finally reached the French fort with his liberated captives. He was received with great rejoicings and returned to his own country, laden with gifts and told with more than usual eloquence of the good dispositions of the French. His return to Onondaga gave some respite to the sufferings of Le Moyne and the captives, but still there was no appearance of willingness to set free the other prisoners.

Winter passed by, and spring was ending, when at last his entreaties prevailed. He himself was to lead back all the Frenchmen, with the exception of one to whom liberty was not given, though his name was Liberté.

"On the last day of August, 1662, the Father made his appearance in a canoe below the Falls of St. Louis, having around him all the happy rescued ones and a score of Onondagas who from being enemies had become their boatmen. They landed amid the cheers and embraces of all the French of Montreal, and, following Father Le Moyne, proceeded to the church to thank God."

Trusting in the good dispositions of the Onondagas, or willing to run the risk, plans were forthwith made to establish regular missions in their country. Le Moyne, of course, was eager to go back, but the ceaseless wars made it impossible. In 1664 we find the old hero asking for the Onondaga mission, but his health was shattered. He was near the end. He fell sick of a fever and died in 1665. The record of the death of this great man merely recites that "Father Le Moyne expired at Cape Madeleine," a place opposite Three Rivers, which rejoices now in its handsome churches and thriving population. We suppose that he was buried there.

Garagontié was then at Quebec, and when he heard that Le Moyne had gone on his long journey, he delivered in Indian fashion a eulogy of his departed friend who had done so much for the Onondaga nation:

"Ondessonk," he exclaimed, "dost thou hear me from the land of souls to which thou hast passed so quickly? It was thou who didst so often lay thy head on the scaffolds of the Mohawks; thou who hast gone so bravely into their very fires to rescue so many of the French; thou who didst bear peace and tranquillity wherever thou didst pass and hast made believers wherever thou didst dwell. We have seen thee on our council mats decide peace and war; our cabins became too small when thou didst enter, and our villages were too contracted when thou wast there, so great was the crowd drawn by thy words. Thou hast so often taught us that the life of misery is followed by one of eternal bliss, now that thou enjoyest it what reason have we for grief? But we deplore thee, because in losing thee we have lost our father and protector. Nevertheless we will be consoled, because thou continuest to be so in heaven, and because thou hast found in that abode of bliss the infinite joy, of which thou hast so often spoken to us."

CLAUDE DABLON.

ONE of the most prominent figures in the first mission to the Onondagas was Claude d'Ablon, or Doblon, or Dablon, or Biblin, as it appears in its various forms. His own handwriting is atrocious and might be made to spell anything. He was born at Dieppe. We are not sure whether it was in 1618 or 1619, or whether it was January or February—the records are lost—but after a brilliant course of studies and teaching in the great colleges of his native country, he landed in Canada when about thirty-six years of age, in 1654 or 1655.

He had been longing from his youth for the Canadian missions. Reading of Paraguay, he saw in his dreams similar conditions in the wild woods of North America. As a preparation for his work, he studied music and was an adept on several instruments. He played *fort bien,* wrote his companion, and although it is not said that the Iroquois swam after his boat as he discoursed on his flute or flagelet while sailing up the Oswego or over Lake Ganentaa, yet his music did wonders with those wild natives. He did not know a word of Iroquois when he got into the canoe at Montreal with Father Chaumonot to paddle up to the Onondaga country—he had no time, for he was commandeered as soon as he arrived,—but he had a power with his instruments which even the eloquent Chaumonot did not possess of drawing those fierce men and women into the little bark chapels, where Chaumonot taught, while Dablon followed or preceded with the marvelous instruments, on which the Indians heard their own weird melodies reproduced.

We do not know if his music enraptured the first great convention in which they took part when they came to Onondaga, though it is probable it did; but in the chapel at Ganentaa and elsewhere the Indians swarmed night and

101

day to listen to him, leaving him scarcely any time for his other work, and they readily lent themselves to learn the hymns which he taught them. The students of American musical archæology, if there is such a thing, will find in these Indian choirs on the Oswego something to interest them. They are our beginnings of ecclesiastical music.

He did not know what was before him when he started on that journey up the St. Lawrence, nor did he ever dream of the terrifying conditions under which he would come down again the following winter. We give a few extracts from his diary.

After describing the Lachine Rapids and telling how the St. Lawrence widens out into lakes on its course, he says: " On the 10th we erected an altar and what might be called a living chapel, for it was formed of foliage. Wine we made from the native grapes, which we found in abundance on the wild vines." They saw Mohawks tracking them, and on the 13th provisions gave out, and " the hunters and fishers *went to seek their living and ours* in the woods and streams. On the 14th we ate a dead cow which had been drowned. The flesh smelled badly, but appetite is an excellent cook, and, although he flavored this dish with neither pepper nor salt nor cloves, yet he made us relish it highly." Eight bears are killed on the 15th, and on the 17th, thirty. " One of the ceremonies of the feast that followed this great slaughter was the drinking of bear's fat, after the meal, as one drinks hippocras in France. Then they all rubbed themselves from head to foot with the oil."

" On the 24th we reached Lake Ontario. Such a scene of awe-inspiring beauty I have never beheld; nothing but islands and huge masses of rocks, as large as cities, all covered with cedars and firs. Towards evening we crossed over from the North to the South side." This was at the head of the Thousand Islands. They had kept on the upper side out of respect for the Mohawks.

They entered the Otithatangue (Salmon River) on the

CLAUDE DABLON.

29th, and the kettle of welcome was offered them there. Dablon noted how the streams were filled with fish, and he carefully described the species. He laments that the Onondagas were not quite what was expected. They were not thinking of embracing the faith at all. It was at best only a business speculation, or, perhaps, a deep-laid plan to strike a blow at the French, for he found, after the first welcome was over, that the Indians appeared discontented. They were glad enough to have the black robes, but wanted something more. They wanted a colony of Frenchmen as well. Why, they would not say, for there was probably a dark design underneath, but on February 29, 1656, a notable council was held declaring that " they had been waiting for three years and were tired of so many postponements." But it was midwinter, and how could anyone at that season inform the people of Quebec of what the Indians wanted? No one would undertake the journey. Besides, it was the hunting season. A novena of Masses was made, in honor of St. John the Baptist, the patron of the mission, and lo! on the ninth day, contrary to all expectation, an Indian named " John Baptist, the *first adult baptized in perfect health,* offered to lead the expedition."

The precious diary of Father Dablon, describing this journey, which virtually meant *walking* in midwinter through the forest from what is now Syracuse to Quebec, records an act of heroism equal to anything we have in missionary annals. It may be found in the *Relations,* xlii. We give a few extracts.

" On the first day we advanced five leagues in spring rather than winter weather, but it soon changed, and we were forced by rain to spend a day and two nights in the woods in a house without doors, without windows and without walls.

" On the fourth of March, after proceeding six short leagues, we camped on the shore of the lake. This was a hard day's journey *through almost uninterrupted snow and*

103

water up to our knees. A day and two nights were spent in this halting place. We wanted to cross the lake, but it was beginning to thaw. However, we accomplished a long league and a half on ice, after which it was a pleasure to walk over the soft snow.

" On the seventh of March, after a light meal, we started in the morning and *walked till evening without eating.* We were unable to cross the great Lake (Ontario), because of the blocks of ice on the shore, but after hunting some bustards, which make their winter retreat there in a little swamp, we made ours in the same place for the night.

" The ninth day was hard. We proceeded over a frozen pool with our feet always in the water, as it had rained in the morning.

" The next day we were forced to cross a vast prairie flooded with water, to make our way over soft and half-melted snow, through woods and across ponds; we waded thrice through rivers. Finally, after walking all day, we found towards evening that we had advanced only three leagues. *In weariness God is strong and in bitterness we find Him indeed sweet.*

" On the 11th day we walked nearly all day over the frozen surface of the great Lake, but with our feet constantly in the water; the ice cracking under us. We were two or three leagues from land. After making seven good leagues we were stopped by rain, which did not cease during the night or next day. It so increased in violence during the second night that *lying as we were on the ground we soon found ourselves stretched in water. . . . Under such conditions a night would seem long indeed did not God illumine our gloom. At any rate the most patient were the best bedded.*

" We left our position after two days and three nights. Our diet was bread and water, but the savages just then shot a deer and some wildcats which restored our vigor.

" We passed all the 17th day with feet in the water;

104

weather rough and road frightful. At times we had to climb with feet and hands over mountains of snow, again to crawl over great ice blocks, pass over marshes, and then to fell trees for bridging rivers, in order to cross streams and avoid precipices. At the day's end we had made barely four short leagues.

" On the 19th, as we were pursuing our course over the ice of the great Lake, it opened under one of my feet. I came off better than a poor Indian, who was swallowed up and lost in the water beyond all possibility of rescue. Having escaped these dangers, we entered an extremely difficult road, with rocks on either side as high as towers and so steep that one makes his way over them with hands as well as feet. After this we were again forced to run three leagues over the ice, never stopping, through fear of breaking through, and then to pass the night on a rock opposite Otondiata. (Beauchamp identifies this as the present Grenadier Island.)

" We made a canoe for crossing the lake; a part of our number (we were twenty) went over first. On nearing the other shore it was struck by an ice floe; and there they were all in the water, some catching at the battered canoe, and others at the ice. They were all saved, and after repairing the boat they sent it back to us that we might follow. We did so on the night of the twenty-first of March. *We had eaten for dinner only a very few roots, yet we were forced to lie down supperless* on a bed of pebbles, with the stars above us, and *under the shelter of an icy north wind*. On the following night we lay more comfortably; our bed being of snow, and the day after, rain attended us on a frightful road over rocks fearful to behold, both for their height and size and as dangerous to descend as they were difficult to climb.

" On the 25th we found a canoe, or rather a whole treetrunk hollowed out, which God seems to have put in our hands for completing the passage of the Lake without fear of the ice.

"On the morrow seven of us embarked in this dugout, and in the evening reached the mouth of the Lake, which ends in a waterfall and turbulent rapids. Here God showed us still another special favor; for on leaving the dugout we found a fairly good bark canoe with which we accomplished forty leagues in a day and a half, not having made more than that on foot during the three preceding weeks.

"Finally, on the thirtieth of March, we arrived at Montreal, having left Onondaga on the second."

Such was the Indian fashion of sending ambassadors. It is inconceivable how the human frame could stand such exposure, especially in the case of Father Dablon, who was only beginning his career.

He succeeded in persuading the Governor-General to send the colonists to Onondaga. What helped him was that refusal to gratify those upper Iroquois might be a motive for a new war, and, moreover, such a settlement might serve to bring the Mohawks to terms. So far they had a monopoly of the trade. Even the other Iroquois tribes could not sell their furs without carrying them through the Mohawk country to Fort Orange and Manhattan.

By the month of May all was ready. With Dablon was the famous Ménard, who was to give an example of heroism in his subsequent career as a missionary, of a kind peculiarly his own, which distinguishes him as a most extraordinary apostle. Father Le Mercier went with the party as Superior, but his stay in New York was brief; Father Frémin's name also appears on the list. Later on, Frémin returned to his post and was one of the conspicuous figures in the second effort to establish the missions. There were also three coadjutor brothers, Ambrose Broard, Joseph Boursier and a third whose name has unfortunately been lost. Ragueneau followed them some months later.

Dablon's return to Onondaga was, of course, not marked

by the same amount of hardship and danger which had attended his journey down the river a few months before, though it was not without suffering. They started from Quebec May 16th in a flotilla of canoes, containing, altogether, fifty Frenchmen, under the command of Dupuis, and many Onondagas, Senecas and Hurons. A larger bark led the rest, and from its bow floated a snow-white banner on which was embroidered the name of Jesus. It was not until July 11th that they reached Lake Onondaga, over which they sailed with as much display as they could make to impress the savages. Cannons and musketry roared their salute as the barks approached the shore; the banner fluttered in the breeze, and songs and cheers resounded over the waters. It was a wonderful sight in the midst of the wilderness. Banquets and speeches followed, and then the French proceeded to erect their blockhouse at Ganentaa, making it the headquarters of the settlers and missionaries. The site is what is known now as Liverpool.

The position of the colony was found to be delightful, as it was almost the centre of the four Iroquois nations, and access to it was easy by canoe from other lakes and rivers. It was filled with fish; eels especially were plentiful, and " as for game, it is always abundant in the winter, and in the spring turtle doves from all the country round flock thither in such great numbers that they are easily caught in nets." In the missionary's letter there is a curious study of rattlesnakes, whose numbers around the salt spring, which they seem to have preferred to the fresh one, must have added an element of discomfort to this Garden of Eden.

" The Jesuits' Well " is still an object of interest, though there is no notice taken of the fact that the Governor of Canada, De Lauzon, had very generously made a grant to the Jesuits of ten square leagues running eastward from the lake. A manuscript copy of the concession is still to be found in the archives of St. Mary's College, Montreal. It was an open-handed gift, but it was easily eclipsed by the grants which the Dutch and English were accustomed to bestow. Thus the jolly old minister, Dominie Dellius, Peter Schuyler and three others got all the land from Fonda to Utica, on condition of one beaver skin for five years. Captain Evans accepted magnanimously all the land on the west side of the Hudson, for forty miles in length and twenty in depth, in all about 650,000 acres, for a quit rent of twenty shillings, and one fat buck yearly. The Van Rensselaers took twenty-four miles square, and Livingston a tract of sixteen by twenty-four miles. The Jesuits, however, in enumerating their holdings, never included the New York grant, which Thwaites thinks was in keeping with their usual prudence.

Thanks to the new accession, the mission was now inaugurated on a grander scale, and everything at the beginning promised well. During the two years of its existence Dablon, like the others, went from place to place, endeavoring to plant the faith. Nothing more than the usual dangers and privations had to be faced during that period, and in his usual lighthearted but observant way he took note of all he saw, and has left us a very exact and graphic account of the physical conditions of the country at that time. Finally the disaster came. Like the rest, he saw the coming danger, and embarked with his companions when they flitted away like ghosts from the land which they had entered with such high hopes two years before. Ragueneau tells us that wonderful story. The figure of Dablon disappears somewhat in the throng of fugitives, but no doubt his experience on the river was of great service in directing the course and helping the party to reach Montreal in safety.

In 1659 we find Dablon in the Residence at Quebec, but in 1660 a wandering Algonquin spoke to him of a number of savage tribesmen far up near Hudson Bay, which in those days was considered to be the North Sea. Thither he and the great Druillettes, the apostle of Maine, determined to direct their steps.

CLAUDE DABLON.

" We have long known," say the *Relations,* " that we have the North Sea behind us which is contiguous to that of China, and all we have to do is to find an entrance to it. In that region lies the famous bay, 70 leagues wide by 260 long, which was first discovered by *Husson,* who gave it his name but won no glory from it other than that of having first opened a way which ends in unknown empire. Upon this bay are found, at certain seasons of the year, many nations, known by the general name of Kilistinons.

" During the past winter, a Nippisirien chief entertained us with a full account of the number of these peoples, the situation and nature of the country, and especially with a description of a general fair in the following summer to which our savages of Quebec and Tadoussac were invited. It was a fine opportunity for us to go in person and gain information which we had hitherto obtained only through untrustworthy sources. Such information is important as well for an exact knowledge of the longitudes and latitudes of the new country—data on which is based in part the assumption that a passage to the Sea of Japan is found there—as also for seeing, on the spot, what means there are for laboring effectively for the conversion of those peoples.

" To this end Fathers Gabriel Druillettes and Claude Dablon with the greater part of our savages started from here in the month of May last; the first Father proposing to winter there to obtain at leisure all information requisite for assuring that mission's success."

It may be remarked here that this plain statement of the purpose of the expedition disposes of Parkman's gibe, that the Jesuit missionaries of this epoch had in great measure lost the apostolic spirit of their predecessors, and were chiefly desirous of making scientific explorations. The missions were indeed scientific and had been from the beginning, but science was only a means to an end. That end was at all times the salvation of souls.

Dablon in an interesting letter tells us of the result of this

109

expedition. We give a few extracts. It is too long to quote in its entirety, and the student may find it in the forty-sixth volume of the *Relations*. It is dated " From Nekouba, one hundred leagues from Tadoussac, in the forest, on the way to the North Sea, this second of July, 1661," and begins with *"Transivimus per eremum terribilem et maximum,* we can well say with Moses. We have passed through forests which might easily have frightened the most confident of travellers—whether by the vast extent of these boundless solitudes *where God only is to be found,* or by the ruggedness of the ways, which are alike rough and dangerous, since one must journey over naught but precipices and over bottomless gulfs where one struggles for his life in a frail shell, against whirlpools capable of wrecking larger vessels. At last here we are, with God's help, half-way to the North Sea. Enclosed is a little journal, written now on the surface of a rock, amid the roar of the falls, and now at the foot of a tree, when one could be found large enough to shelter us from the sun's rays, which here are well nigh unbearable."

The travellers were detained three weeks at Tadoussac by " a contagious disease hitherto unknown which swept away the greater number of those whom it attacked; the victims dying in horrible convulsions." The start was finally made up the Saguenay with forty canoes, but beyond making some observations about the remarkable ebb and flow of the noble river, Dablon leaves us no description of what it was in those early days.

Tadoussac, or Tatoushak, as the Indians called it, from which they started, gets its name from the high sand hills by which the place is surrounded. It is about 120 miles below Quebec, and only of late years have white men settled in that vicinity; but the story of Tadoussac goes back to the first discovery of Canada. Cartier dropped anchor in its harbor in 1531, and the Jesuits established a mission there in 1639. Their little bark hut where Mass was said was replaced by a chapel in 1648, and one hundred years after-

THE SAGUENAY.

wards another was built, which still remains to interest the tourists who are now venturing into the wild regions through which the dark Saguenay flows.

What the Saguenay was in those times can with difficulty be imagined. A writer of the present day says, " It can hardly be called a river. It is rather a stupendous chasm from one to two and a half miles in width, doubtless of earthquake origin, cleft for sixty-five miles through the high Laurentian plateau. Its walls are an almost unbroken line of naked cliffs of syenite and gneiss. Its depth is many hundred feet greater than that of the St. Lawrence. Indeed, if the St. Lawrence were drained dry, all the fleets of the world might float in the abyss of the Saguenay, and yet find anchorage only in a few places."

" It is nature's sarcophagus," says another. " Talk of Lethe and the Styx; they must have been purling brooks, compared with this savage river." Its rushing waters burst out into the mighty St. Lawrence striving to reach the opposite shore.

Two rocky promontories guard the entrance of the gorge: the Pointe aux Bouleaux, as it is now called, and the Pointe aux Vaches, which got its name from the number of sea cows, or walruses, which are reported to have swarmed there in early times when they were hunted by the Basques. The grampus may still be seen at times, disporting itself in the water. Three or four miles up are islands which seem to bar the way, and higher still is the Saguenay's chief tributary, the Marguerite, and further on again, but on the opposite side, the Little Saguenay enters the stream. Beyond this loom two enormous promontories, called " Trinity " and " Eternity "; " three different elevations, and yet but one rock; three distinct heights, and yet each about the same in its own individual extent and proportion; three equal steps, yet each distant from the other, and one great, awful ' Trinity ' of cape and mountain raising aloft its summit to a majestically precipitous height of 1,900 feet. Coming near

111

to the frowning sides of these peaks, the feeling of awe is increased by the remembrance that the still, black water of the river, out of which these mountain capes so abruptly rise, is neary 2,000 feet deep. Cape Eternity is more than a hundred feet higher than Trinity, or nearly six times as high as the citadel of Quebec, and if ever mountain anywhere deserved a name, it is assuredly that of Cape Eternity. The Man of Uz might have had in his mind the birth of the Saguenay when he wrote, 3,400 years ago: ' He overturneth the mountains by the roots. He cutteth out rivers among the rocks.' "

Still ascending the river, we come to what the French explorers called Ha! Ha! Bay, thinking it was the main channel of the Saguenay, and finally, sixty-eight miles from the mouth is Chicoutimi, the head of navigation. There the torrent of that name leaps down into the River of Death, as Bayard Taylor calls the Saguenay, over rocks fifty feet high, after having descended nearly five hundred more in the short space of seventeen miles above, in its course from Lake St. John.

In 1647 the Jesuit De Quen had reached that lake when looking for some sick Indians whom he had converted down in Tadoussac. He was the first white man to set foot on the shores of that inland sea. His description of it is to be found in the *Relations,* and travellers to-day note its exactness. Dablon, however, gives a more picturesque description of it than that left by De Quen.

" The lake presents a beautiful appearance, being dotted with a number of islands near its mouth, while beyond them it gently spreads its waters over a fine sandy beach which entirely surrounds it, forming a circle that tends somewhat towards an oval, and is from seven to eight leagues in diameter. It has the appearance of being crowned with a beautiful forest which shades its shores, and from whatever point we survey it, constitutes a fine natural stage of verdant scenery, twenty leagues in circumference. It is not very deep, considering the numerous rivers that empty into it, and which ought to increase its size, since it has but one outlet, the Saguenay, of which it is the source."

Here the Indians wanted to stop, and advised strongly against proceeding farther on account of the dangers of the route. There was news also of a frightful malady prevailing there which was a combination of lunacy, hypochondria and frenzy, developing a more than canine hunger, and making the victims ravenous for human flesh. But Dablon insisted that they had gone too far to turn back. Before leaving the lake, however, " he had the happiness of taking possession of the new land in God's name by baptizing eight persons. Four were christened in due form on the sandy beach with all the ceremonies that time and place would allow. I fancy that the Angels of heaven had their eyes fixed on this spectacle, and took more pleasure in viewing these holy ceremonies, performed with entire simplicity in a church of leaves and a sanctuary of bark, than those that are celebrated with such pomp and ceremony beneath the marble and porphyry of Europe's great basilicas.

" In the Octave of Corpus Christi we started on our way to enter Satan's dominions in good earnest. We accordingly issued from the lake upon the river Assouapmouchouan, which we named the Blessed Sacrament. It is beautiful and wide, divided here and there by islands and meadows. We did not think that such peaceful waters could be lashed to so great a fury against the rocks disputing their passage." Four great waterfalls soon compelled them to leave the river and to carry their boats above. Later on two more portages so wearied the travellers that they " were forced to seek a hostelry to pass the night. The neighboring woods furnished us a fine one, built of great trees, under which one slumbers more sweetly than under canopies of gold and azure where unrest and sleeplessness make their abode more frequently than in the silence of the forests."

Twenty-nine days after leaving Tadoussac they reached

Nekouba. "We found its latitude to be 49° 20', and its longitude 305° 10'; for proceeding N. W. by W. from Tadoussac, we come to Lake St. John after travelling 35 leagues by the shortest route, and still advancing N. W. by W. from that lake, whose latitude is 48° 30' and longitude 307° 50', we arrive here, having accomplished about 45 leagues in a straight line."

Here they were welcomed with great demonstrations of joy by the Indians gathered for the fair. "The orator, who spoke for all, took his stand on a stump that chanced to be very conveniently at the water's edge, addressing us at great length with many gestures and as grandly as if he had been on a gilded throne.

"There was nothing beautiful, nothing attractive to be seen. The soil was dry, barren and sandy, and the mountains were covered only with rocks or little stunted trees which find insufficient moisture in the crevices from which they spring. The people do not cultivate the soil, but live as the birds do, and are often a prey to famine. There are no mosquitoes, midges or gnats, as they find nothing to live on. It is the sole redeeming quality of these deserts. The air is almost always brown with smoke caused by the burning of the surrounding woods which, catching fire all at once within a circuit of fifteen or twenty leagues, send us their ashes from a distance of more than ten leagues. The trees are pines, spruce and thorns, which are all resinous, and their trunks are coated with a sticky gum that makes the whole forest inflammable. The great conflagrations are caused either by lightning, or carelessness, or sometimes because of the wantonness of some savage. Though the heat is unbearable at times, yet the cold is so intense and continued that snowshoes are used as late as June."

They baptized some poor people there, one of whom especially seemed to have been preserved by God for their coming. "Do not such dispensations of Providence," says Dablon, "compensate with usury the fatigues undergone

THE SAGUENAY.

in coming so far to win souls A single conversation on heavenly themes with a savage in some wooded nook, or on the edge of a rock; a soul won for God; a child baptized; a barbarian at your feet weeping over the sins of many years, although they may be often years of ignorance, impart a joy greater than the trouble of a long and arduous journey."

The same terror that pervaded the regions of the St. Lawrence met the missionaries in those parts. The Iroquois had penetrated these distant regions, and there was a constant dread of meeting them. For that or some other reason which the missionaries do not explain, it was impossible to obtain guides to lead them to the North Sea, and consequently they were compelled to retrace their steps towards Lake St. John and the Tadoussac, and from there to Quebec.

The Saguenay missions were not, however, abandoned. Tadoussac remained the headquarters, and we find Père La Brosse laboring there in 1782, nine years after the Society was suppressed. About him a curious legend is still told to travellers. " The Father," so the story runs, " had been working hard all day, as usual, among his converts and in the services of the church, and had spent the evening in pleasant converse with some of the officers of the post. Their amazement and incredulity may be imagined when, as he got up to go, he bade them good-bye for eternity, and announced that at midnight he would be a corpse, adding that the bell of his chapel would toll for his passing soul at that hour. He told them that if they did not believe him they could go and see for themselves, but begged them not to touch his body. He bade them fetch Messire Compain, who would be waiting for them next day at the lower end of Isle aux Coudres, to wrap him in his shroud and bury him; and this they were to do without heeding what the weather should be, for he would answer for the safety of those who undertook the voyage. The little party, astounded, sat, watch in hand, marking the hours pass, till, at the first stroke of midnight, the chapel bell began to toll, and, trembling with fear, they rushed into the church. There, prostrate before the altar, hands joined in prayer, shrouding his face alike from the first glimpse of the valley of the shadow of death, and from the dazzling glory of the waiting angels, lay Père La Brosse, dead. What fear and sorrow must have mingled with the pious hopes and tender prayers of those rough traders and rougher Indians as, awe-stricken, they kept vigil that April night. With sunrise came a violent storm; but mindful of his command and promise, four brave men risked their lives on the water. The lashing waves parted to form a calm path for their canoe, and wondrously soon they were at Isle aux Coudres. There, as had been foretold by Père La Brosse, was M. Compain waiting on the rocks, breviary in hand, and as soon as they were within hearing, his shout told them he knew their strange errand, for the night before he had been mysteriously warned; the bell of his church was tolled at midnight by invisible hands, and a voice had told him what had happened and was yet to happen, and had bade him be ready to do his office. In all the missions that Père La Brosse had served, the church bells, it is said, marked that night his dying moment.

To this charming legend the Abbé Casgrain adds: " For many years the Indians going up and down the Saguenay never passed Tadoussac without praying in the church where reposed the body of him who had been to them the image of their Heavenly Father. They prostrated themselves with faces to the ground above his tomb, and, placing their mouths at a little opening made in the floor of the choir, they talked to him as in his lifetime, with a confidence that could not fail to touch God's heart. Then they applied their ears to the orifice to hear the saint's answer. In the ingenuousness of their faith and simplicity of their hearts they imagined that the good Father heard them in his coffin, that he answered their questions, and afterwards transmitted to God their prayers. This touching custom has ceased since the removal of the remains of Père La Brosse. The abandonment and ruin into which the chapel of Tadoussac had fallen decided the removal of these holy relics a good many years ago to the Church of Chicoutimi."

After these apostolic journeys far up in the gloomy regions near Hudson Bay, we find Dablon out on Lake Superior with his friends Allouez and Marquette, forming with them what Bancroft calls "the illustrious triumvirate." There seems to be always a brightness in the scene where Dablon enters. His accounts of situations, his descriptions of places and people, are marvellously clear and comprehensive, with a vein of humor running through all he says, and so vivid that the occurrences of over 230 years ago are as real as if they happened yesterday.

Putting before his readers a singularly accurate word-map of Lakes Superior and Michigan, he takes them familiarly by the hand and travels in their company from one station to another all over that vast territory. Michillimackinac and Sault Ste. Marie, he tells you, "are the two doors and locks, one for the South, the other for the North; and therefore all the Indians who do any trading have to pass by one or other of those passages. That is the reason we chose them for our missions.

" Michillimackinac is an island, a league in diameter, and has such high steep rocks that it can be seen a distance of more than twelve leagues. What is commonly called the Sault is not properly a Sault, or a very high waterfall, but a very violent current of waters from Lake Superior, which, finding itself checked by a great number of rocks that dispute their passage, form a dangerous cascade of half a league in width, all these waters descending and plunging headlong together, as if by a flight of stairs, over the rocks, which bar the whole river. Nineteen different tribes gather there to fish, and evangelization of them is comparatively easy."

He discusses the currents, and the winds, and the porous

rocks; describes the different varieties of fish; tells you what dexterity and strength are needed to net the whitefish without upsetting your canoe; guides you along the shores of Lake Superior; enumerates the rivers that run into it; and wonders if the great sea, which the Winnipeg Indians, who have come down to fish, tell him of, is really the North Sea.

"Two reasons," he writes, "have led us to make a journey as far as the region of that North Sea. The first is to see in what way we can apply ourselves to the conversion of those tribes. The second, to discover at last that North Sea, of which so much has been said, and which has not yet been found by land. If we get there we can find by a comparison of its latitude and longitude whether it is the bay to which *Hutson* penetrated in 1612, and then ascertain what part of the sea is nearest to us. Secondly, we can learn whether communication can be had from Quebec all the way to the sea, by following the Northern shores as it was attempted some years ago. If it is found to be Hutson's bay, easy communication cannot be hoped for, since it would be necessary to double a point extending to more than 63 degrees of latitude. Thirdly, we can verify the quite probable conjectures that a passage could be made by this route to the Japan sea. For at some days' journey from the mission of St. Francis Xavier, at the Bay des Puans, is found a great river more than a league in width." This is the Mississippi, which he is eager to explore, and he goes on to describe what the savages had told him of it.

The same informants had spoken of a Western sea beyond Lake Superior, which, he says, "can be nothing else than the Japan sea. So that if we can reach the Northern sea, and the Western sea and go down the Mississippi to the Southern sea, it will be possible to pass from one to the other, and will be most advantageous for commerce." These were not all dreams, for Marquette found the Southern sea, and it is not at all impossible that the Indians who told him of the Western sea had travelled to the lakes from the Pacific or Sea of Japan. Such journeys were not too great for them.

Dablon gives us a detailed account of his travels through Wisconsin with his companion Allouez; tells of their journey inland after leaving Green Bay; the pleasant rivers and lakes, the fertile country on all sides, what animals and birds were found there—the American pelican then comes for the first time before us and its skilful method of fishing is noted; the character of the savages is described; their ridiculous antics in endeavoring to imitate the drill of European soldiers; the mild-mannered, polite and hospitable chief, who was at the same time a great warrior, etc. He tells us of the rock-hewn idol which he took from its base at De Père Rapids and threw into the river; the curious way the savages had of honoring the crucifix by throwing snuff at it, and finally, when the travellers returned, what observations they made of the remarkable parhelion that occurred in the spring of the year 1671. He gives a minute description of all the phenomena connected with it, draws a chart of the different false suns that appeared, and carefully notes the time of the occurrence in other localities.

It is Dablon who first informed the world of the vast wealth that lay yet undiscovered in those distant regions. In the *Relations* of 1669-71 he describes in great detail the rich copper mines of Lake Superior. He had determined even then the principal spots; such places as Thunder Island, Isle Royale, Chagaouamigong Point, as he calls it; the River Nantounagan, etc. He had seen a " ' Rock of Copper ' weighing fully seven or eight hundred livres, so hard that steel can hardly cut it," and he adds in his report, " all this information and more besides, which is not necessary to give in detail, make it worth while to undertake an exact investigation in these matters, and that is what we shall try to do." The world of commerce, especially in our days of copper-wiring, roofing and the rest, owes something to Dablon, who wrote of these treasures as far back as 1670.

An event occurred in those regions while Dablon was there, which, with his sunny disposition, he would not have missed for the world. " It is not our purpose," he says, " to describe this ceremony in detail,"—but the good man does not keep his word, and we are glad he did not.

" When Monsieur Talon our Intendant returned from Portugal, after his shipwreck, he was commanded by the King to set out for this country, to exert himself strenuously for the establishment of Christianity, and to cause the name and the sovereignty of our invincible monarch to be acknowledged by even the least known and the most remote nations." Talon commissioned De Saint Lusson to prepare a solemn *prize de possession* of the Northwest.

In May, 1671, De Saint Lusson appeared at Sault Ste. Marie, and summoned the tribes within a radius of a hundred leagues or more to meet him on June 4th " for the most solemn ceremony ever observed in those regions."

" When all had assembled in a great public council, and a height had been chosen well adapted to his purpose, overlooking as it did the village and people of the Sault, he caused the cross to be planted there and then the King's standard to be raised with all the pomp he could devise. The cross was publicly blessed by the Superior of the Missions (Dablon himself), with all the ceremonies of the Church, and then when it had been raised from the ground for the purpose of planting it, the *Vexilla* was sung, many Frenchmen there present joining in the hymn to the wonder and delight of the savages. Then the French escutcheon fixed to a cedar pole was erected above the cross while the *Exaudiat* was sung, and prayer for his Majesty's sacred person was offered in that far away corner of the world. After this M. De Saint Lusson took possession of those regions while the air resounded with repeated shouts of ' Long live the King ' and with the discharge of musketry, to the delight and astonishment of those people, who had never seen anything of the kind.

CLAUDE DABLON.

" Then Father Claude Allouez began to eulogize the king, told of our incomparable monarch's greatness," etc., what riches he had, what power, what splendor. He is the captain of captains, and has not his equal in the world, with his armies and navies and palaces. " When he attacks, he is more terrible than the thunder; the air and the sea are set on fire by the discharge of his cannon. He has been seen amid his squadron all covered with the blood of his foes, of whom he has slain so many with his sword that he does not count their scalps," etc. The Father added much more of this sort. He had to be " bluggy " to impress the savages. Then M. De Saint Lusson spoke, and " the whole ceremony was closed with a fine bonfire which was lighted toward evening and around which the *Te Deum* was sung to thank God, on behalf of these poor people, that they were now the subjects of so great and powerful a monarch."

After this Dablon went to Quebec as General Superior of all the houses. Talon was about to return to France, but was unwilling to leave America before an attempt was made to discover the Great River, a scheme which, of course, had possessed the soul of Dablon for years. Joliet had just arrived. He had been present at the great ceremony at the Sault, and was pursuing the copper investigations which Dablon had inaugurated. He was to undertake the discovery. Who was to go with him? That depended on Dablon. Willingly would he have thrown aside his superiorship to realize the dream of his lifetime. He could not go, so he appointed his friend Marquette. The result justified the choice, but it has forever linked Dablon's name with the great achievement. Were it not for him, Marquette could not have gone. It was he also who received Marquette's letters and charts, edited them and gave them to the world.

In connection with this journey of Marquette, it is worth while noting that Dablon immediately called attention to an advantage accruing from the discovery which he said "would hardly be believed," namely, that "we could go without difficulty to Florida, in a bark, by very easy navigation. It would only be necessary *to make a canal* by cutting through only half a league of prairie, to pass from the end of the Lake of the Illinois (Michigan) to the River of St. Louis (Illinois). Here is the route that would be followed: The bark would be built on Lake Erie; it would easily pass from Lake Erie to Lake Huron, whence it could enter Lake Illinois. At the end of that lake, the canal which I have spoken of would be made to gain a passage into the River St. Louis, which falls into the Mississippi. The bark when there would easily sail to the Gulf of Mexico." (*Relations*, lviii.)

This was written at Quebec, August 1, 1674. Now in March, 1907, that is, 233 years afterwards, the Governor of Illinois sends a special message to the Legislature advocating the digging of this same canal. Full credit is given to the first projectors, however; for the commission appointed to consider the proposal, after referring to Marquette's and Joliet's journey across the Chicago Divide, reported that Joliet advocated this canal in a letter to Dablon *August 1, 1674*. Here a little obscurity occurs. It is Dablon's letter which is dated August 1, 1674; and as Joliet was then in Quebec, it is not likely he wrote to his friend Dablon, who was in the same place. Joliet's letter, as far as we can make out, was sent to France three months later, viz.: in November. He had written it to Frontenac October 10th, and it is found on a panel of a map forwarded to the home government by Frontenac. But although the map was made in 1674, it did not see the light until our own times, viz.: in 1880, when it was published by Gravier under the title: *Étude sur une carte inconnue*. This information is found in Rochemonteix (viii, p. 23). Nevertheless there is no doubt whatever that all of Dablon's information was given to him by his friend Joliet. He expressly says so, only it was from memory, as Joliet had lost his maps in the wreck at Lachine, and Marquette's papers had not yet arrived. As a matter of fact the idea of the canal was the joint result of the studies and deliberations of these three intimate friends, Joliet, Dablon and Marquette. Nor was Dablon taking his information at second hand. He had travelled all through those regions with Allouez as early as 1670, and had come very near the Mississippi. His foresight as to the commercial possibilities resulting from the opening of the western country is very remarkable.

There is another matter connected with these letters and papers which is of interest, not only to the student of history, but to the general reader. Besides the account written in August, Dablon sent a letter to Colbert in France, dated November 11th, which probably went by the same vessel that carried Joliet's map. In it he says that " Joliet had left at Sault Ste. Marie on Lake Superior in charge of the Fathers, copies of his journal, which we cannot obtain till next year; but in which you will find more particulars about the discovery, *in which he has so well acquitted himself."* Among those papers at the Sault was Marquette's account; a copy of which had been taken by Joliet, but which he lost at Lachine with his own documents. It was more than likely that the original account by Marquette or another copy was sent to Colbert, as Dablon had promised. But, strangely enough, it was published in France *only in 1680,* and then in a very mutilated form and with a systematic omission throughout of Marquette's name. What is the explanation of this delay and mutilation?

Just before Marquette's discovery, difficulties had arisen among the missionaries in the East Indies, which so irritated Cardinal Altieri, who was then the dominant power at Rome, that he forbade the publication of the accounts of the missions of any part of the world, without leave of the Propaganda. This angered Louis XIV, and nearly precipitated a clash between France and the Holy See. The conflict had the effect of suspending the publication of the *Relations* just at the moment of the great discovery, namely, 1673. Hence, when Dablon's report came over, it could not be given to the public without the authorization of the Propaganda, and that authorization Louis XIV refused to ask. It is more than likely, therefore, that Thevenet, who edited the account in 1680, omitted the name of Marquette so as to deprive it of all appearance of a missionary relation, in order to avoid any condemnation by the Holy See. Finally, it is Dablon's account substantiated by Frontenac's letter, which disposes definitely of the claims of La Salle to have been the first discoverer of the Mississippi.

Dablon remained Superior in Quebec until 1680. He was named again in 1686 and remained in office till 1693. He was the wisest and most distinguished and most experienced of all those who were entrusted with the onerous task of providing means to carry on the great work which the Jesuits had set for themselves in Northern America. According to Rochemonteix and Terrien, he died at Quebec on May 3, 1697. Father Martin says it was on September 20th.

JOSEPH CHAUMONOT.

L IKE his companion Dablon, Chaumonot had a very
variable patronymic. He was Chaumonot, or Chau-
monet, or Chaumont, or Calmonoti, as Carayon misprints
it, or Calvonotti, as it also appears in its Italian form, though
he was not an Italian, Charveloix to the contrary notwithstanding. But, no matter how he spelled his name, he was
one of the conspicuous figures in the early ecclesiastical history of New York. Rochemonteix, yielding somewhat to
his propensity for vigorous dissection of character, even
when of his own religious family, for which a Canadian
author takes him to task, tells us that " Chaumonot was of
a very singular spiritual physiognomy. Simple even to
credulity, timid even to fear, of an intelligence that lacked
culture, impressionable, and with nothing in his character
that could confer distinction, he became, under the influence
of divine grace and the austere practice of exalted virtue,
one of the most beautiful figures of the Church of Canada."
It ought to be noted that the concluding words of this description are from the Abbé Gosselin and are only quoted
by Rochemonteix.

Doubtless the harshness of this portrait was not inten-
tional, but resulted from the antithesis employed, which aims
at effect rather than correctness. There may also have been
an unconscious exaggeration of the supernatural at the expense of the natural, though it is hard to reconcile " the
austere practice of exalted virtue " with writing an autobiography which is described as " *un exposé naïf* of a life in
which the marvellous blends too easily with the supernatural,
and is of another age and another world." On the whole
Abbé Gosselin's estimate of this holy man and mighty missionary will suffice.

Joseph Marie Chaumonot was born near Chatillon-sur-

Seine. He was the son of a poor Burgundian vine dresser, and when still a child was sent to live with an uncle, an old-fashioned curé, who had an idea that he might develop an ecclesiastical vocation. The old man was apparently too exacting; for the lad took a notion to run away to study music with the Oratorians of Beaume. It was only plain chant, and someone else tempted him to go. He helped himself to five sous of his uncle's money to defray the expenses of the expedition, and, without breathing a word to anyone, disappeared. Of course, very soon his five sous disappeared also, and then, not daring to return, he became a vagabond, begging something to eat from door to door, sleeping in barns or under the light of the moon, or helped from time to time by some charitable convent where he stopped to ask for food. In that fashion he travelled across Savoy and Lombardy, visited Ancona and Loretto, and at last arrived at Terni in Umbria, barefooted, with his clothes in tatters and his person in a condition which is not generally described in print. In fact Father Chaumonot's own account of it in his Autobiography is somewhat shocking to modern ideas of delicacy. He finds employment at last as a servant in the house of someone fairly well off and settles down to regular life, but happening one day on a book called the " Lives of Some Holy Hermits," he begins to dream of becoming a Capuchin, a Recollect, a Carmelite, or a Hermit. His roving propensity, however, asserts itself again, and a second time he takes to the road and begs his way through Italy to Rome. Chance brought him to the Jesuit College there, and some kindly and intelligent influence was exerted in his behalf, with the result that by the time he was twenty-one—that is, on May 18, 1632—we find him a very holy novice of the Society of Jesus. His long stay in Italy accounts for his being sometimes taken for an Italian. He went through his philosophy and theology, taking only what Rochemonteix describes as a *léger bagage;* but it was heavy enough to explain the difficulties of the Hurons, whom he was going to

LORETTO IN ITALY.

convert. Father Poncet left Rome along with him. It was he who had influenced Chaumonot. They came by way of France and crossed the ocean with the Venerable Marie de l'Incarnation, and had the chance of witnessing the enthusiasm of the colonists when that holy woman and her companions came off the ship at Quebec. That was August 1, 1639. At the beginning of the next month, Chaumonot presented himself to Brébeuf on the shores of Lake Huron.

Daniel, who was afterwards martyred, was one of his first companions in this new work, which Chaumonot probably found was not at all in keeping with his early dreams, for he wrote to the Superior of the Professed House at Rome, Father Napi: "Never could I imagine such hard-heartedness as there is in a savage. You cannot convert him unless you pay him for it. But he is by no means stupid. On the contrary, *he is more intelligent than our average peasant.* The difficulty is with the sixth commandment. Purity is non-existent, even among the women. The chief and the sorcerers are the most licentious, and permanency of marriage is out of the question. Every time I go to their cabins I feel as if I were going to be hanged."

He went, nevertheless, and discovered that he had an unusual facility for picking up their language. He could speak it inside of a month, and he has left some valuable works on the Huron dialects. His Huron Grammar has been translated by Wilkie and published in the Quebec Lit. and Hist. Soc., Trans. vii, 1831. In fact the Indians, who plumed themselves on their oratorical powers and their art of coining words, admitted that Chaumonot surpassed them all.

After a few months Brébeuf took him as companion in an expedition to the Neuter Indians, who lived north of Lake Erie, where the Niagara River formed the only barrier between them and their terrible foes, the Iroquois. Had Chaumonot been "timid even to fear," he could never have kept pace with Brébeuf, especially in this instance. For, though the Hurons were bad enough, the wild orgies of the Neuters, their fiendish manner of executing captives, of which Chaumonot has left us some harrowing descriptions, and the grossness of their immorality made them worse than any Indians he had yet seen.

The missionaries started out in November, and after five days' journey through forests covered with snow, arrived at Kadoucho, which they called All Saints. It was not as pleasant as tramping under the sunny skies of Italy, but Chaumonot never flinched, even when he found that the Hurons had sent messengers to the Neuters counseling murder. Everywhere they were threatened with being eaten alive, but they could not be frightened. They would sometimes force their way among the scowling savages and dare them to carry out their threat. Possibly it was amazement at the audacity of these two lonely white men that made the Indians hesitate, and content themselves with flinging them out of their wigwams to perish in the snow.

There were about 12,000 of those wretched people scattered around in forty settlements. After visiting eighteen of their villages, from most of which they were expelled, or to which they were not admitted, they gave up the work as hopeless. They had devoted five terrible months to the task, and now weary and broken they wended their way back to St. Mary's, though the thaw had set in, making the journey doubly perilous. Chaumonot had suffered everything as well as Brébeuf and displayed the same courage. At one time, while the Indians were howling around him and threatening to drink his blood, one savage stood in front of him with his arrow drawn to head, about to kill him. Though only a novice in missionary life, Chaumonot calmly looked the murderer in the eye, and the astonished warrior turned and went away.

It is several times related, by the Venerable Marie de l'Incarnation, that, during these missionary expeditions, Chaumonot in a vision saw Father Daniel, who had just been killed, and, recognizing the martyr, exclaimed: " Ah!

128

dear Father, why did God permit your body to be so horribly treated after your death, not even permitting us to gather up your ashes?" The martyr replied: "He has regarded my reproach and has recompensed as only He can the labor of His servant. I have led with me to heaven a great number of the souls of Purgatory." Daniel, it is said, appeared another time at a council of the Fathers and exhorted them to labor for the glory of God.

Chaumonot shared in all the hardships and dangers of that Huron mission until it was destroyed. He was there when Brébeuf and Lalemant and Chabanel and Garnier won their crowns of martyrdom. He was at St. Mary's when the panic-stricken Hurons rushed in upon them in thousands. He was one of those who rowed away over the lake as the beloved mission-post was given over to the flames. He was side by side with Ragueneau when pestilence and famine were destroying the poor remnants of the tribe that had escaped the tomahawks of the Iroquois, and when all was given up he came down with the four hundred refugees over the thousand miles of river and forest to ask help and life for them at Quebec, and during the winter he went around from house to house to beg for bread for his famishing people. It was he who was chosen by his superiors to found the Huron settlement on the Isle d'Orleans, and so great was his influence with his flock and so wise his government that opposite Quebec there sprung up a settlement of native Christians whose piety recalled all that had ever been said of the famous Paraguay Reductions.

In 1653 the Iroquois showed signs of wishing to bury the hatchet, and a delegation came to Quebec to ask for the establishment of a mission at Onondaga. Of course, there was danger in accepting the offer; for the Iroquois were a treacherous set, and it was feared that the murders perpetrated on Lake Huron would be repeated in Onondaga. It was thought worth the risk, however, and the one upon whom all eyes turned for this perilous undertaking was

Chaumonot. It was a fine tribute to his heroism and zeal. For the moment, however, it was impossible to leave his heartbroken Hurons on the Isle d'Orleans, and Le Moyne took his place.

After Le Moyne had returned and reported favorably on the dispositions of the Onondagas, it was decided to send two priests to establish a mission. Chaumonot and Dablon were selected, and on October 7, 1655, they started up the St. Lawrence for Lake Ontario, in spite of the news that had just been brought them by an escaped captive, that the object of the Indians was murder. There were two reasons, however, why they felt compelled to go on. One was that if they refused, the Onondagas and Mohawks would unite in a common effort against the French; the second was, say the *Relations,* that " the Fathers of our Society, who thus far have never paled at the sight of their own blood, or feared the fires and the fury of the Iroquois, thought they would surely baptize some people before they themselves were slain." They reached Lake Ontario on the 24th, and on the 29th entered the Salmon River, where a score of captive Hurons, recognizing Chaumonot, ran towards him with the wildest delight; some embracing him, others bringing him presents, and others inviting him to a feast.

We find on the present map of New York, near that place, a Chaumont Bay, and also a town of the same name. Was it called after the missionary, or is it the name of the stout Chevalier de Chaumont, who later on accompanied de Tracy on his raid in the Mohawk country? However, that gallant soldier never ventured so far west. Perhaps it is the memory of the old missionary hero that still lingers.

Reaching Onondaga, the entrance was made between files of Indians, who saluted him with great show of rejoicing. The streets were all swept, and on the roofs of the cabins were swarms of children to see the great man. Chaumonot addressed the assembly in an impressive speech, and all wondered at his eloquence as he strutted up and down in Indian

JOSEPH CHAUMONOT.

fashion, though Dablon thinks it was rather Italian than Indian. While speaking he bestowed presents lavishly for all sorts of sorrows and woes. A splendid wampum belt which he gave on that occasion is still among the treasures of the Iroquois League at Onondaga.

On Sunday, November 24, he began his catechetical instructions, and in the little bark chapel which they had constructed offered the Holy Sacrifice. This place, which is so sacred for Catholics, has been identified by General Clark in Hawley's " Early Chapters," p. 23, as being about twelve miles from the lake, and two miles south of the present village of Manlius. The name given to the church was St. John the Baptist.

It was a beautiful country in those days. " Our Residence," says the *Relation,* " is situated between the 42d and 43d degrees on the shores of the little Lake Ganentaa, which would be one of the most commodious and most agreeable dwelling places in the world, without excepting even the levée of the River Loire, if its inhabitants were as polished and as tractable.

" It has advantages that are wanting in the rest of Canada, for, besides grapes and plums and many other fruits which it has in common with the fine provinces of Europe, it has a number of others which excel ours in beauty, fragrance and taste. The forest consists almost entirely of chestnut and walnut trees. There are two kinds of nuts; one as sweet and agreeable to the taste as the other is bitter, but with all their bitterness an excellent oil is extracted from them by passing them through the ashes, through the mill, through the fire and through water in the same way as the savages extract oil from sunflowers.

The nuts here mentioned are, according to Thwaites, hickory, the " shell bark " variety or the " pig nut," which is sweet, and the bitternut or swamp hickory. Charveloix describes the way the Indians extracted oil from the latter.

The oil of the sunflower was used not for food, but for the hair.

"Stoneless cherries (cranberries) are found there, and fruits which are the color and size of an apricot with blossoms like those of the white lily and with a taste like citron (the May-apple). There are apples as large as a goose egg (the pawpaw). The seeds have been brought from the country of the Cats (Eries) and look like beans; the fruit is delicate and has a very sweet smell; the trunk is of the thickness and height of our dwarf trees; it thrives in swampy spots and in good soil. But the most common and most wonderful plant in these countries is what we call the universal plant, because its leaves, when pounded, heal in a short time wounds of all kinds. These leaves, which are as broad as one's hand, have the shape of a lily as depicted in heraldry, and the roots have the smell of laurel. The most vivid scarlet, the brightest green, the most beautiful yellow and orange of Europe pale before the various colors that our savages procure from these roots."

"The universal plant," says Thwaites, "has not yet been identified, so far as known; though it would seem to be the common sassafras, which has always been prized for its medicinal virtues, and was used by the natives of Florida before the Spanish conquest. Upon its discovery by white men it speedily became a valued drug in Europe and an important article of commerce and is still employed in domestic medicine in the United States. The sassafras is described by Charveloix in *Plantes Amer.*, pp. 9, 10.

"I say nothing," continues the *Relation,* "of trees as tall as oaks, whose leaves are as large and open as those of cabbage, or of many other plants peculiar to the country, because as yet we are ignorant of their properties. The springs are as numerous as they are wonderful, and are nearly all mineral. Our little lake, which is only six or seven leagues in circumference, is almost entirely surrounded by salt springs. The water is used for salting and seasoning meat, and for making very good salt. It often forms into fine crystals with which nature delights to surround these springs. The salt we found at a spring about two days from our residence towards Cayuga is much stronger than that from the springs of Ganentaa; for when the water, which looks as white as milk and the smell of which is perceptible from a great distance, is boiled, it leaves a kind of salt almost as corrosive as caustic. The rocks about that spring are covered with a foam as thick as cream. The spring in the direction of the Senecas is no less wonderful, for its water, being of the same nature as the surrounding soil, has only to be washed in order to obtain perfectly pure sulphur. It ignites when shaken violently and yields sulphur when boiled. As you approach the country of the Cats you find heavy and thick water which ignites like brandy and boils up in bubbles of flame when fire is applied to it. It is, moreover, so oily that all our savages use it to anoint and grease their heads and bodies."

The first of these springs has never been identified. " The burning spring near the Senecas " is in the town of Bristol. " The spring towards the country of the Cats " was probably the noted oil spring in the town of Cuba, Allegany County.

As narrated in the sketch of Dablon, the Jesuits received from the Governor of Canada a grant of land of ten square leagues running eastward from Lake Ganentaa. Of course as the French did not retain their hold on New York this munificence was useless. It is a pity the gift was not from the Governor of New York instead of the Governor of Canada. It would have been more in keeping with the supposed wisdom of the Fathers, especially as the missionary thought that " the temperature of the atmosphere, which resembles that of France, added to the advantages supplied by waters and the earth, greatly facilitated the conversion of the savage. We have reason to hope, therefore, that their capricious and peculiar disposition will be the only obstacle to their blessedness."

Father Le Mercier, the Superior of Canada, who came with the fifty colonists, did not remain long. He was back again in Quebec on the first of June, 1657. He succeeded, however, in establishing a chapel in the town of Onondaga itself, besides the one already built twelve miles away. Meantime Chaumonot and his new associates started out on their expeditions, not only among the Onondagas, but also the Oneidas and Cayugas. Many of the sites of their chapels have been identified by painstaking topographers, and are indicated in the writings and maps of General Clark and the Rev. Mr. Beauchamp, who are ardent admirers of these old missionaries. It was while this work was going on that a tragedy occurred near Quebec which brought to Chaumonot's arms at Onondaga some of the unhappy Hurons whom he had left behind him at Isle d'Orleans.

In May, 1656, 300 Mohawks appeared near Three Rivers and exchanged presents with the French. They said they were returning to their own country. They assured Le Moyne that such was their intention, but instead of doing so they stole down to Quebec and, landing at Isle d'Orleans, concealed themselves in the forests and waited till the unsuspecting Hurons were at Mass. A general slaughter was then begun and kept up until the Hurons surrendered, and consented to divide their tribe; one portion going to Onondaga, a second to the Mohawks, a third remaining on the island. All this was done in full view of Quebec. Those who were dragged to Onondaga had at least the happiness of seeing their old friend Chaumonot. He had been forced to leave them, and now Providence had brought them to him in his own exile. It is astonishing to hear that "our Hurons are doing well. It seems to me that they manifest much more faith and piety than usual, especially *those who belong to the Sodality,* who number eighty, *probati omnes testimonio fidei et pietatis.* They observed the time of Advent

134

with especial fervor, each one endeavoring to make more solid progress in virtue. Many who considered Mass too short to satisfy their devotion heard two every day. Some came to pay homage to the Blessed Sacrament in the morning before the hour of prayer. Others came at noon regularly, and neither cold nor bad weather could hinder their fervor." This is an extraordinary scene from those far-off days in the wilds of Onondaga. But it must be remembered that the Christians here described were not Iroquois, but their Huron prisoners.

Nevertheless, not only did the Huron captives console the missionaries, but high hopes were cherished of converting the Iroquois. " It is difficult," says the *Relation* of 1656-57, " to find an instance in which God has shown himself more absolute master of hearts than in our reconciliation with the Iroquois. We receive as much kindness and as many tokens of good will as we feared to experience baleful results from their cruelty. We dwell and eat in security with those whose shadow and whose very name filled us with dread a short time ago. It is not temporal interest which cements the friendship, for it has not as yet brought them any temporal advantage. Never is there greater joy or greater pleasure in their cabins and in their villages than when they can have us there. They follow us to our dwelling and behave as if God made them find delight in talking to us. The murderers of the preachers of the Gospel, those ravenous wolves who had vented their fury on the fold of Jesus Christ with greater rage and more atrocious torture than any Nero or Diocletian, now embrace our holy religion with more fervor than those whom they exterminated, and assume the yoke of which they were some years ago the oppressors. They repeople the Church which their cruelty had depopulated; they build in their own country more chapels than they had destroyed in that of their neighbors. More Iroquois have become Christians in two months than had been converted in several years."

All this was in the early days when Chaumonot first went among them. It may have been only a ruse to ensure the coming of the colony, for we find the same missionaries writing afterwards: "Every day we feel as if we were on the point of being massacred. If God wishes it, may His name be blessed!" Indications began to multiply that the extermination of all the whites, priests and laymen alike, was not only thought of, but was being deliberately planned. Month after month they waited, hoping against hope, until finally, when there was no possibility of doubt, arrangements were secretly made to escape, and on the night of March 20th all stole away in their boats across the lake, and after incredible hardships reached Montreal. Chaumonot never saw New York again, although the mission in Onondaga was reinaugurated a few years later.

He returned to Quebec, and for the next thirty-five years was entrusted with the care of the Huron colony. His old affection for Loretto, which he visited when a ragged boy in Italy, asserted itself again on his return to Canada. When with his Indians on the Isle d'Orleans, before he went down to Onondaga, he was already laying the foundations of his famous sanctuary by uniting it with all the great shrines of the Blessed Virgin in Europe. Thus he sent to the Sodality of Paris what to the white man must have been a surprising gift: a wampum belt and a letter of congratulation written on birch bark. The belt, which was to be offered to the Blessed Virgin, contained the inscription *Ave Maria* worked out in white and purple beads on a white background. The letter conveyed the information that "we have nothing more precious in our hands or holy in our hearts to be presented to you."

From the Isle d'Orleans the Hurons migrated in 1668 to what is now Beauport, but lingered there only from spring till autumn. They then shifted to a place above Quebec, near Sillery, and which is now known as Ste. Foy. The Abbé Scott in his interesting *History of Ste. Foy* is

LORETTE IN CANADA.

careful to warn us not to imagine that it was a wild district when they arrived. Concessions of land had been granted to many colonists; clearings had been made, and the Chemin Ste. Foy was opened to Quebec. But they left that place and shifted their quarters again to a place three miles from Quebec. There Chaumonot determined to build his Lorette, modelled after the old shrine of Italy. The shape of the building was copied with the greatest exactness; even the stones, says Père Bouvart, were of the same material, which is contradicted by Abbé Lindsay in his exquisite story of *Jeune Lorette*. Brick was employed, not stone. In fact, Chaumonot himself, in his Autobiography, says brick.

From this shrine other wampum belts were sent abroad; first to Notre Dame at Dinant, from which the statue of Notre Dame de Ste. Foy, which was such a favorite in the missions of New York, had been sent. The accompanying letter of the Indians, however, was not on birch bark but on parchment, which robbed the missive of some of its local color. But the Belgians did not mind that, and it will come as a surprise to our modern coldness and lack of enthusiasm to hear how the people of Dinant received the treasure: " Barons under arms, and the clergy in their sacred vestments, and five hundred students on horseback—the cavalry of the Jesuit college—and a countless host of people covering a vast expanse of territory, all accompanied the triumphal car on which was placed the wonderful collar; and while cannons roared their welcome to it the great procession wended its way to the church and, amid the blare of trumpets and the beating of drums, solemn Mass was celebrated and the gift was suspended at the shrine." Of course presents were sent back to the Indians, and they were nothing less than the beautiful robes which had adorned the statue of Dinant and were to be used in the American Lorette.

Another belt was sent to Loretto in Italy, and the French Penitentiary there had it put in a gilded frame and the canons and other dignitaries received it with great marks of respect. In 1819, Mgr. Plessis, the Bishop of Quebec, saw it there, and wrote to his diocese about it. Chartres also received its present, and it can be seen there to-day along with a similar *ex voto* from the Abenakis. Bishop Bourget relates how the sight of those precious offerings filled him with emotion when he saw them in 1841. The documents accompanying these gifts are of especial value as they are the only known examples of the Huron and Abenakis dialects of the eighteenth century. The return letter of the Chapter of Chartres has recently been found in the archives of Jeune Lorette. The famous reliquary representing the tunic of the Blessed Virgin, of which the Indians are so proud, was sent to America on that occasion. Finally the Sodalists of Saumur received their wampum. There were probably others, but we have no record of them.

In spite of all that was done for them in that place the restless Hurons tired of it. Perhaps it was too far from the water, and so in 1697 they started off to establish a new settlement on the St. Charles, which was then and is yet called La Jeune Lorette. Such is the common persuasion, but the fact is that the Bishop of Quebec, St. Vallier, laid hands on it and turned it into a parish church. There were violent reclamations against the act. They are to be found in Rochemonteix. No doubt that was the reason why the Indians strove to take everything with them and would have carried off the walls if they had been permitted. By that time Chaumonot was dead. In fact he had lived a little too long, as Superior of Ancienne Lorette, and the Indians were getting beyond his control.

In his very touching and affectionate story of Jeune Lorette, the Abbé Lindsay, who was born there and grew up with Indian playmates, says that " Fenimore Cooper's romance of the *Last of the Mohegans* might be applied to Jeune Lorette. It represents the last of the Hurons. It is all that remains of a once glorious and powerful people, and is the more to be regretted, as the Hurons gave to the infant Church of Canada examples of piety and virtue worthy of the times of the Apostles. Even its language is dead, and with the exception of a few canticles preserved from old missionary times, or of some glossaries jealously guarded in the archives of our legislatures or religious communities, or the battle names of the chiefs which are proudly proclaimed on some national festival but whose owners have long since been absorbed in the life-current of the whites, there is nothing left of the sonorous idioms which were once heard in the councils of war or the songs of triumph.

"What has lasted in Lorette is the Catholic faith, which was purchased for them by the blood of Brébeuf, Lalemant, Garnier, and Daniel, and which they were anxious to preserve when they asked to be taken to Quebec. 'Let us go there,' they said, 'lest we lose our faith.' The mission chapel is still there; its steeple pointing to heaven still shows the road to the children of the forest; its bell still summons to prayer the last descendants of a people which soon will be no more. Near the church is God's Acre, still dear as of old. The Huron has lost nothing of his care of the dead, but the arrows and the bows which the hunter was to use in the land beyond are replaced by the cross which promises resurrection. Even the St. Charles, the Cabir-Coubat, or 'the winding river,' as they called it, though it delights and fertilizes many a valley in its course, is now used to slake the thirst of the invaders or to drive their mighty machinery by curbing the rush of the waters while the once powerful nation is dying on its banks."

Frontenac used to come to pray at Lorette, but he was for a time under the impression that the conversion of the Indian diminished his prowess as a warrior. The long list of warlike expeditions in which the Lorette Indians took part, which Abbé Lindsay furnishes us with, dispels that illusion. They were splendid fighters, but so well behaved

139

that they were known as " the holy Indians." " I congratulate you, indeed," said Father Vaillant to Davagour; " you
have as many saints as Hurons at Lorette." Douglas, in
his *Old Quebec,* finds that " to this day the Lorette Indians
reflect credit on their teachers. The work of the Jesuit
Fathers still bears its fruit, and whoever knows the Lorette
Indian and has hunted with him can excuse the vein of
exaggeration in which the Jesuits record the many virtues
of their converts."

These were Chaumonot's Indians. He had placed them
especially under the Blessed Virgin's protection and she took
care of them. It was the same devotion to the Mother of
God which prompted him to found the Congregation of the
Holy Family, which is still a potent factor in Canadian religious life. It gave great trouble in Frontenac's days by
the refusal of its austere members to attend the state balls,
which were considered too worldly an amusement—a resolution which Frontenac resented. The old missionary had
established the congregation even among the Onondagas, so
that it has the distinction of being New York's first sodality.

In spite of their hardships and exposure, or perhaps on
that account, these old pioneers generally lived to a great
age if they escaped the tomahawk. *" Le pauvre Hechon,"*
" the man who drags the load," as Chaumonot called himself, gave up his work in 1692, and after lingering for a
year went to heaven February 21, 1693. He had been a
missionary since 1639, that is for more than half a century.

PAUL RAGUENEAU, S.J.

PAUL RAGUENEAU.

THERE is a very distinguished missionary who labored for a time in New York, but who is almost lost sight of in the throng: Paul Ragueneau. It was he who, in 1658, directed the daring escape from Onondaga, which averted the massacre of every white man in the Iroquois territory. His journey thither, a year after Dablon had sailed with his fifty colonists over Lake Onondaga, though not as romantic, has elements of tragedy in it which the other was not called upon to face.

The brief letter which contains the account of his first journey to New York is dated: "On the road from Quebec to Onondaga, August 9, 1657." At what particular point in the woods, or on the shore of the St. Lawrence on this "road" to Onondaga, he indited the epistle, which he thought would be his last, we have no means of determining.

With fifteen or sixteen Senecas, thirty Onondagas, and about fifty Christian Hurons, men, women and children, he started upon what proved to be a bloody pilgrimage. From the first there was evidently trouble ahead, for the Onondagas were surly and protested against taking the Frenchmen and their baggage into the canoes. Indeed, although they yielded at first, much of the freight was flung overboard five leagues above Montreal. "I had difficulty in getting anyone to take me," says Ragueneau, "but at length I discovered an abandoned canoe on the beach which Brother Louis le Boesme and myself took possession of. With us were two Frenchmen and two Indians, the latter not being very willing to go." One of these Frenchmen was the famous Radisson, whom we met at Fort Orange when Father Poncet was there.—"I had no provisions but a small sack of flour; and moreover, menaces of danger multiplied as we went on. Everywhere we met with stranded Frenchmen, and

141

saw discarded goods in the stream or on the shore. What Indians we met received us sullenly, and we heard that the Mohawks were waiting up near Lake Ontario, to capture the Hurons. But, alas! the misfortunes of the Hurons were not to come from the Mohawks, but from the Onondagas, who had, however, been so profuse in their promises of protection.

"On the 3d of August, between four and five in the evening, we reached an island which had been designated as a stopping place. We found the Indians in a state of wild excitement. The reason was that an Onondaga chief had crept up behind a Huron woman and buried his tomahawk in her skull, because she had rejected his advances." Where that island is which this martyr of chastity dyed with her blood we do not know, nor did the Father recall her name. He was too much startled by the storm which had thus suddenly burst upon him, "out of which," he says, "the lightning bolt almost immediately fell. A general butchery of the Hurons began. My eyes were compelled to gaze on that spectacle of horror, and my heart was pierced with agony as I saw them murdered before the eyes of their wives and children. Some of them were stabbed or tomahawked in my very arms and on my breast as I tried to shield them. Seven were killed outright and of the women, who were first robbed of all they had, I saw some with children of three or four years of age burned at the stake. I found then what consolation faith brings in the bitterest sorrows. There was not one of these poor creatures who did not receive with affection the advice I gave, as I reminded them that Christ did not promise joy in this life but in eternity.

"When night came on, I assembled the Onondagas and Senecas in a public council to speak to them about what had happened. I told them that the blows that had fallen on the heads of the Hurons had rent my heart. I had the heart of a father and the tenderness of a mother for these poor Christian Hurons, whom I had under my charge for twenty years. I loved them and they loved me; and that love could end only with death. Kill me, burn me, and let them live, if by my death I can bring them back to life; but since such wishes are in vain, I have these words to carry to you. The ' words ' were, (1st) to stop the slaughter; (2d) to be merciful to the captives; (3d) to continue the journey *as if nothing had happened*. I used for this 6,000 porcelain beads. But the treacherous chief had the effrontery to declare that Father Le Mercier and Father Chaumonot had told him to do the deed. I replied in a loud voice that he lied, and he had nothing to answer except that I did not know all that he knew. Word came to us that on that very night our deaths would end the tragedy. But we were spared. In due time we reached Onondaga."

There, as Superior, he directed Dablon, Chaumonot and Ménard in their labors among the Oneidas, Cayugas and Senecas, but his practised eye soon took in the whole situation. He received secret information that a general massacre was planned; that Le Moyne, down among the Mohawks, was to be released, and when the Indians in Quebec were exchanged for him, the fifty or sixty Frenchmen who were, so to speak, shut up in the heart of the country from which there was no escape, were to be butchered. Indications of this plot thickened during the autumn months, and as early as January the Indians threw off the mask. War parties were sent in all directions. There was no time to lose.

The situation was discussed with Dupuis, the Commandant. Should they attempt to escape? The officer had no choice left, for nine out of his ten soldiers had already determined to desert. Consequently the missionaries in the out stations were called in gradually, and on March 20th, in the darkness of the night, the entire colony stole out in their boats across the lake to the ice-choked river, trusting to their own instinct to find the course, for no Indian could be trusted. They cut their way through the ice and reached

143

Lake Ontario. Tossed for a time on the billows of Lake Ontario, and then flung over the rapids of the St. Lawrence, they finally, after a month's terrible battle with the elements and with starvation, reached Quebec on April 23, seeming to all the settlement, as they passed, like ghosts from the other world. We give an extract of Ragueneau's account of the escape:

" The resolution was taken to quit the country forthwith, even though the difficulties seemed insurmountable. To supply the want of canoes we built in secret two boats of a novel structure to pass the rapids. They were flat bottomed and could carry considerable freight, with fourteen or fifteen men on each. We had besides four Algonquin and four Iroquois canoes. The difficulty was to build and launch them without being detected, for without secrecy we could only expect a general massacre.

" After succeeding in finishing the boats we invited all the savages in our neighborhood to a solemn banquet, and spared neither the noise of drums nor instruments of music to deceive them as to our purpose. At the feast everyone vied with each other in uttering the most piercing cries, now of revelry, now of war. The savages sung and danced in French fashion, and the French after the manner of the Indians. Presents were given and the greatest tumult was kept up, to cover the noise of forty of our people outside who were launching the boats. The feast was concluded, the guests retired and were soon overpowered by sleep, and we slipped out by the back way to the boats.

" The little lake on which we sailed in the darkness of the night froze as we advanced. God, however, delivered us, and after having advanced all night and all the following day we arrived in the evening at Lake Ontario. The first day was the most dangerous. Ten or twelve Iroquois could have intercepted us, for the river was narrow, and ten leagues down the stream it leaped over a frightful precipice. It took us four hours to carry our boats around it through a dense and unknown forest. The perils in which we walked made us shudder after we escaped them. We had no bed at night but the snow, after having passed entire days in icy water.

" Ten days after our departure we reached the St. Lawrence, but it was frozen, and we had to cut a channel through the ice. Two days after, our little fleet nearly foundered in the rapids. We were in the Long Sault without knowing it; we found ourselves in the midst of breakers, with rocks on all sides against which the mountains of water flung us at every stroke of our paddles. The cries of our people, mingling with the roar of the waters, added to the horror of the scene. One of our canoes was engulfed in the breakers and barred the passage through which we all had to pass. Three Frenchmen were drowned there; a fourth fortunately saved himself by clinging to the canoe. He was picked up at the foot of the Sault just as his strength was giving out and he was letting go his hold. On the 3d of April we landed at Montreal at the beginning of the night."

They found out afterwards what had occurred at Onondaga after their flight. When night had given place to day, and darkness to light, the barbarians awoke from sleep, and leaving their cabins roved around our well locked house. They were astonished at the profound silence that reigned there. They saw no one going in or out. They heard no voice. They thought at first that all were at prayer, or in council, but the day advancing and the prayers not coming to an end they knocked at the door. The dogs, which we had designedly left behind, answered by barking." Radisson's account adds that they had attached a bell-rope to the leg of a pig that was left behind, so that every time the animal moved, the pealing of the bell was heard. The Indians, of course, thought that some exercise or other was going on inside the establishment. This is omitted by Ragueneau. " The cock's crow which they heard in the morning," says Ragueneau, " and the noise of the dogs, made them think that the masters were not far off, and they recovered the patience which they had lost. But at length the sun began to go down, and no person answering either to the voice of men or the cries of the dogs, they scaled the house to see the condition of our men in this terrible silence. Astonishment now gave place to fright. They opened the door; the chiefs enter, descend to the cellar and mount to the garret. Not a Frenchman made his appearance, dead or alive. They thought they had to do with devils. They saw no boats; but never imagined we could have been so foolhardy as to face the rapids and run the horrible dangers in which they themselves, who are so expert in shooting the cascades, often lose their lives. They were convinced that we had walked on the waves, or fled through the air. Perhaps, it was suggested, we were hiding in the woods. A search was made but no one was found. They then fancied we had made ourselves invisible, and just as we had so suddenly disappeared, we would just as suddenly pounce upon their village and destroy it."

Radisson in his *Travels* has also described this famous escape. But he dwells mostly on the occurrences at the feast, where the Indians gorged themselves into a stupor. He informs us that the proposition was made to the priest to let the fugitives massacre the Indians who were now helpless in sleep on account of their gluttony. Of course Ragueneau forbade any such gruesome reprisal.

The exodus took place on March 21, 1658. It was the end of the first attempt to plant the Church in New York. The mission had lasted only two years, but it was not altogether a failure. During that time the missionaries had baptized 500 children, who died shortly after; they had converted 400 victims who were burned at the stake; had ministered to a great number of Christian captives; and had sown the seeds of the faith in the minds of many of the far Western Indians who had come down to Onondaga.

We have anticipated events in the life of Ragueneau, and

PAUL RAGUENEAU.

the question naturally suggests itself: Who was this wonderful man that appears as the guiding spirit in that ever memorable retreat from Onondaga? He was one of the heroes of the Northwest, and had already displayed his consummate ability in dealing with disaster by leading ten times as many fugitives to a place of safety over a territory much more dangerous and extensive than that which lies between Syracuse and Quebec. He was born in Paris in 1605, and had distinguished himself as the professor of the Great Condé, establishing an affection with his illustrious pupil which lasted through life. He came to Canada when he was thirty-one years of age.

Preceding him by a few years, Brébeuf and some others had set sail with Champlain, who had come out to take possession of the colony from which he had been driven four years previously. Landing at Quebec, they were met by 140 canoes which carried 700 Hurons, who had come down to ask for missionaries. Brébeuf was chosen for the work, and in the following year he, Davost and Daniel were in the far-off wilderness of Huronia, almost discouraged at first by the brutal treatment to which they were subjected and the hardships they were compelled to endure. On their way they had become separated from each other. Davost was robbed and abandoned on a desert island; Daniel was beaten by his guides and left to find his way alone to some Indian camp, while Brébeuf reached the shores of what is now Thunder Bay, whither he had gone in search of a village, where he had been four years before. But he found it deserted, and he then struggled on through the woods to Ihonatiria, which was on the Eastern shore of Penatanguishene Bay, some miles further on.

There Brébeuf began his work, and about six kilometres from that point, on a little promontory which juts out on the west coast of the Huron peninsula, fringed all around with sombre pine forests, the mission of Ossossané was established. This was Ragueneau's place of work a few

147

years later. With him was Garnier, the future martyr, and from thence both of them travelled south in search of Indians; going as far as Niagara, which Ragueneau speaks of as "a cataract falling from a frightful height." That was fully thirty-five years before Hennepin, the alleged discoverer of the falls, had described them in detail.

Those who are familiar with the story of the Huron missions know the awful experiences of those early years; how, to add to the sorrows of the missionaries, a destructive pestilence swept over Ihonatiria and the adjacent villages; how the medicine men had resorted to all sorts of incantations to put an end to the plague; how hideous and obscene dances, in which the plague-stricken took part to charm away the evil, turned the villages into what seemed almost like abodes of the damned; and how, when the conjurers failed, they turned upon the missionaries and accused them of being sorcerers whose more potent spells made the native medicine useless. Defying danger, Brébeuf and his companions walked into the wigwam where a council was being held to deliberate on their death. To awe the savages they sat down next to the most bloodthirsty among them. "Show us the cloth that produces the malady," cried the savages. "I have none," answered Brébeuf. "It is your sins that have brought this curse upon you," and amid their howls and execrations he strove to give them some idea of Christianity. It was all useless, and as he was going back in the dark to his own cabin, a huge Indian fell dead at his feet; a tomahawk had cloven his skull. "Was that for me?" he coolly asked of the murderer. "No," was the answer, "you can go."

Then came a meeting of all the Indians of the district at the place where Ragueneau was stationed. It was to discuss again the death of the missionaries, though ostensibly for some other object. Brébeuf had come to Ossossané, and in Ragueneau's bark cabin the little group of heroes knelt and prayed. Their time had apparently come, and they wrote what they thought was their last message to their friends. It was signed by each and placed in the hands of a trusty Indian, who carried it to Quebec. It was dated the 28th of October, 1637, and runs thus:

" We are perhaps on the point of shedding our blood and offering the sacrifice of our lives for our good Master, Jesus Christ. It is a singular favor which His goodness confers upon us to make us endure something for His love. May He be blessed for evermore for having chosen us among so many thousands of others to come to this country to help Him to carry His cross. May His holy will be done in all things! If He wishes us to die now, what a happiness it is for us! If He reserves us for other trials, may He be likewise blest! If you hear that He has crowned our little labor here, or rather our desires, bless Him; for we desire to die for Him, and it is He who gave us the grace to do so."

" This superb monument of courage and love," as Rochemonteix calls it, " has affixed to it the names of Jean de Brébeuf, François Le Mercier, Pierre Chastelain, Charles Garnier, and Paul Ragueneau. A postscript added that Father Pierre Pijart and Isaac Jogues in the residence of St. Joseph were in the same sentiments."

So convinced were they all of their approaching murder, that after the fashion of the Indians, they invited the sachems and braves to the farewell banquet; the banquet of death. The savages came in throngs, curious to see how these European sorcerers would face their doom. In the middle of the repast Brébeuf rose amid the group of the Fathers who were there with him, and began to speak. He did not extol his own courage, as was usual on such occasions, but explained to his hearers the perfections of the Great Spirit. The Indians listened in gloomy silence. They uttered not a word of approbation; nor gave any sign of relenting, and when the banquet was over they withdrew, cold and evidently unimpressed.

To all appearances the storm had not spent itself. But

the victims began a novena of Masses in honor of St. Joseph, the patron of the mission, and before it was over they were aware that the danger had passed for the moment. The great disaster came twelve years later.

When Jogues was being tortured and killed in New York, in 1646, Ragueneau was Superior of the Huron Missions, and lived at St. Mary's on the Wye. The mission at that time counted eighteen priests, two of whom were with Ragueneau at St. Mary's. Father Daniel was at St. Joseph's; Brébeuf and Lalemant at St. Louis and St. Ignace, neither of which was far away; and to the south, among the Tobacco Indians, Garnier and Chabanel were at work. The rest were scattered in different places not necessary now to mention. As a Superior, Ragueneau seems to have been ideal. "We have excellent and capable laborers here," wrote Brébeuf to Father-General, "but they are very inferior to Father Ragueneau, especially in matter of government." The work of conversion of the Indians was also satisfactory, for Ragueneau wrote: "I never thought that fifty years of work would have achieved what I have seen of piety, devotion and sanctity among the Indians." Father Jogues' blood in far-off New York was beginning to produce its fruit. These were his Indians of St. Mary's who were being converted.

Such was the happy condition in which they dwelt for two years, when on July 4, 1648, Daniel, who was at St. Joseph's, was startled at sunrise by the cry "To arms." The Iroquois were upon them, and the Hurons, who had been in the chapel praying, were already in mad flight, though some stood their ground, and made a fight at the palisades. While the battle was going on, Daniel hurried from cabin to cabin to absolve the dying, and to baptize the catechumens. Returning to the chapel where the old men and women and children were gathered, he gave them a general absolution, and by aspersion baptized those who asked for it.

PAUL RAGUENEAU.

Outside, the yells of the Iroquois were rising higher. The assailants had scaled the palisades, and set fire to the cabins, and were already engaged in massacring every one they met. " Hurry in that direction," said Daniel to the panic-stricken people in the chapel, " the way is still open," while he went back in spite of their entreaties. He faced the oncoming Iroquois, who, astonished at his audacity, halted for an instant, and then poured on him a shower of arrows, ending their work by a shot from a musket. He fell at their feet and they stripped him of his clothes, dipped their hands in his blood and flung his lifeless body into the flaming chapel. This self-immolation saved hundreds of his people, who in the momentary pause made their escape. But nevertheless the Iroquois took 700 prisoners, and setting fire to the village, which was soon a heap of ashes, they hurried away to their own country, only to return after the wretched Hurons had been led to believe that no further danger was to be apprehended.

They came back next year on the 16th of March, a day most memorable in the annals of the mission. One thousand Iroquois had gathered from the various parts of New York, and crept stealthily up to the mission of St. Ignace, which was under the care of Brébeuf and Lalemant, but from which both of them were just then absent, being engaged at the adjoining post of St. Louis. St. Ignace was given over to the flames, most of the inhabitants were massacred, and some fugitives hurried with the news of the tragedy to St. Louis. But the Iroquois were close behind them. The priests were seized, and carried in triumph to St. Ignace. The horrors of their martyrdom have been too often described to call for repetition here. When the tragedy was over, the bodies of the martyrs were carried to St. Mary's, where the Superior, Father Ragueneau, interred them with the reverence which their heroism and sanctity demanded. The remains of Father Daniel, who had died

151

the year before, were never recovered. They had mingled with the ashes of his humble chapel.

Necessarily, during all this terrible time, St. Mary's was trembling for its existence. Though it was fortified it could not hope to withstand the ever increasing power of the Iroquois, who were now coming nearer and nearer. Another difficulty presented itself. The number of fugitive Hurons who sought shelter there made the question of their sustenance one of startling importance. Would they have to abandon this last defense?

In the beginning of June, 1649, two months after the death of Brébeuf and Lalemant, twelve Huron chiefs came to beg Father Ragueneau to transport the mission to St. Joseph's Island out in the Bay. The Fathers would have preferred Manitoulin, which is far up on Lake Huron, the same place which is now occupied by the successors of these missionaries. It seemed safer and more desirable, but yielding to the persuasion of the sachems, it was determined to emigrate to St. Joseph's; and so on the 14th of June, putting all their live stock and provisions and effects upon rafts and boats, they rowed away from St. Mary's, after setting fire to the beloved mission which had cost so much sacrifice and labor during the ten years of its existence, but which one hour reduced to ashes. The ruins are yet to be seen.

Arriving at St. Joseph's, Frenchmen and Indians alike set to work to dig ditches, fix the stockades and build a fort, which they made mostly of stone. It was 123 feet long and 60 wide, with two bastions at the southern end. " It was easy to defend," says Ragueneau, " and we did not dread fire or escalade or sapping and mining. We also fortified the Huron village next to our dwelling. We threw up redoubts at all the approaches." On the southeast shore of the island you can still trace the lines of the old fortifications, the site of the chapel and the residence of the missionaries. Father Martin, who visited the place in 1845, published a description of it and added it to Bressani's *Relation*.

PAUL RAGUENEAU.

"There are no remnants of the village," writes Father Martin, "but the ruins of the fort have survived all the disasters. It is square, with bastions at the angles. Originally, the walls were five metres high, and at some places there are two metres left. The work is perfect in its regularity, and remarkable in its proportions and correctness of alignment. In the centre is a cistern in masonry 3 metres square and 2 deep. In the middle of the east curtain is an abutting wall which must have been protected by constructions in wood. Doubtless the northwest bastion was part of it.

"Some years ago there were found in the midst of the ruins a number of wampum belts, some white, some violet; and also remnants of copper utensils and human bones. The most interesting of all was the mould for making altar breads. It was of iron, and, being so heavy, was doubtless not put on the backs of the Hurons when they fled to Quebec. It was nearly like what we use nowadays. The stamps on it were in a perfect state of preservation. They adhered to each other, but the rust on the outside had prevented all action of air or water. An Englishman paid a good price for it, and not knowing its purpose, sent it to a museum in London. There were also dug up some pieces of coarse pottery and pipes, which have the merit of letting us know what was the nature of Huron industry. We ourselves found some calumets in the Indian graves."

Work was carried on with such vigor in this new place that when winter set in they were secure from attack; and on March 13, 1650, Ragueneau was able to write to Rome: "Never have we gathered such fruits of our labors; never has the Faith struck such deep roots in the hearts of the Indians; never has the Christian name been so glorious as in the midst of the ruins of this unhappy nation. Last year we baptized 3,000 Indians."

But the sky was already growing black. Hardly was the fort completed when Indian runners brought the news of two more disasters down to the south of them among the To-

153

bacco Indians, where Fathers Garnier and Chabanel had been stationed. The Iroquois had appeared, but confident of their strength, the Petuns, or Tobaccos, had gone out to meet them. Their excessive confidence was their ruin, for the wily Iroquois, taking a roundabout course, slipped by them and, falling upon the undefended town, massacred all its inhabitants. When they arrived, Garnier was teaching catechism in his cabin. He might have escaped, but that thought never came to his mind. On the contrary, he hastened from hut to hut to baptize the children and absolve the dying. While he was hurrying on with his work two musket balls stretched him in his gore; but in spite of that, while bleeding to death, he struggled to his knees to crawl over to a dying Huron who was asking for absolution. The Iroquois saw him and a tomahawk clove his skull. After they had satisfied their fury they withdrew. Then the braves who had gone out to meet the foe came back, and saw with horror the ruins of their cabins and the mangled bodies of their wives and children. All day long they sat on the ground, motionless statues of bronze, their heads bent, their eyes fixed on the earth. Not a cry, not a tear betrayed the agony of their hearts.

A few days before this massacre Father Chabanel had been called back to the headquarters at St. Joseph's Island. Several Hurons went with him. While they were halting in a forest in the dead of night, and when his companions were all buried in sleep, Chabanel heard the noise of approaching feet. It was the Iroquois returning from the massacre. He awakened his Hurons, but they all fled in terror, leaving him alone with an apostate Christian. He was never seen again, and the renegade afterward confessed that he had murdered him. His death and that of Garnier ends the list of the heroes who died for the faith in Canada. No doubt when the intelligence of the tragedy was brought, it dispelled the bright hope that Ragueneau was cherishing for the Church of the Hurons.

OLD QUEBEC.

PAUL RAGUENEAU.

The Hurons outnumbered the Iroquois and could easily
have beaten back their foes, but they had lost heart. Ten
thousand of them had already perished; other thousands
were absorbed by neighboring tribes, and multitudes in a
starving condition came to the missionaries for food. Soon
a pestilence reaped a harvest of death among them. The
famine was so great that even the dead were disinterred and
eaten; and, worst of all, when spring set in, the Iroquois
reappeared. The unhappy Hurons were vanishing from the
earth. At last everything had to be abandoned, and, yielding to the entreaties of the Indians, Ragueneau turned his
face to Quebec and led the wretched remnants of the once
great tribe down to the city on the St. Lawrence, which had
scarcely enough to sustain its own inhabitants. Three or
four hundred naked and famishing Hurons, men, women
and children, presented themselves at the city gates. There
was consternation among the inhabitants, but the colony was
Catholic, and in that supreme test of its charity it did not
fail to give a splendid example of self-sacrifice in saving these
wretched outcasts. The Fathers and nuns begged everywhere for food and clothing during the long winter, until
spring melted the snows, and then the poor unfortunates
were gathered under the care of Father Chaumonot on the
Isle d'Orleans.

After his return to Quebec Ragueneau became the director
of a nun of the Hôtel Dieu, whose life has just been written
by the Jesuit Father Hudon, of Montreal. She was called
Mother Catherine of St. Augustin, and came to Canada at
the age of twenty-three or four. Her recent biographer presents her to his readers as a mystic of quite an extraordinary
kind, to whose sufferings and prayers Canada owed its preservation at a time when the fortunes of the colony were
hanging in the balance. De Brébeuf, who had just been
killed, frequently appeared to Mother Catherine, and directed her in the practices of the supernatural life. Associated with Ragueneau as confessor and spiritual guide was
Bishop Laval. The testimony of these two great men is a

sufficient guarantee that Mother Catherine was not a victim of delusions.

It was to be expected that a man of such prominence as Ragueneau would immediately attract attention on his arrival at Quebec. So it happened, but only to his misfortune.

From the year 1647, the Jesuits had occupied a seat in the Supreme Council of the colony, an honor which had been accepted after considerable hesitation. Father Le Mercier was the first to hold that place, and when he went to France, Ragueneau, whom he had appointed Vice Rector of Quebec, naturally succeeded him. But as the duties of his office brought him into frequent contact with the Governor, De Lauson, a strong personal friendship developed between the two men, with the unfortunate result, however, that whatever the Governor did was ascribed to Ragueneau, so that a good deal of discontent and jealousy was engendered, especially among those who had to be severely dealt with. The Jesuits themselves objected, and forwarded their complaints to the Father General, who forthwith ordered the Provincial to remove Ragueneau to another field of labor, and hence, in October, 1656, the Superior of Quebec wrote to Rome that, "in obedience to orders, he had transferred Father Ragueneau to Three Rivers, notwithstanding the strong protest of the Governor." The letter of Father de Quen to the General, dated October, 1656, says: "Father Ragueneau is a man of great candor and of remarkable virtue, but more immersed in secular affairs than becomes our Society, and is a cause of many complaints and much ill will in our regard. All this will stop if he cuts loose from this business and is sent into the *most remote mission."* There Ragueneau was laboring when a second command sent him to the Onondaga mission.

It was a fine test of virtue, but he was found equal to it; for though no one has written so much about the Canadian mission—he is in fact the author of the greater number of the *Relations*—not a word appears in his voluminous publications and corespondence, which shows that he resented in

156

the least what might seem unnecessarily harsh treatment for
one who had scarcely yet recovered from the sufferings
which he had undergone among the savages of Lake Huron.
Not only did he obey, but he undertook the new work with
enthusiasm. We have seen how he labored at Onondaga.
His submission is all the more admirable as we find a
letter, written by him in 1658 to the General who had
asked for information, that he thought " Father de Quen,
the Superior, was naturally weak and lacking in prudence;
and that better natural parts would be desirable in one occu-
pying his position." Ragueneau's obedience was along supernatural lines. It is worthy of note that Father Poncet,
who was one of those to object to Father Ragueneau's politics, was himself removed from his office for analogous reasons some time later.

When Ragueneau returned to Quebec with the wreck of
the Onondaga mission he, a second time, became an unwilling source of discomfort to his superiors. He was again
marked out for honors by the civil authorities, and we find
in the State Papers of the Great Condé a letter from M. du
Bois d'Avajour dated Quebec, October 13, 1661, which informs His Highness that he had put " at the head of the
Council for the service of the King and the good of the
country the Reverend Father *Ragnaust,* who has the honor
to be known to Your Highness."

These dignities which were again thrust upon him without
any fault of his were still displeasing to his superiors; for
we find that when Bishop Laval, who was his devoted friend,
returned to France in 1662, in the interests of the colony,
Father Ragueneau was his companion. America never saw
him again. All the rest of his life he remained in France
acting as Procurator of the Missions, which he had served
so well. He died in Paris September 3, 1680. Besides the
four volumes of the *Relations* which he edited, he has left
also the Life of Mother Catherine of St. Augustin. His
missionary career in New York was brief, but he occupies a
splendid place in its list of heroes.

RENE MENARD.

RENE MENARD'S American missionary career begins in a wild storm which raged in the very harbor from which he was to set sail from the other side of the Atlantic. He describes it all in a long letter which may be found in the eighteenth volume of the *Relations*. That and the romantic scenes on board the Espérance as it sailed away subsequently over the tranquil ocean, he narrates with the most exquisite taste. The letter does not indeed purport to be his, as the Superior embodies it in the annual report, saying: "Father René *Menart* having arrived at *Kebec,* related to us some adventures of the Fleet this year, which seem to me very worthy to compose this chapter"; but nevertheless it is very likely a transcript of Ménard's own account given in writing to Father Le Jeune. As he had been a student at Paris, La Flèche, Bourges, and Rouen, and an instrcutor at Orleans and Moulins from 1629 to 1639, in the palmy days of the French Jesuit Colleges, he was quite capable of giving it the delicate literary touch it possesses.

"Our ships," he says, "set out from their anchorage on the 26th of March, 1640. Madame the Duchesse d'Aiguillon having increased the endowment of her Hospital in New France, and desiring, consequently, that two nuns of the House of Mercy established at Dieppe should come and give help to their good sisters, Monseigneur the Archbishop of Rouen granted them their dismissal with a love and affection proportionate to his desire for the increase of the glory of our Lord in the conversion of the poor savages." The dignified courtesy in the references to "Monseigneur" and "Madame la Duchesse" is observed throughout the letter, and is characteristic of the courtly gentlemen that most of those first missionaries were. "Mother de Sainte Marie and Sister de Saint Nicholas," he continues, "both professed

DIEPPE.

nuns of this monastery, were chosen, *with a very keen appreciation of their good fortune and with regrets for the many others who were sighing for this cross which they regarded as a paradise.* There were two other nuns also, Mother Anne de Sainte Claire and Mother Marguerite de Saint Athanase, who embarked on the vessel called the ' Espérance ' under the command of Monsieur de Courpon, a very honest gentleman who favored these good souls to the utmost. I do not know whether the demons foresaw some great blessing from this passage, but it seems as if they desired to engulf us from the time we left the roadstead. They raised up the whole ocean, unchained the winds, and excited such horrible and continuous tempests that they almost made us perish in sight of Dieppe. We were in the midst of these dangers from the twenty-sixth of March until the twenty-eighth of April, beaten by rain and snow, *and as near to death as we were to the coasts of France.* A ship of Saint Valéry which was in the harbor with us, detaching itself from its anchors, went to pieces before our eyes, everything that was within being carried away. The men were engulfed in the waves, and of twenty or thereabout who were in this ship, only three were saved. The death that reaped these bodies seemed at every moment waiting to devour us. I heard many people cursing the day and the hour when the thought entered into their minds to go upon the sea and to entrust their lives to the mercy of a cable. *Virtue animates a heart powerfully. These good Sisters, who at other times would have trembled in a boat upon the Seine, mocked at death and its approaches.* This tempest having passed, another arose as furious as the first. As they saw it arising in the sky our sailors cast the second anchor, which saved our lives, for the cable of the first, which until then had secured us, broke in a moment, and our ship would have been hopelessly lost if the second anchor had not held us fast. If we avoided one danger we fell into another. A wave dashed our Vice Admiral towards us with such violence that the most steadfast thought we were lost. Never have I confronted death so near. If this ship had advanced twenty paces we should have been dashed to pieces, and the ocean would have swallowed us in its waves. . . . I do not know that for a hundred years vessels have been so long anchored or assailed by such contrary winds. Yet the fury of the tempest, while chaining us near the port, defended us against hostile frigates equipped for war which were awaiting us outside, so that if we had weighed anchor one day before our departure, we should infallibly have fallen into the hands of the enemy. Madame the Duchesse d'Aiguillon, having been advised of this ambuscade, so arranged that Monseigneur the Cardinal de Richelieu ordered the ships of Havre to act as our convoy. As we were about to go and join them we encountered five Dunkirk frigates. Immediately our men grasp their weapons, cannon are thrust out of the portholes—every one is ready for the combat. Monsieur de Courpon, our Admiral, advances. But these frigates, being hampered by two Dutch ships that had left us the previous night and had been captured a little while before we appeared, turned away from us, seeing from our appearance that we were ready to dispute the victory with them stubbornly. We reached Havre directly afterwards, where we found fifty ships at anchor, awaiting us. I did not think I was on the sea, seeing myself encompassed by so much wood. . . . As we floated along in this security the ships of the King sighted eight hostile frigates, to which they gave chase. But they escaped, owing to a favorable wind. The royal escort, seeing us out of the channel and out of danger, left us. Thus the tempests, ready to destroy us in the port, protected us against our enemies."

The voyage across was as tranquil as its beginning was boisterous. Great piety reigned among the crew. " But the devotion was most profound and most conspicuous on the day of the Blessed Sacrament. A magnificent altar was prepared in the cabin of our Admiral; the crew erected another at the prow of the ship, and Our Lord, desirous to be adored upon this unstable element, gave us a calm so peaceful that we could imagine ourselves floating upon a pond. We formed a really solemn procession. Everyone took part in it, and their piety and devotion caused them to march in excellent order around the deck. Our brother Dominique Scot, wearing a surplice, bore the cross; on either side of him were two children, each bearing a lighted torch; the nuns followed with their white wax tapers, in angelic modesty; after the priest who carried the Blessed Sacrament walked the Admiral of the fleet, and then the whole crew. The cannons made the air and the waves resound with thunder, and the Angels took pleasure in hearing the praises that our hearts and lips gave to their Prince and to our Sovereign King."

They reached Tadoussac on the last of June, and finally " on Sunday morning cast anchor opposite *Kebec.* Monsieur our Governor went down to the wharf with our Reverend Father Superior to receive our Fathers and to escort these truly generous Sisters to their house. They upon leaving the ship fell upon their knees and kissed the ground so long desired and sang the *Laudate Dominum omnes gentes;* and Madame de la Peltrie, accompanied by her little seminarists, neatly dressed, embraced these good nuns," etc.

It is rather a surprise to be told that " they left the ship in better health than when they had entered it. Poverty and discomfort in houses that are built upon land seem palaces and riches to those who come forth from a house of wood floating at the will of the winds and waves." Thus did Father Ménard make his entrance into the New World.

During the next year he studied Algonquin, and his name appears on the baptismal register at Sillery, alongside of Massé's, Pijart's, and others equally famous. Among the sponsors are such dignitaries as Montmagny himself, Le Gardeur de Repentigny, Achille de Lisle, Madame de la

Peltrie and her maid Carola. René Goupil is also there as godfather.

Ménard then started with Father Ragueneau for the Huron country. On the way the Indians informed them of danger ahead, and it was deemed prudent to return to Three Rivers. Messengers meantime were sent to Quebec to ask for an escort, but the Algonquins refused to go. At last a Huron arrived and told them that the road was open, and so they departed, " without any other discomfort than the great fatigues of a most frightful road." As a matter of fact there were five hundred Iroquois on the warpath, and Father Brébeuf, coming down the St. Lawrence, had narrowly escaped them.

In Huronia he was associated with the heroic Raymbault, who had been Jogues' companion in the journey over Lake Huron to meet the throngs of Indians awaiting them at Sault Ste. Marie. It was after he and Jogues had returned to Georgian Bay that Raymbault "immediately re-embarked in another canoe to seek the Nippissiriens in their winter quarters and to continue instructing them." His companion was Ménard.

Lake Nippissing lies east of Georgian Bay. You enter it by the Rivière des Français, but it is very far from the River Wye, where the mission headquarters had been established. The travellers never reached their destination. " The lake was so agitated, the winds so contrary, and the storms so great, that the canoe was compelled to put back to where it had started, and the ice, which formed immediately afterwards, rendered the voyage impossible. But, worse than that, Raymbault fell seriously ill, and Father Jogues had to carry him down to Quebec, a thousand miles away. There Raymbault died. But Jogues never returned to the Huron country. He was caught by the Iroquois, and began his martyrdom at Ossernenon. Ménard, however, did not abandon the Nippissirien project for which Raymbault had sacrificed his life. We read in the *Relations* that " at the end of

RENE MENARD.

April, Fathers Claude Pijart and René Ménard leave us to return to the Nippissiriens in their own country and to continue instructing them, for that nation seems of all these wandering peoples the least averse to the faith."

In the *Journal des Jesuites* for 1650-1651 we find this simple entry: "June 4. I appointed Father *Menart* to be Superior at Three Rivers. *Omnia peculia Huronum et Algonquinorum sublata*"; which means it was all over with the Hurons and Algonquins. The heroic work of those many years had come to naught. Many of the missionaries were killed, and Father Ménard, who had lived and worked with them all, was now down at the Fort of Three Rivers, probably disappointed that he had not been chosen for martyrdom. But we find also in the same Journal the month after: "July 2d. A band of eighty Iroquois appeared at Three Rivers, at first to the number of eight, who, issuing from the wood, rushed upon two canoes which were approaching the land opposite; but our men, having abandoned their canoes and taken to the shallop, there appeared a greater number of Iroquois, who discharged forty or fifty shots upon the shallop." Ménard was still in the midst of war. Finally, on the 3d of August, this entry appears: "Father Ménard baptized the two Iroquois, Pierre and François, who were burned the next day." They had been captured in the foray which they had persisted in making at the very palisades of the fort. Poor Father Ménard could not prevent their execution, but he sent them to heaven.

Then came the call for missionaries to go into the very heart of the Iroquois country. Of course, Father Ménard was sent; for he was known as "the most spiritual of all the missionaries," and as the *Relations* inform us, "he seemed to pine away when not engaged in some perilous enterprise for the salvation of souls." He was chosen to be one of the apostles in the expedition that sailed from Quebec, May 17, 1656. We do not know whether he was one of those who left that city and barely escaped being murdered by 300 Iroquois who were waiting in ambush at the very spot where the party had proposed, the first morning after leaving Quebec, to land and celebrate Mass. Fortunately this they did not do, merely because the pilot forgot all about it. He thus unconsciously averted the massacre. Possibly Ménard joined the party at Three Rivers. At all events he was in one of the canoes that sailed over Lake Ganentaa on the 11th of July with cannon booming and men cheering and banners waving, to take possession of the new region for Christ.

The month after his arrival he and Chaumonot went off to the Cayugas, where after a while he was left alone, not even knowing the language. Nevertheless, he had every reason to expect the triumph of the Gospel. His going there was brought about by a sort of an Indian Constantine.

When Le Moyne first addressed the Onondagas, a Cayuga chief was in the throng of listeners. He demanded baptism. He was going to fight the Eries. Le Moyne, of course, refused. "Are you the master of life and death?" asked the Indian. "Can you prevent the arrows of the Eries from piercing my heart? Unless thou baptize me I shall be without courage. Baptize me, and I will obey thee and give my word to live and die a Christian." Le Moyne instructed and baptized him and the chief set out for battle. He met the foe and his braves were inspired by his fervor. When they saw themselves surrounded by the Eries, four times their number, they invoked the God of the Christians and won the day. Many kept their promise, but many forgot it.

By these warrior-Christians Ménard was led to Cayuga, but he received the reverse of a welcome from the rest of the tribe. Even the children attacked him, and till his dying day his scarred face showed how cruelly and how freely they had used their knives. "Without trembling," says the *Relation* of 1662-64, " he saw the Iroquois fall upon him to cut his throat when he was laboring for their conversion. Others at the same place raised their hatchets against him to split

164

MGR. LAVAL.

his head, but he was not frightened. The children hooted
at him and ran after him as after a madman. But little by
little his patience triumphed. The purity of the Huron captive women, whom he taught, amazed the Cayuga squaws,
and soon his little chapel began to be frequented. Children
were baptized, as were many women. The men held back.
Of them he gained only a few; the first an old man on his
death-bed, and the second a once famous chief who had tried
to prevent the burning of Brébeuf years before in the Huron
country, and who now, half eaten by a cancer, received the
gift of faith. His influence was often valuable in saving
Ménard from death, especially in the beginning, but after
two months Ménard was a favorite, and when called away
deputations were sent to entreat him to return. He did so,
and went afterwards to the Oneidas, who were still harder
to deal with than the Cayugas. When the crash came two
years later he and the other missionaries disappeared in the
middle of the night from Onondaga. His going, he said,
was like tearing out his heart.

In the catalogue of 1659 we find under the heading
" Three Rivers " three illustrious names: Ménard, Fremin
and Le Moyne. In that year Bishop Laval wrote to Pope
Alexander VII: " This summer a priest of the Society of
Jesus left for a mission five hundred leagues from Quebec.
The country is inhabited by numberless nations who have
never heard speak of the Catholic faith. Seven Frenchmen
go with him; they to trap beavers, he to gain souls. He will
have much to suffer and everything to fear from the winter,
from hunger, from sickness, from the savages. But the
love of Jesus Christ and zeal for souls triumphs over everything."

That priest was René Ménard, Superior of the Residence
of Three Rivers. " On his way back from Montreal to
Quebec," says Rochemonteix, " the bishop had met a flotilla
of sixty canoes with 300 Ottawas going up the stream, after
leaving their peltries at Three Rivers. In the midst of the

Indians he perceives Father Ménard, and asks him whither he is going. " To Lake Superior, or perhaps beyond; wherever the glory of God may call." The bishop was startled. Ménard was already fifty-five years of age, his health shattered by labors, fatigue and excessive penance, and he was bent like an old man.

The missionary understood the anxious look of the bishop. " What should I do, Monseigneur?" he asked. " Father," was the answer, " there is every reason for you to remain, but God, who is stronger than all, wants you there." The words were consoling, and later on in the Far West Ménard wrote in his journal: " How often I have recalled them, amidst the roar of the rapids and the solitude of the trackless forests." The memory of that meeting on the St. Lawrence prompted the bishop's letter to the Pope. Douglas in his " Old Quebec " fancies that Ménard's question to the bishop indicated a fear about going, but Douglas, not being a Catholic, could not appreciate the import of the words of either the bishop or the missionary.

Kneeling for the blessing of the holy prelate, Ménard set out with his savages, trusting to God. He had no baggage, no presents for the savages, and no provisions. He went with his faithful John Guerin, a *donné,* whithersoever the Spirit of God might guide, only convinced that he would never return. Before he left Three Rivers he wrote a farewell letter to one of his friends: " I write to you probably for the last time, and I want this last word to be the seal of our friendship until we meet in eternity. In three or four months you can put me in your *Memento* for the dead. The life among those people, my age, and my poor health " (he calls it *ma petite complexion*) " make it certain. Nevertheless, I felt so impelled to it, and find so little of the natural in the call, that I could not doubt that if I missed the chance I should be punished by an eternal remorse. We were a little surprised not to have been provided with clothes and other things, but He who feeds the birds and robes the lilies of the field will have care of His servants, and if it happen that we die in misery, it will be for us a source of happiness."

It is worth noting that one of the seven Frenchmen who went out on this daring expedition was the famous Groseilliers, whose history has been told in the life of Father Poncet.

Three years afterwards thirty-five canoes manned by Ottawas came to Montreal. With them were the seven Frenchmen who had gone out into the wilds with Father Ménard, but when they beached their canoes near the fort on that 26th of July, 1663, Father Ménard was not with them. From them some meagre information was gleaned of what had happened to him, and the account forms one of the most pathetic narratives in all the wonderful *Relations*. We can only quote from it here and there.

" The poor Father and the seven Frenchmen, his companions, setting out with the Ottawas from Three Rivers, on the 28th of August, in the year 1660, reached the Ottawa country on the 15th of October, Saint Theresa's day, after enduring unspeakable hardships, ill treatment from the boatmen and an extreme scantiness of provisions." He tells us in a letter that reached his brethren how they made him paddle all day long, sometimes without even breaking his fast; how he had to drag his canoe through the shallow streams or carry it on the long portages while sinking with weakness and fatigue; how anxious he was never to omit saying his breviary, which was very difficult, for they started early in the morning and stopped only at night. Once they snatched the book from his hands and threw it into the river, " but by good fortune," he said, " I had another, which I took good care they did not lay hands on."

" Finally, overcome by fatigue, his already delicate constitution almost shattered, he arrived at his destination; but ' as a man spent with toil can still go a good distance after growing weary ' he had spirit enough to drag himself to the

167

wretched cabin where he was to stay. It was owned by an Indian known as *le Brochet* (the Pike), a chief excessively proud, extremely vicious and troubled with four or five wives. He treated the poor Father very badly, and finally forced him to leave and make himself a hut out of fir branches. Heavens! what an abode during the rigors of winter, which are well-nigh unendurable in those regions? The food was scarcely better, as they commonly had for their only dish one paltry fish to be divided among the four or five of their party, and this, too, was a charitable offering made by the savages, some one of the Frenchmen waiting at the water's edge for the return of the fishermen's canoes, as poor beggars wait for alms at the church door. A kind of moss growing on the rocks often served them in place of a meal. They would put a handful of it into their kettle, which would thicken the water ever so little, forming a kind of foam or slime, like that of snails, and feeding their imaginations more than their bodies. Fishbones, which were carefully saved, also served to beguile their hunger. There was nothing that these poor starvelings did not turn to some account. The bark of oak, birch, linden, and that of other trees, when well cooked and pounded and then put into the water in which the fish had been boiled or else mixed with fish-oil, made them some excellent stews. They ate acorns with more relish and greater pleasure than attend the eating of chestnuts in Europe, yet even of these they did not have their fill. Thus passed the first winter.

" In the spring they fared better. In the second winter they tried to fish, and it was piteous to see those poor Frenchmen in a canoe amid rain and snow, borne hither and thither by whirlwinds on those great lakes. They frequently found their hands and feet frozen, while occasionally they were overtaken by snow so thick that the one steering the canoe could not see his companion in the bow. But while destitute of bodily refreshment they were comforted by heavenly favors. As long as the Father was alive, they had Holy Mass every day and confessed and received Holy Communion about once a week. While the Father was wintering there, he began a church among those barbarians —very small but very precious, since it cost him much exertion and many tears." "The church" was only two old men and some women. One of the women whom he baptized was "a wonderful example of purity among a people wholly given over to lechery."

Gloomy and discouraging as it was, he had no thought of abandoning his post. "I would have to do myself violence," he wrote, "to come down from the cross which God has prepared for me in this extremity of the world in my old days. I know not the nature of the nails which fasten me to this adorable wood, but the mere thought that anyone should come to take me down makes me shudder, and I often start up from my slumbers imagining that there is no Ottawa land for me, and that my sins will send me back to the spot from which the mercy of my God had by so signal a favor drawn me."

This place was, as his letter informs us, 100 leagues west of Sault Ste. Marie; in all probability at Keweenaw.

At last, seeing that the brutality and polygamy of these people precluded all hope of their conversion, he proposed, as we see in a letter he wrote in July, 1661, to evangelize the Dacotahs, *who lived 300 leagues further on.* But he changed his plans, for he heard that there were some unfortunate Huron Christians in those parts who had fled thither from the pursuing Iroquois. Shea locates them on or near the Noquet Islands, in the vicinity of the mouth of Green Bay.

Before setting out, however, he asked three of his French companions to go to find them and give them presents so as to prepare the way. The scouts accepted the perilous task, but they found only a wretched remnant of the tribe. It was in its death agony. Entering the cabins, they found nothing but sick people, almost like skeletons, and in such a state of weakness as to be unable to move or stand.

Unable to do anything for them, the messengers returned, suffering much more on their return journey than on their way thither. Had they not been young men they would certainly have perished. They told Ménard that it was madness for him to attempt the journey; they explained to him the difficulties of the road; the great number of rapids, the cataracts; the long and perilous portages; the precipices to be passed, the rocks over which he would have to climb and the arid tracts where there was nothing to support life. " God calls me," he answered. " If I die it will be like St. Francis Xavier. ' Farewell,' he said to them, ' and it is the final farewell that I bid you in this world, since you will not see me again.' "

He started on the 13th of June, after nine months' stay with the Ottawas. Some Hurons went with him, but deserted him near a lake. There he waited two weeks for them—Shea says " a month "—and he then struggled onward. "On the 10th of August, while following his companion, he went astray, mistaking some woods or rocks for others which had been indicated. His companion searched and called and discharged his musket, but in vain. He was never seen again. Some time afterward a savage found the Father's bag, but would not admit having found his body, fearing lest he should be accused of killing him—an accusation perhaps too well founded, since those barbarians did not scruple to cut a man's throat when they met him alone in the woods. He was probably murdered at the first rapid of the Menominee. Some of the furnishings of his chapel were afterwards discovered in a cabin, and his breviary and cassock are said to have been used by the Sioux in their solemn incantations."

So died this holy man; alone in the wilderness, no one knows where or how. The " Pater Frugifer " he was called, the Father who made each moment bear fruit. He had, as the *Relations* tell us, " the consolation of dying in the quest for new sheep, having traversed five hundred

RENE MENARD.

leagues of rapids and precipices in that work; being the one
of all the missionaries who approached nearest to the China
Sea, going as it were to meet his dear Apostle of the Indies,
St. Francis Xavier—by a different route indeed, but by a
last journey that was almost identical with that of the Apostle of the Indies, both having died in solitude and on the
way toward fresh conquests which they purposed to make
for heaven."

We find in Justin Winsor's *Narrative and Critical History
of America* (iv. p. 171) a passage relative to Father Ménard's last journey which is well worthy of being noted.
" Just beyond the Huron Isles and Huron Bay," he says,
"on the southern shore of Lake Superior, is Keweenaw Bay;
and on the 15th of October, Saint Theresa's day, in the cal-
endar of the Church of Rome, the traders and René Ménard with the returning Indians, stopped, and here passed
the winter. Discouraged by the indifference of the Indians,
he resolved to go to the retreat of the Hurons, among the
marshes of what is now the State of Wisconsin. He set out
on June 13, 1661, but about August 7, while Guerin was
making a portage around a rapids, Ménard lost the trail and
there was killed or died from exhaustion. Perrot writes:
' The Father followed the Ottawas to Lake Michigan, and
in their flight to Louisiana (Mississippi), as far as the upper
part of Black River.' Now if Perrot's statement is correct,
Ménard and his devoted companion *saw the Mississippi
twelve years before Joliet and his companion looked upon
the great river.*"

Thus did Ménard, while in quest of souls, win earthly
glory also, though it came two centuries after his painful
and heroic death. But would he have ever returned from
those distant regions to tell the story of his discovery? He
did not want to be taken off his cross.

171

JAMES FREMIN.

FATHER JAMES FREMIN had the air of a military man; a fierce colonel of dragoons. He could swagger through an Indian council; hector the chiefs, and threaten the tribe with the wrath of the Governor, the army, the King, etc., till they got to look at him as some mighty potentate who never could be touched. And yet this fierce ecclesiastical mustachio was the apostle of the babies. During his apostolate of thirty-five years he baptized 10,000 of them, and sent them to heaven. He was so beloved at La Prairie that when there was question of his being replaced as Superior, young and old were in consternation, and mournful prophecies were made about his succesor. Rochemonteix is very careful to tell us that he was not generously equipped with theological science, but that there was no doubt about his sanctity; that if he were not an exquisitely cultured scholar, he had the saving grace of common sense, and possessed to an eminent degree the master gifts of an apostle: piety, perseverance, and courage. Surely that sufficed. Treatises on sanctifying grace would have availed little with the Wolf, the Bear, and the Tortoise.

He was born in Rheims, March 12, 1628, entered the Society at Paris in 1646, and started for Canada in 1655. In the following year he went with Dablon and the fifty Frenchmen to Onondaga, and remained there till the mission collapsed in 1658. To what particular tribe he was assigned we do not know, but on his return to Quebec the Superior thought it opportune to send him to France for his tertianship. He pronounced his last vows when he returned to America in 1660. To have been on such a dangerous mission prior to his profession is a tribute to the solidity of his virtue.

Six years elapsed from that time till he made his second

entry into New York. He is mentioned as having been, meantime, with the Micmacs at Cape Breton, which is as far from Quebec, on one side, as Onondaga on the other. Again he was stationed at La Prairie, which he was to evangelize later; and probably he was laboring at Cape de la Madeleine, opposite Three Rivers, when the call came for volunteers to re-establish the abandoned Iroquois missions after the peace of 1666, and we find him with Bruyas and Pierron accepting the worst tribe of the Federation, the Mohawks, and coming down to Gandaouagé, around which were still clinging the bloody memories of Jogues, Poncet and Bressani. Frémin describes it as " the exact spot " where Jogues had been martyred. It was consequently not on the other side of the river, six miles away, as some pretend.

They welcomed its shelter, for the Mohegans were pursuing them. That is the reason, perhaps, why they delayed two days before visiting Tionnontoguen, the capital, fifteen miles up the river, the place which the readers of Jogues' *Life* will remember was one of the stations where the martyr was tortured in 1642. Its resemblance to Gandaouagé or Ossernenon is very striking in its strategical advantages, for in both places you can look far up and down the river. Though the scenery at Ossernenon is remarkably beautiful, Tionnontoguen surpasses it. As on the St. Lawrence at Quebec, the river seems to end in the mountains that close it in far below towards the East.

The reception at Tionnontoguen was remarkable for the enthusiasm which characterized it. Two hundred warriors met the missionaries outside the village, and conducted them to a place where they were formally welcomed by the orator of the tribe. " The hoary heads," says the *Relation,* " and the sachems proceeded with admirable gravity to the entrance of the palisade, where we were received with a discharge of all the artillery available, each one firing his musket from his cabin, and two swivel guns doing duty at both ends of the village."

The feast of the Holy Cross, September 14, was chosen by the missionaries as the proper day for presenting their gifts and explaining the motive of their coming. They opened the proceedings with a prayer and the singing of the *Veni Creator,* which delighted the savages, but the musical instruments which accompanied the chant quite captured them. Frémin was the orator, as he was the only one who could speak Iroquois, having learned it while he labored in the Onondaga country, ten years previously. He purposely assumed a very imperious tone, reproached the Indians bitterly for having broken the peace, and threatened all sorts of things if they did it again. "But, in order to inspire them with greater terror and to make a deeper impression on their minds, as these peoples are greatly influenced by external phenomena," says the writer, "the Father caused to be erected in the middle of the place where the council was being held a pole of forty or fifty feet in length, from the top of which hung a porcelain necklace. He declared that in like manner should be hanged the first of the Iroquois who should kill a Frenchman or any one of the allies."

"It is incredible," he continues, "how this present, suspended in the air, astounded them all. They remained for a long time with their heads down, not daring to look at it or talk about it, until the most prominent and eloquent of their orators, having recovered his spirits, arose and performed all the apish tricks imaginable around the pole to show his astonishment. It is impossible to describe all the gesticulations made by this old fellow, who was more than sixty years of age. What looks of surprise he pretended at the sight of it as if he did not know its meaning! What exclamations upon finding out its secret! How he seized himself by the throat with both his hands in a horrible manner, squeezing it tightly to give a picture, and at the same time to inspire a horror of this kind of death! In a word, he employed *all the artifices of the most excellent orators,* and ended by delivering to us the captives for whom we had asked, and giving us the choice of a site for a chapel." It was fine play between the civilized and savage politician.

Tionnontoguen was a difficult place to live in at any time, for the Iroquois, at his best, was a brute, but when drunkenness was added to his power of evil, the missionaries had death continually staring them in the face. On the other hand, a number of Huron captives were found there, who, in spite of having been left so long without spiritual aid, had bravely adhered to the faith. In one village of that district, forty-five of them were discovered who had the custom of meeting in some secluded spot, to rehearse what they had heard in their Huron homes, and to repeat what they could recall of their former religious practices. Some of them regularly assembled for the rosary, and one of their number kept track of the days of the week, so that they might observe Sundays and holidays by some act of devotion. They were like the Jews weeping at the waters of Babylon, though the North American savage, strictly speaking, rarely wept.

On November 10, 1668, a delegation of Senecas arrived at Montreal to ask for priests, and a similar embassy was sent to Father Frémin, who was then the head of the New York Missions. He accepted the offer for himself, and started for the Seneca country early in October, 1668, arriving there on All Saints' Day. As he was a sort of ambassador he was received with great ceremony, and a chapel was immediately built for him. But a general war was going on with the Ottawas, Andastes or Susquehannas, and the Mohegans, and so the Seneca braves who were out murdering their enemies were left untouched by the missionaries' zeal. But there were multitudes of Christian Hurons to be looked after; there were dying babies to be baptized; there were Christian captives burning at the stake to be shrived, and an epidemic was ravaging the towns at the same time, so that work was not lacking. Frémin's influence grew apace, and in spite of the wrath of the medicine men and the unconcern of the depraved people around him, the Indian stoicism began to give way to better dispositions.

In August, he set out for the home of the Cayugas, who were in three towns about a mile from each other, near Lake Tiohero, which is a mile east of the present Cayuga. It happened in the natural course of his work, but his departure just at that time has been made the subject of a historic reproach. He is accused of deliberately deserting his fellow countrymen in distress. In this instance the countrymen were no other than the illustrious La Salle and his party, who had come to the Seneca town for assistance.

La Salle had been a Jesuit scholastic in France and was known simply as Robert *Ignace* Cavelier. It was only in America that he assumed the high sounding appellation of Cavelier de la Salle. His restless disposition prompted the Superiors to dismiss him, although he was extremely eager to devote himself to the American missions. As a teacher in the colleges he had completely failed, in spite of his magnificent presence, or perhaps because of it. Coming to America, he allied himself closely to the Sulpitians, his brother happening to be one of them. His unfriendliness to his former associates, the Jesuits, showed itself on all occasions. His purpose, he said, was to discover the passage to China, and possibly it was for that reason that when the Sulpitians gave him a large tract of land near the Sault above Montreal it was called in derision La Chine. It is not true that he ever built any fortifications there.

When in 1667 a deputation of Senecas came to Montreal to ask for missionaries, they stopped at La Chine and told La Salle of the Ohio River, which emptied, they said, in the South Sea. La Salle immediately took fire, sold part of La Chine to the Sulpitians, who had given it to him for nothing, and set out for Quebec to ask permission to organize an expedition. There he met the Abbé Dollier, who was planning the discovery of the Mississippi, and they were induced by the authorities to unite their forces. They set out with a small flotilla of canoes, the Intendant Talon thanking God that the Government did not have to bear the expense of the expedition. He had strong doubts about its success.

La Salle gave Dollier the impression that he knew all about the country and was familiar with the Iroquois languages. Both assertions, however, lacked foundation, and that explains why a short time afterwards La Salle found himself in the Seneca country looking for a guide and an interpreter.

When he arrived there, Frémin had already left, to visit the Cayugas and prepare for the coming synod at Onondaga. Whether he knew that La Salle was coming or not, it was fortunate that he absented himself. He knew the character of the man who, as Parkman says, had a great esteem for priests, *except Jesuits.* There might have been some explosion of anger which would have been uncomfortable, at least in the presence of the Indians. Charlevoix speaks very kindly of La Salle, but B. Sulte in his " Compte de Frontenac " describes him as taciturn, gloomy, at times brutal, like a man who sees ghosts, repellant and solitary." Frémin did well to avoid him if he knew of his coming.

The Indians, however, received him cordially when, as Parkman relates, " they found themselves in the midst of a disorderly cluster of large but filthy abodes of bark, about a hundred and fifty in number, the largest of which was assigned to their use." But other things met their gaze, and we have from the pen of Galinée, La Salle's chaplain, a picture of conditions there.

" A young captive was brought in to be burned, and I wanted to buy him, but was refused, and I saw the most miserable spectacle I ever beheld in my life. The prisoner was tied to a stake and tortured for six hours with diabolical ingenuity, while the crowd danced and yelled with delight, and the chiefs and elders sat in view smoking their pipes

12   **177**

and watching the contortions of the victim with an air of serene enjoyment. The body was at last cut up and eaten, and in the evening the whole population occupied themselves in scaring away the angry ghosts by beating with sticks against the bark sides of their lodges."

Such was the scene which met these chance visitors to Gandougaré. They were common occurrences for Father Frémin. Unfortunately La Salle's chaplain was unable to help the dying wretch, who may have been a Christian Huron; whereas these burnings furnished abundant harvests for the missionaries, who often risked their lives in assisting the victims.

After waiting for a couple of weeks, La Salle had to depart without a guide; but it is unjust to impute his failure to any desire on Frémin's part to thwart his work of exploration.

Whether La Salle returned to Montreal or not we do not know, but there is a Memoir, purporting to be his, which says that he reached the Ohio, though no date is given, that he followed its course until he reached one of its tributaries coming from the Northeast, the Miami or the Scioto, and that finally he stopped within 300 miles of the Mississippi at the rapids of Louisville in Kentucky. What he did until 1673, the year of Marquette's discovery, is not known. In 1670 Perrot met him hunting on the Ottawa, and, according to B. Sulte, he was at Sault Ste. Marie June 14, 1671, when the French Representative took possession of those countries. It is only an anonymous account published in 1678 or 1680, which makes him go by Lakes Huron and Michigan to the Illinois River, by which route it is claimed he reached the Mississippi. La Salle's own Memoir, written in 1677, never even mentions the name Mississippi. Whither, therefore, the traveller directed his steps after leaving the Senecas no one seems to know.

Frémin's visit to Cayuga was of short duration. He arrived there on the 10th, and on the 26th of August he was presiding at a general meeting of all the missionaries. They assembled at Onondaga. There were present Bruyas from Oneida, Pierron from the Mohawk, de Carheil from Cayuga, and Garnier from the Senecas. They remained there for a week, praying and planning for the success of their missions. Even while they were discussing their plans of spiritual conquest, the air was full of threats. Some Iroquois had been murdered near Montreal, and the people were wild with excitement. Only a word from some furious or drunken Indian was needed to have every priest butchered on the spot. That 26th of August, 1669, should be a memorable day in the annals of New York Ecclesiastical History as that of its First Ecclesiastical Synod.

Why did they choose Onondaga for this meeting? Because it was the capital of the Iroquois Confederacy. It had a great council house, to which the delegates of the Five Nations came to discuss the affairs of State. It had streets regularly laid out, which for an Indian town were faily well kept. It was situated on what is now known as Indian Hill, opposite Pompey, and between the ravines formed by the west and middle branches of Limestone Creek. "It was there," according to Hawley's *Cayuga,* "that the first chapel was built in the State of New York." At least, it is probable that Father Le Moyne drove his stake at that place; a ceremony equivalent to the laying of a corner stone. We do not know if Frémin saw there the same horrors which de Lamberville was compelled to witness thirteen years later.

From Onondaga, Frémin returned to the Seneca town of Gandougaré, which, however, had been mostly given up to the captives from other tribes, among whom were many Christian Hurons. Father Garnier was with him, and it was there they were both set upon by a drunken savage. Frémin describing it, says that Garnier was in considerable danger of being killed, but he conceals the fact that he himself came off worse than his companion in that encounter, and bore the marks of the fight a long time afterwards. But, in spite of this episode, he went on with his companion to a more distant post, and after a spell of sickness, probably the result of his ill-treatment at Gandougaré, returned to his mission, where his faithful Hurons by their excellent lives atoned for the wickedness of the pagans around them. The innate vice of the savage would supply trouble enough, but the Dutch and English were deluging the place with firewater.

Added to the evil of drink was the dream superstition. What an Indian dreamed, he performed as a religous duty, no matter how hard or horrible. Fortunately, no one just then dreamed of killing the priest.

However, it was not only the Huron captives who consoled him. He made wonderful converts among the Senecas themselves, in the short time he was there, notably a famous chief, who had been Le Moyne's host twelve years before, and who spent his life afterwards in winning converts to the faith. The usual burning of captives went on, however, satisfying the hate of the Senecas, but giving the missionary a chance for many a baptism. One of the victims, he tells us, was a Susquehanna Indian, who had come under the influence of the Maryland Jesuits and was well instructed in the faith. The poor wretch never thought he would meet some of the brethren of his old spiritual guides to stand near him at the stake when he was burning to death in the wilderness of New York.

The dreadful surroundings in which the converted Indians were compelled to live, and the extreme difficulty of their remaining true to their teaching necessarily prompted the early missionaries to look around for a remedy. An attempt had already met with success in a settlement of the Abenakis at Sillery, and of the Hurons at Isle d'Orleans, so Father Raffeix proposed to establish an Iroquois settlement near Montreal. The Jesuits had some land at La Prairie, and there the first feeble effort was made. Its

CAUGHNAWAGA INDIANS.

JAMES FREMIN.

small success, however, prompted the desire to place it on a solid foundation, and at the request of the Governor de Courcelles, Frémin was recalled from New York and put in charge of the colony. A glance at his work there may help us to understand the spiritual capabilities of the New York Indians. In fact, that settlement of La Prairie, or Caughnawaga, was a piece of New York territory, so to say, transported to the St. Lawrence.

Frémin's military instincts immediately found an opportunity for their exercise in fighting the liquor traffic, an evil of which the French were as guilty as the Dutch or English, but he never ceased till he had secured a complete victory. Father Chauchetière's Report to the Superiors tells us: " We have here no other demon to contend against but liquor and drunkenness, which make a hell of all the Iroquois villages, where life is a continual suffering. The French are responsible for the trouble here, for in order to strip the savages to their very shirts they follow them everywhere to make them drunk." " It is admirable," he continues, " how some of our Christian savages distinguish themselves in repressing this evil. They spill the liquor, they break the bottles with incredible courage, exposing themselves to insults and blows of which some still bear the marks; but in spite of all that they do not lose courage. I know three or four who would endure martyrdom to prevent anything from being done to offend God. They are no longer guided by the French, whom they had hitherto considered good Christians, but who, they now see plainly, are not."

Some of the fine old chiefs, like Kryn, " The Great Mohawk," and Hot Ashes and a relative of Kryn, a remarkable young Indian, who was like an Aloysius in his piety and purity, were strong temperance apostles, going around everywhere, not only at La Prairie, but in their old home in New York, to induce their people to stop drinking and become Christians.

PIONEER PRIESTS OF NORTH AMERICA.

In spite of the great occasions of sin which were deliberately thrust upon the red men by the whites, the accounts that have come down to us about the Christanity of Caughnawaga are little short of amazing. The success of the undertaking was chiefly due to Frémin. He made it a rule that no one could be admitted to the colony who would not abstain from polygamy, successive or simultaneous, and from drunkenness; and who would not give up the dream superstition. Every one had to make a public profession of faith on these three points. Chiefs were appointed to enforce the law, and culprits were summarily dealt with by ignominious and immediate expulsion. Even transient visitors were compelled to submit to these laws. The result was that Dablon did not hesitate to compare Caughnawaga to Paraguay. This satisfactory state of things endured long after Frémin's time, and we have an official letter of Bishop St. Valier which says that "the piety I saw there surpassed anything I had imagined, or that had been reported to me." He gives instances of virtue little less than heroic, and adds: "What I say is not said to please. It is an exact account of the actual state of things. The French are so charmed with what they see that they often go to unite with the Indians in prayer, and to revive their own devotion by the sight of the fervor which they wonder at in a people who were savage such a short time ago." These Caughnawagas were known among the Indians as " those who do not drink and who pray to God right."

Their fervor is not surprising when we remember that Catherine Tegakwitha was there, and Anastasia, and Catherine Ganeaktena, all remarkable for their exalted virtue. Nor was piety the exclusive prerogative of the women. Omitting others who might be mentioned among the men, was the young Mohawk Aloysius Skandegorhaksen, a handsome youth of twenty, who is described by the missionaries as " born solely for sanctity." As soon as he arrived at La Prairie, only religious matters interested him; and his intelligence of the doctrines of the Faith was such that Frémin baptized him after two months' instruction, although two or three years' probation was the usual time for an Indian brave. In his case there was no mistake of judgment. For the fervent young Indian was in the chapel every morning at 4 o'clock and heard two masses; he repeatedly came to adore the Blessed Sacrament during the day at fixed hours, as if he were following a rule of a religious community, making as many as four visits in the course of the day, the last one as late as nine o'clock at night. His devotion in the chapel astounded the French who saw him, and what time was not given to good works outside he spent in praying and singing hymns in his cabin, in which practice he induced many Indians to join him. His conscience was as delicate as a nun's, and his purity like that of an angel, though he was constantly exposed to the most frightful temptations. He even dared to go down to his old home on the Mohawk to preach in the cabins, and especially to reclaim an old companion from an evil life. He contracted a sickness while hunting in mid-winter, and died in the bloom of his youth. To those who gathered around him he spoke of the happiness of heaven, expressed his hope of soon enjoying it, and exhorted them all to be faithful to the practice of their religion. During his delirium he was constantly repeating the " Hail Mary " and making acts of virtue which revealed the habit that had been the practice of his life. His only regret was that he had not the happiness of dying in the arms of Father Frémin, who was absent at the time, and he gave minute directions to pay out of the poor effects he possessed some little debts which he had contracted.

The Fathers made use of this occasion to change the custom prevalent among the Indians of burying the goods of the dead or using them for superstitious purposes. They induced the relatives to give them to the poor, and in this instance invested the distribution of them with more than

usual solemnity.   The chiefs assembled and made grand
speeches about the virtues of the dead; they gave belts to the
people, which they called the voice of the dead, to engage
them to imitate the virtues of the deceased; and then bestowed upon the most needy whatever they found in the
cabin.   Father Frémin had returned by this time and presided at the ceremony.

This young brave was only one of the many examples
that made Caughnawaga so beautiful in those days.   The
very fervent ones went almost to excess in their practice of
piety.   They had, for instance, heard of the austerities practiced by the nuns and religious, and they determined to imitate them, and secretly began a series of penances such as
scourging themselves, plunging into icy water, standing
naked in the snow and the like, sometimes with fatal results,
until the Fathers found it out and regulated their excess of
fervor.   The cases of conscience proposed to the priests
amazed them, as did the wonderful appreciation of spiritual
truths by these savage hearts, such a short time before brutalized by all sorts of vice.   They became gentle and patient
and forgiving, and found delight in helping each other and
working for the poor and the sick, visiting them in their
cabins, consoling them in their sorrows, and assisting them
at the moment of death.

All this seems idyllic, but it is vouched for in the *Relations;* and perhaps we can get a composite picture of it all
in the detailed description that Dablon has left us of two
famous visits which were paid to Caughnawaga in these
early days.   The account is too long to quote in its entirety,
but the exquisitely simple narrative which may be found in
the LIX volume of the *Relations* will repay the perusal.

The first tells of the pastoral visit of the holy Bishop de
Laval.   The village streets and public square were cleaned,
the houses were made ready, and great branches of trees
were brought from the forests to make an archway of green
all the way from the landing on the river to the village

church; along which at intervals were bowers where the bishop was to stop to receive the solemn welcome of the tribe.

At the appointed time the canoe of the bishop was seen out on the wide expanse of water that separates Caughnawaga from the other side. As the great prelate was apostolic in all his surroundings, he came in very simple attire, attended by only one ecclesiastic. Any one who has travelled the six miles of river which separate La Chine from the Reservation knows that making such a crossing in a canoe was fraught with considerable danger. But the weather that day was exceptionally fine, and as soon as the frail bark was sighted the church bells began to ring and Father Dablon embarked in his own canoe and saluted his Lordship a quarter of a league from shore. Every one hastened to the landing place. They were arranged in order and Father Frémin stood on the right with the red men, while Cholenec was on the left with the whites. " When Monseigneur's canoe was within speaking distance the chief of the Hurons, who had taken his place with his sachems on the landing station, cried out: " Bishop, stop thy canoe, and hear what I have to say to thee." The bishop, somewhat amused at the order, obeyed and heard a eulogy of his talents, his virtue and his office pronounced by the chief. Another orator followed in the same strain. He then landed and donned some of his episcopal robes, and when he had given his blessing to the kneeling Indians, Father Frémin intoned the *Veni Creator* in Iroquois, the men and women taking up the strain. The procession then moved up the shaded walk. When they reached the first bower, an Onondaga and an Oneida sachem addressed the prelate, and at the third station, which was at the door of the church, a Mohawk made an address, which was particularly solemn. Taking off his hat, he made a great sign of the cross, and raised his arms to heaven to thank God for having sent them the bishop, following with the usual praise of the illustrious visitor. They then entered the church, singing the *Pange lingua, Ave Maris Stella* and *Domine salvum fac regem,* after which the Indians in alternate choirs of men and women sang the *Tantum Ergo.*

Then followed the reception. The people all knelt to kiss the bishop's hand; while he addressed a kind word to all, especially to those who had been reported to him as being particularly fervent and devout. Early next morning he baptized some and married others, and then celebrated mass "during which our savages," says the account, "sang hymns and received Holy Communion; the bishop preaching, and Father Frémin interpreting." A grand feast followed in the principal lodge, which the Indians did their best to make as splendid as possible. During the banquet "there were addresses and songs and similar ceremonies," and then the good bishop visited the houses of the village, each of which had branches, handsome mats, fine blankets and costly furs spread to do him honor. He charmed them all by his sweetness and benignity, and then conferred the sacrament of Confirmation on those who were prepared. Some Frenchmen profited by the occasion to be confirmed. Finally next morning he said Mass for the people again, at which they all assisted "and sang very well, as they usually do," says the story; and then, wearied but delighted, he set out for Montreal. When he was on the point of stepping into his canoe the people all knelt to receive his benediction, and "they followed him with their eyes as far as they could see. He carried away all hearts while leaving them his own." It was the first episcopal visitation to the Indians of New York.

This very interesting account informs us that during the Mass on the first day of the bishop's arival a messenger arrived from Quebec " with the saddest news that could be brought to an Indian village "—namely, that some of their hunters, about whom they had long been anxious, had been killed. Ordinarily, upon the receipt of such tidings the

186

STREET IN CAUGHNAWAGA.

relatives of the dead shut themselves up in their cabins and give way to lamentations. Nevertheless, not only did they not do so on this occasion, but attended divine service, at which they received the sacraments of Penance, the Eucharist, and Confirmation. Even the wife of the chief of the party, afflicted as she was, not only attended to all her devotions, but offered the *pain benit* to the congregation, and, adds the missionary, "she took up the collection in the church with all the good breeding of a French lady and with infinitely greater modesty and self-possession and resignation to God's will." Happily it turned out to be a false report.

The other visit was that of a layman, Monsieur l'Intendant, whom Dablon styles "that illustrious minister of His Majesty, whose coming has been so fortunate for New France, and who by his piety, his kindness, his integrity, as well as his anxiety to oblige and his application to business, so worthily fulfills his great office." Unfortunately, "this illustrious Minister of His Majesty" was from the outset at odds with Frontenac, and the unfriendliness quickly developed into positive hostility. After trying to adjust their differences, Louis XIV at last lost patience and recalled both to France, May 10, 1682. The Intendant was Jacques Duchesneau, the Sieur de la Doussinière, who came to Canada in 1675.

It was before the controversy with the Governor had become acute that he visited Caughnawaga. With him were "his eldest son and Perrot, the Governor of Montreal, and also fifty notables of the country, among them Monsieur le Curé of Montreal. The Indians were delighted to see him arrive in the evening, in very fine weather, followed by twelve or fifteen canoes. They met him at the beach and led him to the church, where he first knelt in prayer before the Blessed Sacrament. He then went to their village, which is a short distance from the church, and visited their cabins, giving a thousand proofs of his friendship and virtue, returning afterwards to the church. Thence all walked in procession to the bonfire prepared for the feast of St. John, which fell on the following day."

It was a very solemn affair. " Father Frémin marched at the head of his Indians, followed by the cross bearer and two boys in surplices, carrying lighted torches. Then came the priests in their vestments," Monsieur le Curé of Montreal officiating, Monsieur l'Intendant coming next, followed by Monsieur the Governor of Montreal and a great number of Frenchmen. On both sides of this long procession the youth were marshalled in two files, under arms; on the left, the Indians; on the right, the French, with the son of Monsieur l'Intendant at their head. They fired several volleys when Monsieur l'Intendant began to light the bonfire and when the officiating priest intoned the chant, which was taken up alternately by the French and Indians, the former in Latin, the latter in Iroquois.

The narrative goes on to say that " if Monsieur l'Intendant showed that he was charmed by the singing, and above all by the devotion of the savages, who had assisted at the procession silently and in prayer, our savages were no less edified to see him bareheaded, his rosary in his hands, and with evidences of that profound piety which he professes in so exemplary a manner. He gave us still further proofs of it both by the little he ate at collation that day, which was the vigil of St. John, and on the following day by the devotion with which he heard Mass and received the sacraments of Penance and Eucharist."

The illustrious visitor then held a great council of the Indians, praised their zeal and fidelity in worshiping God, gave them fine presents and at a splendid banquet drank the health of the chiefs and asked them to drink his. He remained in the lodge two hours, though the heat was unbearable. Next morning he stood sponsor to a little child, to whom he gave the name of Francis Xavier. As at the reception of the bishop, he also was accompanied to the

188

river bank at his departure, and " all followed him with their hearts and with their eyes." He came again a second time with less solemnity, but " it cost him much more, owing to the rain and storm that overtook him on the road. Nevertheless, all the water that fell did not in any wise cool the fire of his charity and of his zeal for the welfare of our poor savages."

Frémin remained at Caughnawaga till he was worn out by his labors, and then died at Quebec, July 2, 1691. Father Chaumonot saw him in a vision, but that dear old soul had many visions, and his assurance was not needed to convince the world that Father Frémin had attained eternal glory.

JAMES BRUYAS.

F ATHER JAMES BRUYAS was particularly obnox-
ious to at least one of the Governors of New York
for thwarting the English plan of detaching the Iroquois
from the French allegiance. He is also regarded as one of
the oldest and foremost authorities in Mohawk philology,
and his works, even in the early days, were esteemed so
highly that Hennepin came down all the way from Quinté,
north of Lake Ontario, to copy his Grammar; while good
old Cotton Mather in Boston spelled out his " Mohawk Catechism," not, of course, for the religion it contained, for that
to him was idolatry, but for its linguistic treasures. His
Grammar, the oldest known, was published from the original MSS. by the Regents of the University of the State of
New York in the sixteenth Annual Report of State Cabinet
(Thwaites). His " Mohawk Roots " still remains in MSS.
  What is surprising about all this is that when Bruyas was
elaborating his Grammar, digging up his Roots, and com-
pounding his Catechism in the woods and wigwams of the
Mohawk, he was pretty well advanced in years. Nor had
he much help, for his companion found great trouble with
the language, though fancying at the same time that Mohawk had elegances which made it equal to Greek—a statement which the average student will not challenge. Besides these claims to distinction, he was at one time Superior
of the Indian Missions; was chosen as French ambassador
to the Governor of New England, and to Onondaga in 1701
and 1702, and had been Superior of all Canada from 1693 to
1699, and yet, strange to say, with all these claims to re-
nown, Shea tells us that " *apparently* he was a native of
Lyons "; and that his death was subsequent to 1703. Rochemonteix informs us that he died at Quebec, June 5, 1712,

190

but Charlevoix says it was among his Iroquois converts at
Sault St. Louis. Such is glory!

He arrived in Canada in 1666, and in 1667 he, with Frémin and Pierron, entered the cabin of Tegakwitha's uncle at
Gandaouagé, which he and his companions declared to be
the place where Father Jogues was murdered." Assuredly,
no place could have appealed to him more strongly than that
one, but, on the other hand, it is to be regretted that neither
he nor any other of the missionaries who labored there have
left us any description of the old town or, as far as we know,
obtained any of the precious relics of the three heroes who
glorified it: Jogues, Goupil, and Lalande.

On the journey down to New York the three Jesuits ran
considerable danger, for a war was going on with the Mohegans, or Loups, who had come up from the Hudson. A
detailed account of the journey is to be found in the *Relations* of 1666-68, which appears to have been written by
Pierron, but that is not certain. It is said: " They kept a
journal, from their departure up to the time of their fixed
and permanent abode in the Iroquois village," and Thwaites
tells us that in the archives of St. Mary's College, Montreal,
there is an apograph by Martin of a letter written by Pierron during the stay of the missionaries at Fort St. Anne,
dated August 12, 1677, in which he describes his recent
voyage from France, his impressions of the country, the
relations of French and Iroquois, characteristics and customs of the savages, etc. But that letter is not the journal.
It matters little, however, who wrote of the adventures in
which they were both concerned.

" The long delay in the fort," says the annalist, " gave us
an opportunity of rendering some service there to the soldiers by a kind of mission we gave them. But at last, on
the eve of St. Bartholomew's Day, about four o'clock in the
afternoon, we embarked to go and take shelter at a league's
distance from the last fort of the French, and thereafter

we went on our way both day and night without any mishap and without discovering the enemy."

To the uninitiated it is unintelligible how they could seek shelter a league away from the last fort of the French, just as it is incomprehensible how they could travel so light-heartedly day and night with enemies skulking everywhere around them.

"We admired, at the outset," says the letter, "the care that our Christian Iroquois had to pray to God, all together, immediately after embarking"—unlike their white successors—"although they had been present at Holy Mass, which we celebrated very early every morning." Where those precious places are along Lake Champlain where early Mass was celebrated every morning in the woods we do not know. It is a pity that they can never be identified.

"The prayers finished, we all set about paddling like poor galley slaves, from morning till night. Not one of us three had learned this *exercise,* but because we had so few men we had to take our share of the work. We *gaily* crossed this entire great lake, which is already too renowned by reason of the shipwreck of several of our Frenchmen, and quite recently by that of Sieur Corlart, Commandant of a hamlet of the Dutch near Agniè (Schenectady), who on his way to Quebec was drowned while crossing a large bay where he was surprised by a storm.

"Arriving within three-quarters of a league of the falls by which Lake St. Sacrament empties, we all halted, without knowing why, until we saw our savages at the water-side gathering up flints, which were almost all cut into shape. Our Iroquois told us they never failed to halt at this place, to pay homage to a race of invisible men who dwell at the bottom of the lake. These beings occupy themselves in preparing flints for the passers-by, provided the latter pay their respects by giving them tobacco. If they give much they get a liberal supply of stones. These water-men travel in canoes, and when their captain proceeds to throw himself into the water to enter his palace he makes so much noise that all are terrified who know nothing about this great spirit and these little men.

" The occasion of this ridiculous fable," says the missionary, " is that the lake is frequently agitated by fearful tempests. It was in this basin that Corlart met his death. The presence of the stones is explained by the fact that the wind coming from the lake tosses up the flints on the beach. When I asked why they did not offer some tobacco to the Great Spirit of Heaven the answer was that ' He did not need any as do people on the earth ' "—an answer which shows how men are alike everywhere.

" We passed a fine slate-quarry, five leagues from Lake St. Sacrament, a cannon shot from a little islet of about 200 feet in diameter. This quarry is not of the nature of those I have seen on the seashore, or in the neighborhood of Quebec, which have only the appearance of quarries. This one is quite like those I have seen in the Ardennes of our France; its color being of a beautiful blue, and its laminæ easily detached, large or small as one wishes—very fragile and very soft."

They landed at the end of Lake St. Sacrament. " We gladly came ashore and carried our baggage and canoes, happy that there remained only *thirty leagues* of the journey by land, to reach the goal to which we had so long aspired." Leaving the lake, however, they fell into an ambuscade, but fortunately of their friends, who were concealed there watching for the Mohegans. With this party they proceeded by short marches to Gandaouagé on the Mohawk.

They arrived in time, for they were hotly pursued by the Mohegans, who very shortly after made a dash at the very gates of the village scalping a miserable squaw and then retiring. Frémin was engaged at the time in baptizing some dying children when this horrid deed took place before his eyes. He hurried to the poor wretch, but four times she turned away from him with scorn; at last, however, she yielded, was prepared for death, and expired with the prayer of mercy on her lips.

Tionnontoguen was a wild place just at that time, and though the missionaries were received with great honor, they had a chance of seeing the noble savage at his worst, in the midst of his wild debauches when maddened by liquor, which was plentiful there at that time. Not even the chapel would be spared, the drunken savage tearing everything to pieces and flinging firebrands at the heads of the priests.

After three months' stay, Bruyas travelled up to Oneida, in the company of a French trader, Boquet. What kind of a place Oneida was then may be learned, at least to some extent, from a letter of the missionary.

" It is situated on the 44th parallel of latitude upon an eminence whence one could see a great deal of the country, if the woods which environ it were cleared away. There is no river or lake except at five leagues distance from the town, where there is a lake twelve leagues long and two wide. This place is fairly pleasant, and if one would take trouble to plant some vines and trees they would yield as well as they do in France; but the savage is too fond of wandering. Nevertheless, apple, plum, and chestnut trees are seen here, but they have not the same taste as in France. There are also vines which bear tolerably good grapes, from which our Fathers formerly made wine for Mass. The mulberries and strawberries are so abundant that the ground is all covered with them. Both are dried in order to season the sagamité, when there is no fish. The Oneidas have the reputation of being the most cruel of the Iroquois. They will travel 300 leagues and more to remove one scalp. Drunkenness, dreams, and impurity are destroying them."

After describing some of his work he continues: " All that we need fear is being burned or beaten to death by some hothead, but life with these barbarians is a continual martyrdom; and the fires of the Iroquois would be easier than

194

the trials one endures among them. One must expect to have all his senses martyred daily; the sight, by the smoke of the cabins—I have almost lost my eyes from it;—the hearing, by their annoying yells and wearisome visits; the smell, by the stench that is incessantly exhaled by the oiled and greased hair of both men and women; feeling, by cold, as severe at at Quebec; and finally taste, by the food, of which it is enough to say that the daintiest and most delicate piece would be refused by the dogs of France. If the sagamité be without seasoning, it is without taste; if it be seasoned—this is done the greater part of the year with rotten fish—the mere odor of it at first turns one's stomach. I say nothing of the contempt that must be endured; of the frequent raillery to which a person exposes himself when he speaks incorrectly; of the trouble and chagrin occasioned by the study of a very difficult language, above all to persons advanced in age. There is a great difference between meditating upon the Canadian mission in one's oratory and finding one's self exercising the duties of a Canadian missionary. I do not say this to disgust those in whom God has inspired such purpose. On the contrary, why should they lose courage when the meanest and most unfit man in the Province, not only in mind but also in body, manages to exist among these difficulties?"

Nevertheless, in these sordid surroundings Bruyas did great work, and the people thronged to listen to his instructions. His chapel he called St. Francis Xavier's of the Oneida. The place in which he built it has been identified by Beauchamp as two miles northeast of the present Munnsville. But how did he make the Oneidas understand him? He was a linguist and philologist indeed, but as yet could have known very little of the language, for he had only arrived in America the preceding year. It is astonishing with what serenity these men faced the impossible. The solution of the difficulty came by the aid of a remarkable Erie squaw whom he met at Oneida, and who afterwards became very famous in the history of the mission as one of the saints of Caughnawaga. She had been captured in a raid on the Eries and had married an Oneida chief. Even before the arrival of Bruyas she was admired by every one for her virtue, her modesty and gentleness, but a feeling of bitterness was beginning to show itself because of her openly avowed desire to embrace Christianity.

Bruyas' coming was a god-send to her, and she immediately sought him out to inquire about the faith. He welcomed her for that reason, of course, and also because she was able to make out his meaning and act as his interpreter; setting herself to work very vigorously to teach him Oneida. He was very happy until Boquet, the French trader, made up his mind to return to Quebec; for with him went not only Catherine, but her husband, his friends and protectors. Both of them became conspicuous for their holiness in Canada.

A year or so passed with the Oneidas, and then Millet came to take his place, while he went down the valley to Tionnontoguen, which he had left some time before, and which he found as wicked as ever. However, it began to pick itself up when the famous statue of N. D. de Foy was erected in the village.

While Father Bruyas was at that place he formed the acquaintance of one whose family name has always been conspicuous in the history of the State of New York, Robert Livingston, a Scotchman who had established himself at Albany and married one of the Schuylers. This acquaintance at first appeared to be friendship, as would be inferred from a very remarkable document communicated in 1879 to *The Magazine of American History* by B. Fernow, late Keeper of the Archives of the State of New York. It is entitled: *The Papers of Father Bruyas,* and begins with the remark that " Governor Leisler had an excuse to proceed against Robert Livingston, because being a Scotchman and *a friend of the Jesuit missionaries among the Mohawks and*

196

JAMES BRUYAS.

Oneidas, he was easily accused of leaning towards the cause of the dethroned Stuarts. Under the plea that he had not accounted for the revenue of the King during twelve months, his house was searched. Livingston succeeded in making his escape, and in taking all his accounts with him, so that the Commissaries *found only a chest containing papers, etc., of the Jesuit Vaillant.* Several people were got to swear that Livingston had spoken against King William, and an indictment was forwarded to Leisler at New York, saying ' We send your Honor herewith six affidavits against the aforesaid Livingston, and with them goes a package of papers which were found in an old chest, with some jewels formerly the property of the Jesuit Vaillant, from Canada.' "

These papers and " jewels " of Vaillant are labelled as the papers of Bruyas, because he was there with Vaillant at the time; and in fact was the Superior of the mission. The " jewels," which were " inventoried in His Majesty's behalf," are described as catechisms, blank books, Huron paradigms, *hosties of all sizes,* crucifixes, paper bags, raisins, prunes, tobacco, rosaries, &c.

The whole package was sent to Boston, and someone whose name fortunately for himself is not known indulges in a disquisition on the " find." We hope it was not old Cotton Mather. As a matter of fact, he had Father Bruyas' Iroquois catechism and dictionary. Whoever he was he has thought proper to leave in writing his opinion of the gentlemen to whom the property belonged.

He is horrified, for instance, at the immorality of the one hundred *cases of conscience* which he found in the bundle; he ascribes a most indecent meaning to a letter from the nuns at Quebec; is shocked at the Father's illustration of heaven and hell, in which the capabilities of the savage mind had to be considered, and is indignant at the permission given to the Mohawks to hunt on Sunday, &c. The formula of Father Millet's vows, which had been sent on to Bruyas, quite obfuscates him. " I must not omit," says this stern old Yankee Inquisitor, "to mention here the Latin manuscript which covers the third cahier of the Indian dictionary." (This reference to the dictionary seems like an assurance that we are dealing with old Cotton Mather.) *"It is a declaration,"* he says, "demanded by Père Millet, *General of the Jesuits in New France, of P. Bruyas to make him Prefect of the Order."* Poor old parson! He was most wofully muddled and was quite at sea in his Latin and his sense.

The vow not to accept a prelacy is an overwhelming proof in his eyes of the deepest hypocrisy. "Do you not admire," he asks, "the Jesuitical spirit expressed here? Look how he advances gradually. At first he will not violate the vow of poverty, *that is being secularized;* then he will not aspire to any prelacy, but if," &c. "Father Bruyas," he continues, "is one of the most distinguished members; he is Père Proféz (sic), Chief of the Missions, a great converter of the Iroquois, Hurons, and Oneidas; so great, in fact, that another Jesuit dares to speak of his endeavors as Apostolic labors." He concludes with the pious wish: "May God soon deliver the Christian world from these *grasshoppers,* and let a strong *east wind* come to make them disappear. Amen." The *east wind* puts the post-office address on this communication unmistakably.

Cotton Mather was clearly not a friend of the Jesuits, and we fear that Governor Leisler was also doing Livingston an injustice for persecuting the official on that account. In fact, later on we find proclamations over Livingston's signature as Secretary for Indian Affairs exhorting the savages to "make prisoners of the priests as often you can and bring them to me, and for every such Popish priest and Jesuit which you shall bring to this town and deliver up to the Magistrates you shall have one hundred pieces of eight, payed you down in ready money as a reward."

This does not look like "friendship" on the part of Livingston, but possibly he was merely acting as scribe for the

JAMES BRUYAS.

rancorous young Orangeman, Governor Bellomont. It is not recorded that any Indian ever brought any " Popish priest or Jesuit to get the one hundred pieces of eight." Their " friendship " was more sincere than Livingston's.

Meantime, the old " grasshopper and great converter of the savages," Father Bruyas, kept at his work. It was while he was at Tionnontoguen that Boniface fell sick and had to be sent to Canada to die. Bruyas went to Gandaouagé about the time that the " Great Mohawk," Kryn, drew so many after him to Canada; so that when the Indians broke out into a rage about this defection of their best fighters, Bruyas had to bear the brunt of it.

A council was held at Tionnontoguen, which was then their chief town, and the priest was summoned before the sachems and accused of helping the depopulation of their country. He answered in the most vigorous fashion; protested that he knew nothing of the purpose of Kryn; insisting that it was Kryn's own doing; then turning upon his accusers he showed them that their own vices of drunkenness and debauchery were ruining the tribe.

Bruyas continued at his difficult work, going from mission to mission as Superior until 1679, when he seems to have been called to Caughnawaga, where he remained till 1691. By that time the quarrels and ambitions of de Denonville and de la Barre on the one hand and Dongan on the other, all of them Catholics, had made it impossible to go on with the missions. Frontenac had afterwards moved against Schenectady, in 1690, and for a time was dreaming of capturing New York. It was a blank for the missionaries, and only one priest was left in the whole of New York territory: Father Millet, but he was in captivity among the Oneidas.

During all that time Bruyas was laboring for peace, and we find a letter from him in 1691, addressed to Frontenac: " You are aware," he says, "that 140 Mohawks have deputed three of their chiefs to know if you would receive them, as they are desirous of making an inviolable treaty of peace.

These three deputies have come to the fort unarmed, and as friends, and were well received by our Indians. If you will permit me to express my opinion, and it concurs with the most reasonable view taken here, they are sincere, and their coming looks to the cementing of a solid peace with them, and through them with all the others." Father de Lamberville was not as credulous in this matter as Bruyas, nor was Frontenac. The war continued.

In 1693, Bruyas succeeded Dablon as General Superior, and remained in that office until 1699. Describing his labors in this exalted office, Rochemonteix says: "All the Religious of the College of Quebec lived, at the end of the century, under the successive government of four superiors of unequal merit: Theodore Beschefer, Claude d'Ablon, James Bruyas, and Martin Brouyard. Bruyas is known; he succeeded d'Ablon in the month of August, 1693. Indefatigable missionary, hardy traveller, he understood the savage, his manners, his language, and he managed them with intelligence and skill. Interpreter, orator, deputy of the Governors of Quebec to the English and Iroquois, he formed part of every congress and every embassy. *He possessed the art of governing savages better than that of administering a college.* His nomination as Superior of the Fathers of Canada was a fortunate thing, however, for the colony; for this Jesuit by exception was most friendly with the Count de Frontenac, and he was able to help M. de Callières to prepare a general peace among the savages in 1701." Altogether Bruyas can be rated among the great men.

As the College of Quebec must at that time have been very rudimentary, it is clear that extraordinary scholastic requirements were not necessarily called for in the General Superior, who could employ others as professors and teachers. On the other hand, it was great wisdom to have chosen as Superior a man of such wide experience in missionary work; of such admitted diplomatic skill in guiding the decisions of councils and embassies; and, above all, of such influence with

JAMES BRUYAS.

the difficult Governor Frontenac, who disliked all Jesuits except Bruyas.

Shortly after arriving at New York as Governor, Bellomont received an order from the King of England, in consequence of the treaty of Ryswick, to suspend hostilities with the French; de Callières at Quebec being notified at the same time to the same effect. This implied a change of relationship, which necessitated an embassy to Boston for the arrangement of details, and also an exchange of prisoners. Father Bruyas and Major Vallière were sent down to New England as the French representatives. What they did or how long they remained there we cannot ascertain. As Bellomont was a pronounced bigot, the presence of this clerical ambassador was probably not very acceptable, as one may be permitted to surmise from the anti-papist law which the Governor forced the New York Assembly to pass in the following year. It is possible, however, that diplomacy kept personal dislike in the background while the Conference lasted, and that Bruyas was received as courteously, if not as cordially, as Druillettes had been fifty years before.

The Bill which Bellomont sent to the New York Assembly was directed against all priests and Jesuits, excluding them from English territory. As most of the old burghers and military men who composed the Assembly knew the missionaries personally, and were favorably disposed in their regard, the Bill was rejected. But the Governor insisted, and sent it back a second time. As the ballot resulted in a tie, His Excellency voted twice, once as a member of the Assembly and secondly as Governor, so that on November 1, 1700, the law was made declaring every priest in the colony of New York " an incendiary, a disturber of the peace, and an enemy of the Christian religion, to be punished by perpetual imprisonment if caught, and in case of escape and recapture, to be condemned to death. It was decreed also that any one harboring him was to be fined and pilloried."

Besides making it clear that there were to be no more Indian missions, this Bill implied that the English

201

claimed dominion over the Iroquois tribes. Against that the Iroquois protested. They maintained that they were an independent nation, and could make treaties with France or England as they chose. They therefore proposed to send six delegates, two Onondagas and four Senecas, to Montreal asking the Governor to have Father Bruyas, MM. de Maricourt and Joncaire meet them at Albany to make a treaty and exchange prisoners.

Was this a trick or not? Frontenac had just died, and de Callières had succeeded him. As the Indians had never been able to deceive Frontenac, they were now apparently exploiting his successor. Albany was English territory. Moreover, in the delegation there were no Mohawks—the tribe nearest to Albany. So de Callières suspected treachery and insisted that he would not consider a treaty of peace unless it was signed in Montreal. The Indians agreed, abandoned their request about Albany, and asked for one at Onondaga.

To arrange the terms of the treaty the ambassadors named by the Indians were sent. They were Bruyas, who, according to Le Roy de la Potherie, " was in great veneration among them; Maricourt, who was the son of a Frenchman adopted by the Iroquois, and Joncaire, who had married an Indian woman and who acted as chief interpreter."

The delegates arrived at Onondaga August 4. On the 10th there was a grand reunion of the five Cantons. The main object which Bruyas had in view, of course, was to reorganize the missions. He opened the proceeding with an invocation to the Holy Ghost, and then, in a very florid speech which delighted the Indians, invited them to always obey the Governor of Canada, in spite of any reason which the Governor of New England might allege to the contrary. He spoke of Achiendasé (the Jesuit Superior, at that time, Father Bouvart), " who has always loved you, always considered you as his children, although for a long period the sun has been darkened between you and him. He wants to bring back to you the ideas he had given you of the Great

LORD BELLOMONT.

JAMES BRUYAS.

Spirit, the God of armies, and the Master of the Universe. You are worthy of compassion. Since the Black Robes have left you, your children die without baptism. Your old men, your warriors, your women knew how to pray, you knew the Master of Heaven, you have forgotten Him. Your Father now exhorts you to consider if you wish the return of the Black Robes. There are several ready to come to you. Do not refuse the offer he makes to you."

These words embarrassed the Iroquois. The English Governor had promised them " a gunsmith " if they would reject the priests and take a parson. They did not trouble themselves much about the parson, who was the easy going Dominie Dellius of Fort Orange, but the " gunsmith " was a useful man to have among them, and so the words of Bruyas provoked no enthusiasm, and he thought it prudent not to insist. But an incident occurred which gave him his opportunity.

De la Potherie says that Bellomont had sent up a young Dutchman to persuade the Indians not to listen to the French. The envoy apparently forgot himself and informed the assembly that his master wanted to see them at Albany. " What does your Governor want? " they asked in great anger. " Is not peace concluded in Europe, and is he still singing the war song? " " Perfectly right," interjected Bruyas; " the English Governor treats you as slaves. When did the Governor of Quebec ever forbid you to speak to the Governor of New England if you wanted to? " Then Joncaire made a speech to the same effect which was greatly applauded. The Dutchman was defeated, and left the assembly in anger. He returned to the charge, however, at the next meeting, but was unable to disturb the friendly feelings which the Indians entertained for the French.

Toward the end of August the Council broke up, and in the beginning of September the delegates started for Montreal with nineteen deputies from the Onondagas, Senecas, and Cayugas. They had with them ten French prisoners. The others could not or would not return.

PIONEER PRIESTS OF NORTH AMERICA.

On the 8th, the Governor received them in a most imposing manner, but would make only a temporary peace, as he insisted upon the return of all the prisoners, and was aiming, besides, at a union of all the tribes. To attain that object he announced a general assembly for August of the following year, to which the Indian delegates readily assented, but protested that though acceptable to them, they could not speak for tribes other than their own. To persuade those who had not yet entered into the convention the Governor sent Bruyas and his two associates back to Onondaga; while Father Enjalran was commissioned to persuade the Ottawas and Bigot the Abenakis.

When Bruyas reached Onondaga on this mission he found the agents of Bellomont endeavoring to influence the Iroquois against the French, whereupon he set to work a second time to thwart them. He solemnly warned the Iroquois that if they did not present themselves at Montreal for the General Convention, and also send back all the prisoners, they could expect nothing in future from the Governor of Quebec. This the Indians could not afford to do; and they agreed to go to the meeting in spite of the threats of Bellomont that he would hang any priest he found in New York. The result was that when the famous assembly of all the Indians from the east and west met at Montreal, where the old converted traitor, the Huron Chief known as " The Rat " made his wonderful plea for peace and died, the Iroquois were present and signed the treaty which let the priests back again into the territory of New York. Thus Bruyas won his fight with Bellomont. That year Fathers James de Lamberville, Julien Garnier, and Vaillant de Gueslis revived the old missions, and remained at their work until the English were able to reassert their mastery over their old rivals. They were not, however, able to hold their own. By 1708 it was impossible for a Catholic priest to live in New York. Four years after that Bruyas died at Quebec, June 15, 1712.

JOHN PIERRON.

JUST where the West Shore Railroad going west comes up to the Mohawk at Hoffman's Ferry the beautiful valley widens out, leaving long stretches of fertile fields on both sides of the river. It is the scene of a memorable battle in former times between the Mohawks and Mohegans. The Mohegans had ventured on a raid as far as Auriesville, or Gandaouagé, but were repulsed after a fierce fight and were in full retreat when the Mohawks stole upon them under cover of the night and next morning massacred most of them. It was the last of the Mohegans in the Mohawk Valley.

Two days afterwards the victors took up their march homeward, waving the reeking scalps of the dead, and singing songs of triumph as they drove forward their prisoners of war who were to be burned at the stake. In that blood-stained throng was a priest, Father Pierron, who had hurried down to the scene of conflict from Tionnontoguen; for some of the Mohawks were Christians, and if wounded would need help. Moreover, there was a chance of converting the hapless prisoners before they were led to the stake The Christian Indians, who knew about hell, endeavored to stop him. They wanted their enemies to burn beyond the grave as well as on the Mohawk, but the priest persisted and baptized some of the prisoners on the way up to the town.

The missionary's description of the fight is worth reproducing, at least in part. " One of the most important things I have to write," he says, " is the attack on Gandaouagé, which is one of our best villages, and situated nearest to the enemy's country. On August 18, 1669, three hundred of the Nation of the Loups—who live along the sea toward *Baston,* in New England—presented themselves at daybreak before the palisade, and began such a furious discharge of

205

musketry that the balls, piercing both the stockades and cabins, soon awakened men, women, and children, almost all of whom were at that time sound asleep. The men at once seized their muskets and tomahawks to defend the palisades, the women meantime making bullets or arming themselves with knives and other weapons for a hand-to-hand fight if the enemy entered.

" Four Iroquois were killed at the outset, and two were wounded. The terrified people in the neighboring village took flight in all directions, and carried the news to Tionnontoguen, which was distant four leagues from those two forts. They said that the whole country was lost; that Gandaouagé was besieged by an army of Loups; that all the young men had fallen, and that Gandagaro, which is the neighboring fort, was in most desperate straits.

It was eight o'clock in the morning when the news had spread through all the district. Our warriors, *without becoming disconcerted, dressed themselves in all the most precious things they had, according to the custom observed by them on such occasions,* and advanced on the enemy.

" I was among the first to march, to see if I could not save some one in the midst of the carnage. . . . At our arrival we heard only mournful cries over the death of the bravest of the village. The enemy had already retreated after two hours' obstinate fighting. There was only a single Loup left in the place, and I saw that an Iroquois had already cut off his hands and feet, skinned him and separated the flesh from the bones and was preparing a detestable repast.

" When all our warriors arrived and found the enemy no longer there, they promptly had a supply of cornmeal prepared that they might start in pursuit of the enemy. The provisions being ready, they immediately embarked in *canoes on our river, which is very swift, and as they followed the current, they made very good progress.* When night came, they sent out scouts, who were almost entrapped by the pickets of the Loups.

206

JOHN PIERRON.

" Then the Iroquois made a wide détour and laid an ambuscade in a precipitous place, a very well chosen spot, from which the entire road leading to the Dutch was controlled. In the morning, the Loups broke camp, and as they were marching in single file, as savages usually do, they walked into the trap and a shower of balls put to flight those who were not killed. Frightful yells arose on all sides of the forest. The Loups, however, rallied in the place where they had encamped during the night. There they were furiously assaulted by the Iroquois. At first they made a vigorous resistance, but the cowardice of some of their number forced them to yield. However, ten out of the entire band threw up a trench, intending to fight to the last. There the battle raged until night put an end to the contest. Next morning the enemy had fled. It was said that there were nearly a hundred warriors on the side of the enemy who perished. They were either slain in the fight or drowned in the river. The victors, following the custom of the savages, cut off the heads of the slain in order to remove the scalps, but I find it difficult to believe that the number was so great as the Iroquois brought back only nineteen scalps."

Apart from the historical interest of this chapter it sets at rest a very important question of topography.

Gandaouagé signifies " rapids," but at the present time there are no rapids in the Mohawk between Little Falls and Cohoes. This letter of Father Pierron, however, settles beyond any doubt that such was not the case 240 years ago. He says explicitly that the river just there was *fort rapide,* and that they made the trip down the stream *avec une fort grande diligence parcequ-ils suivaient le courant de l'eau.* Gandaouagé, or Auriesville, therefore was the village of the *rapids.* The actual sluggish condition of the stream is easily accounted for by the fact that the main body of the water has been drawn off to make the Erie Canal, the factories all along the shore have drained it also; the railroad embankments have cut off supplies from the hills, and the hills themselves, denuded of forests, now no longer feed the streams that once tumbled down the slopes.

It would be historically incorrect to say, as some maintain, that Gandaouagé received its name because the Indians of the Mohawk went to Caughnawaga, on the St. Lawrence, for Gandaouagé existed long before Caughnawaga was established.

Finally, the name is not derived from Kanewagé, or " flint," which was the symbol of the Mohawk tribe, as Sir William Johnson suggests. Father Melançon, S.J., who was a missionary among the Iroquois at Caughnawaga, shows that Kanewagé and Gandaouagé are radically different. To sum up, there were rapids at Gandaouagé in former times, and another letter to be quoted in the course of this sketch confirms that conclusion. This phrase therefore in Pierron's war-letter apparently settles a long disputed point.

Pierron was born at Dun-sur-Meuse, September 28, 1631. He became a Jesuit, November 21, 1650, and after a brilliant course of studies and teaching came to Canada in 1667. Almost immediately he set out for the Mohawk country with Frémin and Bruyas, getting his first taste of danger as he hurried away from the pursuing Mohegans, who chased his party to the very gates of Gandaouagé.

He was left alone at Tionnontoguen, for Father Frémin started shortly after for the Seneca country, entrusting to this raw recruit the care of the new post. The braves were away scalping the Mohegans, but the squaws and old men listened to his stumbling discourses and grew interested in what he was trying to tell them. Some of them, however, refused, and Pierron resorted to a device which is worth recording, as it made him famous all through the valley. He invented a game which he called "From Point to Point," one point being birth, the other eternity.

It is hard to be perfectly sure of what " Point to Point "

JOHN PIERRON.

was from the description given in the *Relations* of 1670, for he tells us, " it was composed of *emblems* representing all that a Christian should know. I painted the seven sacraments, the three theological virtues, all the commandments of God, and the principal mortal sins, and even the venial sins which are ordinarily committed; each expressed *according to its rank,* along with the marks of horror that one ought to have for them. Original sin has a particular place, followed by all the woes it caused. I represented there the four ends of man, the fear of God, indulgences, etc. In a word, all that a Christian should know is depicted."

The idea had come to him while he was still a scholastic in France when hearing of the wonders achieved by Father Maunoir with the people of Brittany by means of pictures, and he devoted all his spare time to drawing, painting and copying the great masters. Rochemonteix says " he never became a master himself, but there was no need of being a Raphael for the purpose in view." At any rate, " Point to Point " caused a sensation all along the river; it was talked of in the councils and discussed in the wigwams. Everyone wanted to see it. It was commended even in Canada, and the Venerable Marie de l'Incarnation goes into ecstacies over it and describes it in detail. What particularly amuses her is the picture of " the squaw stuffing her ears while a whole lot of devils are pouring fire into those organs and torturing every part of her body. The Father is looked upon as an extraordinary genius," says the Venerable Mother, " and the rest of the missionaries are sorry they are not painters."

" From Point to Point " was not merely a tableau. It was a game not of chance, but of knowledge and skill. As the Indians are inveterate gamblers, this pious device caught them by their weak point. Directions for playing the game were printed at the bottom of each section, and the game was so popular that he had to have it engraved at Quebec to meet the demand for it. He says with delight: " There are some of our Iroquois to whom I have taught it only twice, and who have learned it perfectly; others to whom I have shown it only four times, and who are so skilful that they have obliged me to play it with them. We passed the Easter holidays agreeably with this game, which is equally holy and profitable. All our savages have an extreme passion for playing it. I have written a little book on it, and I hope to have it next year, with another game—a wordly one—that I have invented for destroying all the superstitions of our savages." This pious Monte Carlo in the woods of the Mohawk affords a refreshing revelation of the character of this distinguished professor of the great colleges of France resorting to such kindergarten methods to catch the fancy of those degraded souls.

He has another claim to distinction; not a great one, but interesting as a matter of history. In the " Frontiersmen of New York " it is recorded that *" the first schools* in the Schoharie settlements began to be taught prior to 1740; *one* Spease kept the first, *one* Keller the next; one in Dutch, the other in German." But anent this piece of belated educational history it is worth knowing that one Pierron tried to teach reading and writing to Indian boys near the Schoharie almost a hundred years before Keller and Spease gathered their young Dutch and German lads around them. The little red school house of the Mohawk can point to him as its founder. Unhappily his pupils preferred the chase to the class room, and their fathers frowned on his efforts to make the boys use a pen instead of an arrow, or to learn the alphabet instead of tracking the deer, and so Pierron, after a while, like so many other schoolmasters, gave up his work in despair. His pupils wanted manual training.

One may easily imagine that a man of such engaging personality as Pierron certainly was, would attract the attention of any of the distinguished white settlers who happened to be in those sparsely inhabited regions. Such was the case. Later on we shall find him hobnobbing with the old Puritans of Boston, among whom he came like an apparition; and so,

JOHN PIERRON.

although the *Relations* make no mention of it, a little scrap of paper, all brown with age, but apparently very lovingly preserved, which is signed *Jean Pirron de la Compagnie de Jesus,* and was lately discovered among the Schuyler papers, informs us that very pleasant and cordial relations existed between that family and the lonely man who lived among his savages fifty miles further on in the wilderness.

It is written in French and is from *Tinniontogen,* as Pierron spells the name of the village, and dated 1667. That was after the Dutch had lost their grasp on the territory. It is addressed to *Monsieur Rünselaer et aux autres Messieurs, Les Commissaires d'Albanie, à Albanie,* and every word of it shows the courtly French gentleman. He says among other things: " I hold myself so obliged for the honor I received from you at *Schennecté* (Schenectady) that I shall eternally guard my affection for you as well as the desire to be of service if ever the occasion presents itself. Neither white nor black, nor difference of religion, will interfere with that friendship, and during all our grand disputes, which made us perhaps appear in the eyes of our savages as foes, I preserved that affection in its integrity, and I beg you to do the same in my regard." Some little business matters are then mentioned and afterward apparently there is a reference to a controversial subject : " I have given Mons. de Hinsse some nuts to crack. Will you not take your share, especially you *mon Antagoniste,* from whom, however, I ask *toute la considération de vos bonnes graces;* every consideration of your kindest favor." The *Antagoniste* was probably *M. Rünselaer.* The letter ends: " To you, Gentlemen, I am, with the assurance of being always such, Your very humble and very obedient servant, Jean Pierron." The seal on the letter looks like a heart with a crown of thorns.

Perhaps those kindly acts of the old Patroon had something to do with the gift of faith of some of his descendants, as well as with the religious vocation of one of them to the same Order of which Pierron was such a distinguished representative.   The little scrap of paper comes like a blessed and comforting messenger from the forgotten past.

It is of interest to know that Pierron was a more than usually energetic though unsuccessful apostle of temperance. The great curse of the Indians was the liquor which poured in torrents through the Iroquois country from the inexhaustible casks of the Dutch and English traders.   The Indian is bad enough at any time, but when filled with firewater he becomes an incarnate fiend.   The scenes that occurred in the orgies following immediately on the distribution of the liquor cannot be described.   He preached and prayed against it, and the old chiefs, who saw that it was destroying their people more rapidly than the tomahawks or musket balls of the enemy, helped him in his crusade.   But in vain.   Finally he determined to resort to Government prohibition, and for that purpose sent a solemn delegation of Mohawk sachems to Governor Lovelace, at Manhattan, to beg him to stop the traffic.   It is not said that he went with them.   Perhaps it is well that he did not.   He would have lost heart.

Lovelace was an easy going man; a courtier who tried to steer his way amid the domestic difficulties by which he was surrounded.   President Roosevelt in his *New York* calls him " an archetypical cavalier."   He was Governor in the stormy days when the English were taking possession of the colony; so that he was very wary of offending any of the magnates of Manhattan, who might be making money by selling liquor.   But, worst of all, he himself had established a tavern in the very walls of the Stadt Huys.   Mr. Roosevelt calls it a " social club," but John Innes, in his *New Amsterdam and Its People,* is more severe.   He tells us that " in 1670 Governor Francis Lovelace, who had acquired a plot of ground immediately adjoining the Stadt Huys, upon the west, commenced the erection of *an inn or ordinary,* and asked permission to build the upper part of the house something over the passage of the town which lieth between

JOHN PIERRON.

State House and the lot; *and to make a door* to go from the upper part of the house into the Courts' Chambers. The term 'chambers' used in the communication is hardly likely to have referred to the private rooms of the magistrates, because tavern connection, though possibly very convenient in some cases, might have led to public scandal against those high officials. The tavern of Governor Lovelace is shown upon the Danker and Sluyter map of 1679." Had poor Father Pierron suspected that the Governor was slaking the legislative and judicial thirst of the Province and putting money in his purse by means of it, he would scarcely have organized that prohibition petition at all. Lovelace commended the temperance proclivities of the delegation, promised to do all sorts of things to stop the evil, but did nothing. How could he? He is praised in the *Relations,* however, for his benevolent disposition.

Had Father Pierron applied later on to the Catholic Dongan instead of the Protestant Lovelace, he would scarcely have had better luck, for Dongan's ideas on the liquor question seem to have been influenced by the character of the beverage. Writing to Denonville, September 29, 1686, he asks, indignantly: " Think you, Sir, that religion will progress whilst your merchants supply, as they do, *brandy,* in abundance, which converts the savages, as you ought to know, into demons and their cabins into counterparts and theatres of hell?"

In fact, two months later Denonville puts down in a Memoir that " Governor Dongan sent emissaries among our savages at Montreal to debauch them and draw them to him, promising them missionaries and assuring them that he would prevent *brandy* being conveyed to their villages." At first sight that seems very creditable for Dongan, but unfortunately he writes in the following month, December 1, 1687, to Denonville: " Care would be taken to dissuade the Indians from their drunken debauches, though certainly *our rum* doth as little hurt as *your brandy,* and in the opinion of

213

Christians is much more wholesome. However, to keep the Indians temperate and sober is a very good Christian *performance,* but to prohibit them all strong liquors seems a little hard, and *very Turkish."* Evidently Dongan was badly informed about the conditions, and even if it were " Turkish " he should have tried to keep the Indians sober.

As a matter of fact, New York ways at that time do not seem to have been far removed from those of the Indian camps in the matter of temperance, though, as Fiske suggests there may be some exaggeration. " It was said that one-quarter of all the houses were places for retailing beer and spirits, and the streets were noisy with tipplers. Andros tried his best to stop it, resorting to such drastic measures as fining every house in the street where a drunken man was picked up, if the magistrate could not discover who sold the liquor." So that poor Father Pierron's Indians must have had a fine exhibition before their eyes of the benefits of civilization.

There is one glory that can especially be ascribed to Pierron, viz: that of having delivered the first blow in the destruction of the worship of the cruel god of war, Agreskoué. At the imminent risk of his life he started the movement which did away even with the mention of the name Agreskoué, and forced the substitution in its stead of that of Niio, the God of the Christians, which is now almost universally used even by the pagan Indians in speaking of the Great Spirit. Possibly it was in the designs of Providence that this revolution should have been effected on the very spot where Father Jogues was martyred and where he constantly manifested contempt for that deity. That the triumph was really won at Auriesville we are certain, for we find in " New Amsterdam and Its People," already referred to, and also in " The Dutch and Quaker Colonies," by Fiske (vol. II, p. 55), that when Governor Andros came to the Mohawk, in 1674, to settle the question of Jesuit intrigue, he found " the first Indian castle on the *west bank* of the Schoharie Creek, at its junction with the river." That is the exact spot.

This defeat of Agreskoué took place during a solemn feast of the dead. As is well known, it was customary for the Indians to watch over the remains of their departed with the greatest solicitude, generally placing them upon lofty scaffolding, to protect them from the wild beasts, and when the flesh decayed, arranging the bleaching bones, but especially the skulls, in some place outside the camp, the squaws making it a sacred duty to protect them from desecration. Every ten years a general entombment of those who had died in the interim took place, and was made the occasion for the most solemn and splendid ceremonies. We have a description of one of these festivals, in which Jerome Lalemant, Pijart, and Raymbault participated at Lake Huron, thirty-two years before Pierron witnessed it on the Mohawk, and we quote it here as a description of what occurred on the occasion of which we speak.

On the appointed day, we are told, the Indians all gathered at the end of a deep bay on the eastern shore of Lake Huron. You could see their canoes coming from all points of the horizon, and when near the shore ranging themselves according to their tribes in order of battle. When they were all assembled the chief arose and in a loud and solemn voice announced the purpose of their meeting, and in token of welcome flung into the lake the most precious objects he had, tomahawks, peltries and the like, which the young braves plunged into the water to seize, bringing them up from the bottom amid the joyous shouts and cries of the spectators. It was the first part of the programme.

Coming ashore, there was a grand display on the beach of all their treasures; namely, the skins of beaver and otter and caribou and wild cat, hatchets and pots and belts of wampum. Some of the furs, writes Lalemant, would have cost forty or fifty thousand francs in France. The allied nations then made their presents to the tribe, the Jesuits bringing

215

theirs. Then the festivities begin. They start with a dance representing a battle, the braves keeping step to the beating of a drum, the men singing meantime in excellent accord; another graver dance by the women follows, and finally the planting of a pole, which is flexible and well greased, at the top of which are two prizes, a deer skin and a pot to be won by the successful climber.

Unusual solemnity marks the programme of the second day. A cabin one hundred metres long is prepared. It is shaped like a cradle. The women deck it with the finest furs, and the men carry to it the bones of the dead in bark coffins. In the evening the braves sing the funeral hymn, and the women weep and lament. On the morrow there are melancholy farewells to the dead and advice from the old chiefs to the warriors. The women, with branches in their hands, chase from the cabin the souls of the dead, and all the bones are placed in an immense pit lined with furs, belts of wampum and the arms of the dead warriors. The festival ends with banquets where dog meat is the favorite dish, and finally, after games of strength, agility, and skill, the Indians disperse and the ceremony is over.

At such a ceremony Father Pierron assisted at Ossernenon in 1674. He occupied a place of honor. An Onondaga chief was about to hold forth when some of the Mohawks began to discuss among themselves their various beliefs about the other world, the divinities worshipped by the tribes, etc. To the consternation of all, Pierron, who knew that a tomahawk might cleave his head for his audacity, contradicted and ridiculed them. There was an immediate outburst of wrath, and a conspicuous chieftain, once a friend of Pierron, bade him hold his peace and withdraw, forcing him to stand among the Onondagas and women. Pierron feigned intense indignation. He had been five hours at the ceremony, and now refused to wait for the chanting of the dirge which was about to begin. Declaring himself grievously insulted, that he would abandon the country, and that the Governor would take it as a personal affront, he left the assembly amid the consternation of all. Breaking with the French meant leaving them to the mercy of the Mohegans.

The chief who had driven him from his place came to atone for the offense. " We shall call a council," he said; " you will offer wampum to our three families and you will say what you have on your mind." Next day the greatest haste was made to prepare for the meeting, the chief himself, though sixty years of age, hurrying everywhere to summon the sachems. The council met. " I then began to deliver my speech," says Pierron. " You have received my word that I was going to Quebec. It is true. After all I have sacrificed for you, you have done nothing to be of the same heart with me. You still believe your Agreskoué," etc. After this speech I threw down a great belt of wampum, saying: " Agnié, my brother, if it is true that thou wilt listen to me, there is my voice, which warns you to renounce Agreskoué. This speech was received with great applause. Then I threw down another belt and warned them against jugglers. The last present I made was to warn them against the superstition of dances. Then I was told I would be given the answer in another council."

The difficulty was not yet arranged, and two other councils were held, both of them in presence of the Onondagas, who had come back from the Dutch colony. " As soon as I entered, someone presented me with a great piece of meat, to make me favorably disposed. I accepted it and shared it with those nearest me. Then the great Garagontié spoke indorsing what I had said, but they told him to be silent. They accepted the words of the Frenchman. They would do what I told them.

" I went forth from the assembly," he writes, " filled with joy. It was the feast of the Annunciation."

On the next day the second council was called, and there was a complete surrender. " The promise was made to renounce Agreskoué, and I was presented with as much porce-

lain as I had given.   I thanked them, and some days later
I saw the sorcerers throwing into the fire their tortoise-
drums and other instruments of their calling; they were no
longer summoned in sickness, no dance was allowed but with
my permission.   When a man who did not belong to the
country or who was drunk invoked Agreskoué he was re-
proved and ordered to be silent, and was informed that the
demon was no longer invoked among the Agniers.   The
whole face of things is changed," he adds, "and we have now
a field for several fervent missionaries."

Soon after this Pierron was summoned to Quebec to give
an account of the condition of the country to Talon and de
Courcelles.   He was then sent to La Prairie and afterwards
we find him far away in Acadia.   That was between the
going thither of Druillettes and the arrival of Father Rasle.
He did not, however, minister to the Abenakis, but to the
French, though there is no record of what he did or whither
he went.   From thence he sets out on a very daring venture.
He travels in disguise through all the English colonies, Boston and New York, until he finally arrives among the Jesuits
of Maryland.   What was his purpose we have no means of
ascertaining.

At Boston he created a sensation, and the memory of it,
we are told by Dablon, remained for some years.   The
Catalogue, which never indulges in flattery, describes Pierron as a subtle theologian, a distinguished literateur and
rhetorician, and we know him as a tolerable draughtsman.
That explains how he immediately attracted attention, was
received everywhere, and even had the audacity to engage
in religious discussions with the ministers.   Possibly he had
a tilt with Eliot.   Then it began to be bruited about that he
was a Jesuit, and he was cited before the General Assembly.
That he could not afford to do, and probably in another disguise he disappeared from public view.   He was not pursued, for Boston could not concern itself over much with a
religious inquisition just then.   Its relations with the mother

country were strained; the Royal Commissioners had sent home a very unfavorable account of it; even speaking of Harvard as a " wooden college "; a fleet had appeared in the harbor to awe the colonists, and, worst of all, the Pequod, King Philip, who had been baptized a Christian, was on the warpath and massacre was the order of the day. The good people of Boston were displeased, of course, by Pierron's sudden flight, but were not so much annoyed, as we learn from the Labadist diary, that he was a Jesuit as that he was disguised.

We are at first puzzled to explain how this hard working missionary, who had only a short time before arrived from France, and who since then had lived in the woods, could discuss science and literature in Boston. Could he speak English? We get the answer from a letter written to him by Col. Nicolls, a conspicuous lawyer of those days, who had married into the Van Rensselaer family. It is dated Fort Albany, October 24, 1667, and says:

" Sir: Having seen your very agreeable letter to Madame de Corlart of the 13th of September, and also another to Mr. Hains, I feel very glad to communicate briefly my sentiments to you thereon; but, seeing by the commencement of yours to Madame de Corlart that you have *thoroughly* learned the English language, I dare no longer hazard my bad French style, fearing to appear very ignorant before you, as I am, in fact, of your tongue. Therefore it is I now begin in plain English to let you know that if you please to give me a meeting at Schonestade, I shall be glad to see you and to serve you in what you seem to desire towards your winter provision."

The colonel then communicates to him all the news he had about the war going on in Europe; how the French had taken some towns in Flanders, etc., and then continues: " However, to a person of your profession and merit, I should at any time willingly accept an interview without entering into discourse of politique affairs. Therefore this present letter is expressly sent in place of a passport to give you full assurance of your freedom to come to Schoneistade and to return at your liberty, and if you please to bring one more in your company upon the same terms I shall endeavor to answer your desires. Be pleased to come with all expedition, as I have little time to spend there, and you will find me next *Munday* and till Tuesday attending your answer. You may easily and with the most expedition make the voyage in a canoe down the river, otherwise I would have sent horses for your accommodation. If you cannot lay hold of the present opportunity, *bee* pleased to send *mee* your speedy answer by this bearer in case you are not disposed to take so *suddain* a voyage.

"I am,
"Your very humble servant,
"R. NICOLLS."

"À Monsieur
"Monsieur le Reverend Père Jean Pierron,
"au Chasteau Tionnontogon,
"Soit donné."

It may be worth noting here that the Colonel reminds Father Pierron that the quickest way of travelling from Auriesville to Schenectady was by canoe. "You can make the journey with *most expedition* in that way, otherwise I would have sent horses." The current must have indeed been swift, for the trails in that part of the country were well beaten and direct roads on which a horse could travel fast.

We have no record of his doings in New York. Andros, who sniffed Jesuit intrigue even in the Long House of the Mohawk, was then Governor, but the people of Manhattan were very little concerned about religion. The Home Government was informed that the ministers were so scarce that no account could be given of children's births and christenings. Scarcity of ministers, and the law admitting marriages by justices prevented also any account of the number married.

JOHN PIERRON.

It may be of New York that Pierron speaks when he says "I found naught but desolation and abomination among the heretics who will not even baptize children, still less adults." He saw persons thirty and forty years old and even as many as ten or twelve in a single house who had not received baptism. He had the happiness of preparing a heretic for abjuration.

He did not, of course, see Philadelphia, for, although the Quakers were being scourged and pilloried in New England, William Penn had not yet inaugurated his "holy experiment," though doubtless the traveller passed through the Swedish colony on the Delaware. Of it, however, he does not speak.

"In Maryland," says Dablon, "I found two of our Fathers and a Brother; the Fathers being dressed like gentlemen, and the Brother like a farmer. In fact, he has charge of the farm, which serves to support the two missionaries." Consulting the old catalogues, the Fathers must have been Fathers Clavering and Waldegrave *alias Pelham*. The good "farmer's" name is not recorded. Three years later, however, these Jesuit missionaries had received some help, so that the number of Jesuits laboring there were eight. Newton Manor was their principal place of abode. They did not seem to be concerning themselves much just then with the Indians, and Pierron proposed to undertake that work, but his offer was not accepted, the reasons alleged being that he belonged to another "Assistancy" and that there was no money available; both of them futile excuses. Possibly they were not comfortable about Father Pierron's presence, and perhaps even a trifle suspicious of him.

A little later a curious trail crosses the path of the traveller. In Europe, Labadie, who had been first a Jesuit scholastic, then a Carmelite, and subsequently a Calvinist, had established his ridiculous communist society and sent out his two principal adherents, Dankers and Sluyter, to find a suitable place in America for a settlement. Mr. Henry C.

Murphy has left us the diary of these two men in the first volume of the Long Island Historical Society, and we can follow them step by step in their journey. Arriving at New York, July 27, 1683, they won over to their views an individual then conspicuous in society there. He was the grandson of the Augustyn Hermen or Herman or Heermans who had established Bohemia Manor on the Delaware. The persuasive Labadists induced him to make over to them a portion of this great estate, and thither they repaired to examine it. They took with them also a prominent New Yorker, Peter Bayard, which will explain how the Bayards came to be identified with Delaware.

Arriving in Maryland, Dankers and Sluyter record their impressions: " The priests of Canada take care of the region, and hold correspondence with those here as well as with those who reside among the Indians. It is said there is not an Indian fort between Canada and Maryland where there is not a Jesuit who teaches and advises the Indians, who begin to listen to them too much, so much so that some people in Virginia and Maryland, as well as in New Netherlands, have been apprehensive lest there might be an outbreak." In spite of this dangerous propinquity, however, the socialist colony was established at Bohemia Manor. It did not last long. It was too absurd a scheme, and it is comforting to note that long after, namely, in 1704, Father Thomas Mansell paddled up Bohemia Creek and founded a Jesuit mission, not exactly on the same spot, but near enough to be known as Bohemia Manor, a name which it still retains. Later on, " Jacky " Carroll, afterwards Archbishop of Baltimore, went to school at that Bohemia Manor with the Neals and Brents and other children of the Maryland Catholic families.

After establishing their colony, the Labadist envoys retraced their steps and visited Boston, where they discovered the tracks of Father Pierron. Of the city itself they give us a very discouraging picture.

JOHN PIERRON.

Describing its religious condition, they say: " There was less devotion even than in New York; no respect, no reverence; nothing but the name of Independents, and that was all. In one church one minister made a prayer, two hours long; after which an old minister made a sermon for another hour, and the service continued for three or four hours; when one minister was tired, another went up into the pulpit. We heard preaching in three churches by persons who seemed to possess zeal, but no just knowledge of Christianity." They visited John Eliot, who was then seventy-seven years old. " He could speak neither Dutch nor French, and with our little English and some Latin we managed to understand each other. He deplored the decline of the Church in New England, especially in Boston. We went to Cambridge, where is the only college, or would-be academy of the Protestants in all America. We saw eight or ten young fellows smoking tobacco, with the smoke of which the house was filled, and smelt so strong of it that when I was going up stairs I said: 'Certainly this is a tavern.' We asked how many students there were. They said at first thirty; then came down to twenty; I understood afterward that there were probably not ten. They could hardly speak a word of Latin. They took us to their library, where there is nothing particular. We looked over it a little. They presented us with a glass of wine. This is all we ascertained there." (Quincy's History of Harvard, I, 472, admits this description as not far from the truth.) Speaking of the soil of New England these harsh censors say: " We regard the poorest in New York superior to the best there," and adverting to the English character, they express their opinion in words too severe for us to reproduce.

They were about to depart when they discovered the Jesuit trail. " We went to Mr. Taylor to ascertain if he had some wine and also some brandy. We found him a little cool. He said we must excuse him if he did not admit

223

us into his house in consequence of the suspicion people had of us. They said we were certainly *Jesuits* who had come for no good; *for we were quiet and modest and entirely different sort of people from themselves;* that we could speak several languages; were cunning and subtle; and had come for no traffic, but to see the country. The suspicion seemed to have gained strength because some time ago a Jesuit arrived here from Canada who came in disguise. There was much murmuring about it, and they wished to punish the Jesuit, not because he was a Jesuit, but because he was in disguise, which is generally bad, especially for such as are the pests of the world." This was Pierron. The envoys then departed after carefully noting that "they paid Mr. Taylor for the brandy."

What became of Pierron? Father Dablon tells us that " he returned to the Iroquois," very likely going up through the Susquehanna region and thus reaching one of the missions. Dablon's letter, as Thwaites points out, was never meant for publication, and he quotes Martin, who says: " These apostolic men had been traduced to the ministers of Louis XIV, to their own Provincial, and the King's Confessor. The letter of Dablon to the General is in discharge of his duty to establish the truth, and he informs the General that " Fathers Garnier and Raffeix are among the Senecas, who are the farthest from us and who also seem as remote from the faith; *Father Pierron* has gone to join them to take charge of a large village for which we have hitherto been unable to provide. He is a man of great and rare virtue. I must here mention, in confidence, something about that Father which will console you and which proves his great virtue. Before leaving us to return among the Iroquois— *for whom he has a great natural repugnance which he bravely overcomes*—he came to me, and kneeling in my room with bare head and clasped hands, desiring me to remain covered and seated, he asked me for permission to make two vows; the first, ever to comply unquestioningly with the

JOHN PIERRON.

orders of his superiors, and never to propose anything contrary to them; the second, to bind himself never to return to France, or to secure that privilege in any way. I would not permit the former, but I allowed the latter, in so far as consistent with obedience. He afterwards thanked me for firmly adhering to my intention of sending him among the Iroquois, because in that I had acted against his own feelings."

The scene is a trifle dramatic, but, of course, it was with his Superior and in private. It helps us, however, to understand the man who had a repugnance for the Iroquois, but who nevertheless made himself so familiar with them as to teach school to their restless children, to paint pictures for them and play games with them, and who had succeeded in winning such an influence over them as to be able to inaugurate among them an enthusiastic movement for abandoning the superstitions to which the whole race had given itself up for centuries. Possibly Pierron was a trifle pessimistic.

Apparently, after having labored among the Senecas and Cayugas in 1676 and 1677, Pierron was relieved from his vow with regard to returning to France, for we find in a note by Thwaites in the *Relations* of 1664-1667 that he returned to France in 1678. At that time the missions all through New York were breaking up. He died in France, but of the exact time and place we have no record.

JOHN DE LAMBERVILLE.

THE greatest figure that appears in the final crash of the missions is that of John de Lamberville, elder brother of James. The latter was mostly laboring among the Mohawks and is especially conspicuous because of the conversion of Catherine Tegakwitha. John's whole missionary career, on the contrary, was with the Onondagas.

John de Lamberville first came into prominence when Governor Frontenac was about to establish Fort Cataroqui, the present Kingston, in Canada. The idea of putting a fort at that place originated in the brain of La Salle, who first went down to Onondaga to consult the missionary about it. In the *Relations* we find no details of what happened on that occasion, but we learn that Frontenac arrived at Cataroqui soon after, and we are told he quite captivated the Indians. He not only assumed all the lordliness and martial airs which he knew dazzled the imagination of the savages, but went around preaching to them. De Lamberville wrote to thank him for his evangelical efforts, and we find, in the *Relations* of 1672-3, a pious wish expressed by the grateful missionary when writing to his Superior at Quebec: " May God grant that the powerful exhortations of Monsieur the Governor to the assembled Iroquois to embrace the Faith— *supported as those exhortations were by numerous presents* —will have the effect that we hope from a zeal which so thoroughly unites the interests of the King of Heaven with those of our monarch."

Neither Louis XIV nor Frontenac could complain of the compliment. It is a pity that neither of them enabled poor Father de Lamberville to have some of those " numerous presents " to help out his exhortations to the Onondagas. He often moans over his poverty in this respect.

ROUEN.

JOHN DE LAMBERVILLE.

Times were very hard spiritually in that difficult mission of *St. Jean Baptiste à Onnontagué*. De Lamberville gives the reason: " If legislation and souls were of old found incompatible in the most flourishing empire in the world, it must in the same way be very difficult to establish the laws of God in a land of savages where the demon of war, of pride, and of intemperance has full sway. Faith holds the understanding captive and strives to subject man to the duties of a true Christian, but the Iroquois cannot endure the slightest thing in the world that trammels him. The nature of the savage is to live as he pleases and to follow the maxims of others only in so far as they suit him. It must be understood that *the Iroquois are not capable of reasoning as do the Chinese and other civilized nations,* to whom we prove the truth of faith and the existence of God. The Iroquois is not guided by reasons. The reasons for credibility are not listened to here, and our greatest truths are called falsehoods. As a rule they believe only what they see. To convert the upper Iroquois it would be necessary to subdue them to the Faith by two arms, one of gold, the other of iron. I mean to win them by presents and to keep them in subjection by fear of arms. Missionaries have neither the attraction of one nor the strength of the other. Only the fear of some evil or the hope of some good can determine them to embrace our religion. It is nevertheless a great honor for us to be God's agents and to cause Him to be adored by a small Church in a country where the Devil is so completely the master through unbelief and profligacy. Hell, however, does not swallow up the souls of all those who die in these forests. During this year and in this place I count over thirty who now pray in heaven for the salvation of their country."

Father Millet had introduced the custom of public penance at Onondaga, and de Lamberville continued it, but always with a touch of exquisite delicacy. Thus a poor Huron squaw who was living among the Iroquois got drunk.

She had been invited to a brandy feast and forgot herself. She was broken-hearted over it and implored the priest to admit her into the church services again, promising to submit to any penance. De Lamberville held her off for some time, until, as he says, " Father Millet having given me the pleasure of paying me a visit, she applied to him," and so it was arranged that " after praising her courage I reconciled her and then admitted her to a modest feast which I gave to all the Christians to make the festival a more solemn one."

Barring this single lapse, de Lamberville was able to say that " all the Christians are completely exempt from the vice of intemperance." It is true that they were not all fervent to the same degree. " I am not surprised at it. I am much more astonished to see that in the midst of the iniquity they so well resist the torrent of bad example." Nor was it the women alone who were good; and here de Lamberville takes occasion to pronounce a eulogy of the wonderful old Garagontié, who told the priest that after he had promised to observe the commandments of God he could not remember having ever violated any. " As to marriage," said the old Indian with a touch of humor, " of course you know my wife's ill-temper. Had I not been a Christian I would have sent her away long ago, as the Iroquois do, that I might take another." Garagontié is described as praying with " saintly effrontery," not only among the savages but when he visited the Dutch at " *New Yorch.*" The Indians held him in the greatest esteem. " No ceremony takes place without Garagontié speaking. They say " he knows everything and is as clever as a demon." He is the sanest and the best counsellor they have. I have no doubt he will win the esteem of Monsieur the Count de Frontenac, the King's Lieutenant-General in Canada—to whom he is going to pay his respects at the entrance of Lake Ontario, and congratulate him upon his safe arrival in the country."

De Lamberville's pictures of Onondaga domestic life are

very vivid and very valuable. In the *Relations* we have scenes between a dissipated husband and a patient Christian wife; and next to it the reverse of the medal: a fierce harpy who strives to prevent the conversion of her husband; another of a poor old widower who was so harried by the women of his establishment that he hanged himself, Christian and all as he was; and to omit the rest, that of a poor old cripple of a woman at the point of death assaulted by a drunken brute who beat and stabbed her and left her for dead.

It was with these drunkards that he found most of his trouble. Thus we find him struggling hand to hand at midnight in his chapel with an infuriated savage who was endeavoring to brain Father James de Lamberville. James had just come up from the Mohawk country. Again, he is perched on a high rock looking down at a bloody fight that was going on beneath him for the possession of a captive. Half the mob was wild with liquor and were cutting and slashing each other while murdering the unhappy victim. At last the wretch was carried off to a lodge, where they treated him with such atrocity that he strove to kill himself. A little later de Lamberville entered the wigwam to see a sick person. The captive had meantime been led out and was being roasted to death at the door of the lodge. The savages then cut him in pieces and ate him. Such were the accompaniments of his administrations of the Sacraments. This particular case had an added horror. Before de Lamberville withdrew, a drunken brute entered with the victim's thigh and began to skin it to give to the sick squaw. " I don't want that; I want his liver," screamed the fury; and the liver was brought in after being torn from the teeth of another monster, who was devouring it. Delivering this dainty morsel to the woman the savage cavalier upset the cauldron and so scalded himself that he was crippled for six weeks afterwards.

Such were some of the amenities of Onondaga life. Drink

resulted in daily murders, and people were going around without noses and ears and hands and fingers. They had been cut off in drunken brawls. The eating of human flesh prevailed to such an extent that 600 victims, according to de Lamberville, were devoured in a single expedition against the Illinois.

And yet we find this delicate and sensitive man never losing his patience with them. He writes to his Superior: " When I returned after my absence, the notabilities came to salute me and I gave them presents, exhorting them at the same time to maintain peace with the French, to become Christians, not to annoy me with their drunkenness, to let me baptize the dying and the captives who were going to be burned.

" I showed them a topographical view of the city and environs of Paris, with the portraits of the five principal personages of the kingdom. They admired the skill of Europeans in representing persons to the life. *One of them asked me whether when those whose portraits I showed them died, their images did not also close their eyes.* They could not gaze enough at the picture of Paris and wonder at its vast extent. They were surprised that houses should be built on stone bridges, under the arches of which passed boats laden with all sorts of merchandise. They could not understand how, for the subsistence of so large a town, everything came to it from all sides by land and water. The Louvre, the Bronze Horse (a statue) ; the King's palace, and the houses of the great ; the general hospitals ; the number of inhabitants ; the rare animals brought from every part of the world that are to be seen there ; the superb churches where three or four thousand people pray to God ; the cemeteries ; the colleges where five or six hundred persons lodge ; —these are great marvels in a country whose people know almost nothing."

De Lamberville became a successful medical practitioner among his Indians. " I had brought a great supply of drugs, which the Maréchal de Bellefonds had the kindness to procure for us from Monsieur Pellison, and we also increased our stores from medicines which the King causes to be so liberally given to the poor." It would not be very reassuring to his patients had they heard him say: "We must learn how to use these drugs." But he gave an "orvietan" here, and a "theriac" there, whatever they may be; and his forceps did wonders in proving that the decayed teeth which he vigorously pulled out were not *okis* or demons that had settled in the jaws of the patients. The holy man was in despair when his pharmacopœia was exhausted.

His rivals were the medicine men, and he gives us an account of their methods of dealing with the sick, which reveals the extent of their intelligence in such vital matters. It is like an anticipation of Catlin's account of a similar scene among the Mandans in the Far West, two centuries later.

"In the village," he tells us, "there was a sick girl who was also half crazy. The medicine man was summoned to cure her. He approaches and takes up his position in the centre of a ring of bark. Eight or nine assistants stand around rattling small gourds filled with peas. After a while these savage Galens entered the circle and burned tobacco to propitiate the evil spirit, some in honor of the stag, others in honor of the owl, others in honor of the bear, each imitating the cry of the animal to which he sacrificed. Then the chief juggler made incisions in the patient's temples, whence he sucked some blood and spat it out, mixed with bear's teeth, human hair, stag's bristles and the like, all of which he had concealed in his mouth, pretending that they were the spells which had been cast on the sufferer. Hearty thanks were given to these worthy physicians, but the crazy girl became no better for their treatment." Failure, however, did not disconcert them. It was to their advantage, and they announced that nine feasts were necessary to cure

her completely, for "the design of these disciples of Escu-
lapius," says de Lamberville, "is always to fare well and
eat their fill."

"The first two feasts began with a ceremony which is
quite usual among them. Everyone who had dreamed of
any article during the year came to sing for two nights in
the girl's cabin, and then went around and demanded from
anyone they met the article dreamed of; such as corn, meat,
mats, pots, &c., which were immediately given. One woman
was impudent enough to dream of my cassock, and to send
someone to demand it. Of course I turned the messenger
out. The third feast was a masquerade of men dressed like
bears; the fourth a sham fight, in which they threw ashes on
each other; the fifth an ordinary dance; the sixth one in
which they were all covered with feathers from head to
foot. After a general mêlée they rolled over on the ground,
writhing and frenzied, until the victorious party cured the
others, who pretended to be bewitched, by counterfeited
vomitings, poultices and the like. The seventh dance was
a *pas seul;* a warrior dressed like an Indian from the far
south; the eighth and ninth were too indecent to describe.
All this was to cure the girl. Of course she died."

De Lamberville had spent nearly fourteen years among his
Onondagas when the arrival of de la Barre as Governor of
Quebec gave him the first warning of the approaching storm.

The new official had seen hard military service in various
parts of the world, and had something of a reputation to
support. At first he turned his thoughts to peace in the
management of the restless Iroquois. But it happened that
a few weeks after he had arrived, fourteen Frenchmen on
their way to trade with the Illinois were captured and robbed
by some Senecas, and Fort St. Louis was attacked. No one
but a newcomer would have been disturbed by such trifles.
It was all in the usual course of events and reparation could
have been easily exacted. But de la Barre's military blood
was up, and after the example of de Tracy, twenty years

before, he determined on an invasion of the Seneca country. His Memoir says that Father Bruyas and the Superior of the Sulpitians approved of the war.

De Lamberville heard of the project with dismay, and he began to assail the Governor with letters. They may be found in the *Relations;* and O'Callaghan has reproduced them in his *Documentary History of New York.* They make most interesting reading. He begs de la Barre not to fight; informs him that the Iroquois are all federated; he is astonished that Charles Le Moyne had not told him that war cannot be made against the Senecas without involving the other four cantons; he quotes them as saying that they are sorry he is going to war; that they will slip off from their villages and retreat into *Merilande* and Virginia; that they think the French have a great desire to be stripped, roasted and eaten, and that they will see if their flesh is salty on account of the salt they make use of, and is as good as that of other enemies whom they devour. He informs the Governor in detail of everything that is going on among the savages, and how efforts are being made to tranquillize them. On August 17, 1684, he writes " your people brought my brother back with the greatest possible diligence, having been weather-bound three days at one island. They arrived here *at midnight and having passed the rest of the night* in conferring together, we had the chiefs and warriors *assemble at daylight,* after having obtained information from Big Mouth and Garagontié," and so on. The correspondence is very voluminous.

His efforts, however, were unavailing, and de la Barre pronounced for war. He organized a little army in great haste, and led it without discipline up the St. Lawrence. The progress was slow and painful. On the 21st of August, they arrived at what is now called Famine or Hungry Bay, on the north shore of New York, where Lake Ontario becomes the St. Lawrence River. Already out of provisions, because of a long delay in Montreal, de la Barre found himself encamped in a pestilential swamp with a great number of soldiers down with sickness, and looking more like a routed army than one going to conquer a foe. Without striking a blow the Governor appealed to de Lamberville for help, humbly entreating him to make peace for him with the Iroquois.

Charles Le Moyne, one of the famous family of that name, who exercised great influence over the Iroquois, hurried to meet the missionary. Thanks to de Lamberville's skilful handling of his people, Le Moyne found them ready to grant anything, even to giving up their war with the Illinois, who were allies of the French, but when their deputies arrived at Famine Bay and saw the pitiable condition of the French, they changed their tone and insisted that de la Barre should immediately withdraw, and not dream of interfering in the quarrel between them and the Illinois. To the shame and indignation of all the Governor was compelled to accept all their conditions, and in the early part of September he set out, crestfallen, for Quebec, only to find himself recalled in disgrace to France, as soon as his desertion of the Illinois became known.

In 1685 M. de Denonville came out as Governor, with orders to crush the Iroquois. He kept his own counsel; spoke of his plans to no one; but began building 200 flatboats for the transportation of troops. He fortified Montreal, provisioned Cataroqui, and gathered in arms and ammunition from all quarters. Durantaye at Mackinac, Tonti at Fort St. Louis, among the Illinois, Perot at Green Bay, Du Luth and the others were ordered to meet at Niagara with as many warriors as possible at the beginning of July, 1687.

At that time the only two priests in New York were the two de Lambervilles. The fact is revealed by a very peppery letter form Denonville to Dongan. "When you arrived in your present government, did you not find, Sir," he asks, "in the whole of the five Iroquois villages all our Mis-

234

sionaries, almost all of whom the heretic merchants have caused to be expelled, even in your time, which is not honorable to your Government? It is only three years since the greater number has been forced to leave; the Fathers de Lamberville alone bore up against the insults and ill treatment which they received on account of the promptings of your traders. Is it not true, Sir, that you eagerly desired to induce them to abandon their mission," &c.?

Strange to say, no one seemed to suspect the meaning of the Governor's warlike preparations, not even the two missionaries, who would certainly be murdered by the Iroquois if hostilities began. Not only did he not tell them, but he made use of them in a manner which has brought irreparable disgrace on his name. He summoned de Lamberville to meet him at Quebec, and commissioned him to send Iroquois deputies to Cataroqui to arrange the terms of a treaty. Denonville announces this in a letter to the Minister of Marine, November 8, 1686. In this official communication appear the ominous words: " This poor father does not suspect our design. He is a clever man; but if I recalled him from his mission, our purpose would be suspected and the storm would burst on us."

Returning to Onondaga, de Lamberville assembled forty of the principal chiefs of the Iroquois tribes. He assured them that the Governor, being a Christian gentleman and one specially chosen by the King, could not possibly fail to keep his word. They acquiesced and promised to be at Cataroqui in midsummer.

Meantime Denonville was leaving Montreal with two hundred boats and as many Indian canoes. He disembarked at Cataroqui on the last day of June, and immediately afterwards the Iroquois deputies arrived with a great number of presents. Hardly had they landed when they were made prisoners, and their canoes, peltries and arms were confiscated. A few days afterwards the prisoners were sent to

Aix in France, as galley-slaves, where many of them died in misery.

While all this was going on, Father de Lamberville, in complete ignorance of the trick, was visited at Onondaga by a number of mounted men, who were sent by Dongan, the English Governor of New York, to tell him of de Denonville's treachery. They had found it out some way or other in Montreal, and advised the priest to go with them to New York. They had in fact brought a horse with them for his use. If he did not consent, they assured him he would lose his life.

De Lamberville refused to believe them; and not only rejected their offer with indignation, but set out for Cataroqui with eight of the most distinguished Iroquois chiefs. They had gone but a day's journey when some of the deputies who had escaped from Cataroqui gave them the awful news of the treachery. The rage of the Indians knew no bounds. Was not de Lamberville the chief offender? It was he who had led them thither. But it speaks voluumes for the trust the Indians reposed in him that, instead of cleaving his head with a tomahawk, they said to him: " We know that you did not do this, and that you detest the crime as we do. But you must leave the country, for there are many who will not regard this deed in the way that we do." Guides conducted him to the frontier, and not far from Cataroqui he met the Governor. What passed between them is not known. De Lamberville says not a word except that he induced the Governor to liberate seven or eight of the deputies. But he saw the complete ruin of all his work and hopes.

The fight was now on. The army set out on July 12, and invaded the Seneca country. Two days' march brought them within a league of the chief village. Seven hundred Tsonontouans or Senecas attacked them fiercely, and the issue was for a time in doubt. The Western savages took to flight, but the Christian Indians stood firm, sometimes

JOHN DE LAMBERVILLE.

fighting in their own fashion, sometimes in the open, like Europeans. The Canadians behaved well, but the French troops disgraced themselves. Finally, the Governor arrived with reinforcements, and, though beaten back at first, he rallied his men and then swept the Iroquois before him, killing forty-five and wounding sixty. It is said that the Ottawas, who had fled, returned at night and roasted and ate the dead bodies. The place of this battle, according to Indian authority, is Boughton's Hill, in the town of Victor, Ontario County. The Indians still call it Dyagodiyu or the Place of Battle..

On July 24, de Denonville withdrew and built Fort Niagara, giving it a garrison of 100 soldiers. He then left for Quebec, which he reached in the beginning of September, and wrote to the Minister of Marine: " I have re-established the reputation of the French, which was dishonored among the Indians, and thanks be to God, I hope things will go well now." It shows how little he knew of Indian methods.

The very next year at the instigation of the English the war was renewed. As an Indian told de Denonville, " you have stirred up a nest of hornets; you have not crushed them." And so towards the end of August, Cataroqui itself was attacked, Chambly was besieged, and fires lighted up the course of the Richelieu, and even reached the St. Lawrence at Verchères and Contre Cœur. What was to be done? Nothing but to ask the missionaries to help to make peace with the Indians. There was only one priest who could be of assistance and that was de Lamberville. Where was he?

He was in Fort Cataroqui acting as chaplain, and at the same time had to provide for the spiritual needs of the soldiers at Niagara, so that his " parish " consisted of the whole of Lake Ontario. Going from one post to the other meant each time facing a terrible death.

A manuscript of Father de Lamberville recently discovered in the British Museum gives us a description of one of these journeys which is as graphic as any of the pages of Fenimore Cooper.

"The day before our departure from Cataroqui," he writes, "the Iroquois, who were hemming us in, had fired on the crew when yet at the wharf, and wounded a sergeant, who died after receiving the last Sacraments. Hardly had we doubled the point than an Iroquois fired at us. It was the signal for the Indians to leave their camp, where they had been for several days enjoying the good cheer they had taken from the French near the Rapids. A great number had been invited to witness the attack on our barque. If they took it they would starve out our friends at Niagara. Several canoes pursued us and made for a little island, intending to intercept us, for on account of the shallows we had to pass very close to it. Other Indians ran along the shore to capture us in case we landed. Suddenly the wind dropped and we were becalmed. The savages were all around, but out of gunshot. We prayed, and I exhorted the men to fight to the death rather than be taken and tortured. We had four cannon called *pierriers* for discharging stones, twelve muskets, with two arquebuses and six grenades. We determined not to fire all at once, but one after the other; while two of us were to keep loading. Our deck had no guards, so we had to lie down while fighting. A shower of bullets swept over us. We replied by a volley from both sides of the barque. Some of the Indian fell in their canoes and were carried off, but their place was taken by others. Four canoes bolder than the rest came close up to us, but we stopped them with our arquebuses and the *pierrier,* which had thirty stones in it. That discharge riddled the canoes and made them draw off to the island to attend to the wounded and repair the damage to their boats. They came again to the charge, not doubting that half of our number had fallen under their furious fusillade. But no one had yet been hit. Just then they remarked that there was no fire from the stern and they made for it, but a cry, ' they are boarding us!' from one of the soldiers caused a rush in that direction with swords and grenades, but at that moment a slight wind sprung up and we began to move. I was engaged in loading the muskets and sticking out two arquebuses from the stern to scare the invaders. The puff of wind gave us courage, and we drifted slowly past the island. Just then a chief started out with five or six canoes to head us off. He stood up brandishing his weapons and then aimed at the pilot and a sailor who were defending the bow, but they dodged in time and escaped the shot, and immediately aimed at him and tumbled him over with a shot in the neck and another in the body, as I afterwards learned. But his companions would not withdraw, when one of our soldiers, a Breton, who had been in the German wars, rushed to the *pierrier* and at the risk of his life, for he had to stand up, applied the match, and in a flash a shower of stone balls sunk the canoe to the bottom. The Breton was not hurt, but two Indian bullets passed through his hat. It was the last effort of the savages. The wind freshened, and the distance widened between us, and they, fearing to go out in the open, withdrew. The fight had lasted three-quarters of an hour. Three hundred bullet holes were in our sails; many of the ropes were cut, but thanks be to God, none of our halliards was injured. We were a league away and were again becalmed, but the Indians did not follow us. Next morning we started with a west wind and a cloudy sky. Off in the distance we saw the fires of the Iroquois. We kept out in the lake for a storm was approaching. The lake was soon like the ocean in its fury. Great waves washed over us, but we did not dare to put in, for fear of the enemy. Often we thought we were going to the bottom. Finally, after fourteen days of hard weather, we saw in the distance the flag of Fort Niagara. Our joy may be imagined. We could see the Iroquois skulking around as we landed. We had scarcely unloaded when the Commandant thought it would be advisable to return, because the wind was favorable and our friends at Cataroqui would be anxious. On the 18th of October we reached Cataroqui. The Indians had been hanging about the fort all the time, behind 200 cords of fire wood which we had heaped up. They were waiting for our return, but lost patience and decamped the day before we arrived, after setting fire to all our wood and killing a soldier, whose death revealed their ambuscade."

It was here that de Denonville's messenger found de Lamberville and entreated him to go down to Onondaga to get them to call off the dogs of war. We may well admire the magnanimity of the man who could forget the outrages of which he had been the victim, and wonder at the courage that could dare to go down among the indignant savages to what might be a bloody death. But he went. To the complaints about the seizure of the sachems at Cataroqui he replied as best he could, assuring them that the captives were in Quebec and would be soon sent back to them; being quite unaware of their having been sent to the galleys of France. The perfidious de Denonville had concealed that fact from him and so exposed him a second time to be killed. The Onondagas treated him with the greatest consideration, and received from him two wampum belts, one to engage them to treat the French prisoners well, and the other to drop the subject of the Seneca invasion. These two wampum belts will figure later when Dongan enters on the scene.

Having succeeded in securing a lull in hostilities, de Lamberville withdrew to his old work at the forts, and we find him there sick of the scurvy. We are not sure if he was already afflicted with the malady when he made this journey to Onondaga, but one account describes his being carried down in a litter. At all events, while ministering to the sick he caught the disease, and was soon brought to death's door by it. The method of his cure may give modern medicine material for reflection. We find it described in a letter which de Lamberville wrote from Paris later on, and sent to a friend in China. It is dated 1695.

JOHN DE LAMBERVILLE.

After telling the whole sad story about Frontenac, de la Barre, and de Denonville, as well as his own relegation to garrison work, he says: " The soldiers of the Fort were struck down with scurvy, and while I was attending to them I caught the sickness and had a day or two to live. Just then an officer, a friend of mine, came with some French and Indians to investigate the condition of the fort. Being told by the surgeon that I had only a day or two to live unless I was removed, he determined to carry me with him to Montreal. I begged him to let me die and to take some one else in my stead. He absolutely refused. As I could do no more, I consented, and they lifted me in their arms and I gave a last absolution to the dying soldiers. I was bundled up and placed on a sled drawn by two dogs. Going over the lake the ice broke and we fell in. Fortunately the dogs clung to the cakes of ice, but while we were being dragged out, the rope broke and I came near being drowned. At last they got me out and we hurried on, for the Iroquois were after us. There was no means of making a fire to warm me until nine at night. When the dogs gave out, the men dragged the sled. They never stopped, for the pursuers were close at hand. Whenever we could we had to keep on the ice so as to conceal our tracks. We went so rapidly that in seven days we reached Montreal. They hurried me to the hospital, putting my mattress close to the fire, and for four hours I was on the point of giving up the ghost. Next morning the gentlemen of St. Sulpice took me to their house, and there I remained for two years and a half before I was cured of the strange malady of the scurvy."

From which fort was de Lamberville carried? Niagara or Cataroqui? Charlevoix seems to pronounce for Niagara, as that place was then the most afflicted. Rochemonteix, with de Lamberville's own letter in his hand, of course corrects him. Cataroqui was the place from which he was taken. It would have been impossible to make the journey from Niagara to Montreal in seven days, and de Lamberville explicitly says it was to Montreal he was carried. When he had this adventure he was about sixty-four years of age.

It will be remembered that when de Lamberville went on his perilous mission to the Onondagas he gave them two wampum belts. They received the presents, but afterwards sent them down to Governor Dongan, who in turn made haste to despatch them to de Denonville to inquire what they meant. Both those cunning old politicians knew perfectly well what this transfer of the sacred wampum implied.

Dongan had been instructed by the King to keep on friendly terms with the French. Possibly he had received secret instructions to do the very reverse. At all events, he is credited with the ambition to expel the French from New York, to reach out into the regions of the Ohio, to establish a line of posts as far as Hudson Bay, to take possession of New Foundland, and drive the French out of Maine. For that purpose he kept up an active intrigue with the Iroquois, urging them to lay down the hatchet, but not to bury it, promising them assistance in case they got embroiled with the French, reminding them continually of the treachery of which they had been the victims, and, Catholic though he was, doing all in his power to expel the French Jesuits from the territory claimed by England, promising the Indians, however, to send English Jesuits in their stead; a promise which was possibly never meant to be kept, for there were no English Jesuits who had ever lived with the Indians.

On the receipt of the wampum belts at Quebec, Father Vaillant de Gueslis was sent down to Manhattan, to sound the Governor as to his intentions. After considerable fencing, Dongan bluntly said that he would do nothing to keep the Indians quiet except on certain conditions which the French must comply with, viz:

1st, to send back the Indians who had been condemned to

the galleys; 2d, to compel the Iroquois in Canada to return to their country, *i.e.,* destroy the settlements at Caughnawaga and elsewhere; 3d, to abandon Cataroqui and Niagara; 4th, to restore the booty taken from the Senecas.

These conditions were insisted on in a blunt and positive fashion, and while so expressing himself to de Gueslis he repeated it to the Onondagas. He thus simply tore up de Lamberville's wampum belt, which had stipulated that the affair of the Senecas should be forgotten; and at the same time he revived in the heart of the Onondagas all the fierce memories of de Denonville's treachery. It was a summons to war.

With this sad news de Gueslis returned to Canada, but instead of going to Quebec he stopped at Montreal to consult with de Lamberville, who was just coming back from death's door after his almost fatal illness. At the same time de Denonville arrived, and implored de Lamberville in spite of his physical condition to betake himself to Onondaga. The request could not, however, be entertained for a moment, but the resourceful de Lamberville bethought him of a scheme. He talked to one of the Indians, who had come back with de Gueslis, and so wrought upon him that he was induced to go down to Onondaga and to protest or plead against the threatened war.

Arriving home the Onondaga found a thousand Indians assembled. They had been worked into a fury by the English, and all prospect of restraining them seemed out of the question. Nevertheless, he succeeded in preventing immediate action, and they concluded to send an embassy to Montreal. Fearing another trick, however, they assembled near the city, a thousand strong, but only one hundred went to the council. The chief speaker was Big Mouth. He was rude and insolent, though he boasted that he had been always a friend of the French, and insisted that Dongan's conditions should be accepted. Though almost in a dying condition, de Lamberville had dragged himself to the meeting. Everyone heard the Indian's ultimatum with despair. It meant the ruin of the colony. But de Lamberville skilfully took the matter in hand and succeeded in modifying all the conditions except the one that demanded the destruction of Niagara. As it was impossible to hold it on account of the sickness of the garrison, no one felt much regret. Thus de Lamberville got the better of Dongan all along the line. This was on November 6, 1688, and de Denonville wrote to Seignelay in France: " Only God kept this country from ruin this year. I deserve no praise. You will be told by M. de Callières how necessary Father de Lamberville is, and with what skill he averted the storm that threatened us, and how clever he is in controlling the Indian, who is shrewder than you imagine. If you cannot send all these Fathers back to their missions, you may expect great misfortunes for this colony. For I assure you that it is their skill that has kept the colony alive by the number of friends they have with all the tribes, and by their ability in governing these people, who are savage only in name."

Hostilities were over and preparations were made for a definite treaty, when down from Michigan came The Rat, the famous Huron, who would not hear of peace with the Iroquois on any terms. He attacked a number of the delegates, killed some and told the rest he was commissioned to do so by the Governor. All the work of de Lamberville was ruined. On the 4th of August, 1689, 1,400 Iroquois landed above Montreal at La Chine. In the middle of the night, they fell on the colony and massacred men, women, and children. Two hundred persons were killed and 120 taken prisoners. They even went up to the very gates of Montreal, and were not attacked; the whites were paralyzed with fear, and forever after, 1689 was called the year of the massacre.

By this time poor Father de Lamberville was shattered in health. He was already old, and out of pity for him his Superiors sent him to France, as Procurator of the Mission.

JOHN DE LAMBERVILLE.

His hold upon the hearts of the Indians is shown by the fact that his fierce old Onondagas later on sent a request to have him come back to America and live among them. But his work was over, though we find in a letter to a friend that he would have gladly returned to the missions: "I am here," he said, " as Procurator of our mission, awaiting the happy moment which will cause me to recross the sea, that I may end in our dear Canada the few days that remain to me. Entreat God, I beg of you, to show me this mercy."

The "mercy" was not granted, and he died in Paris, February 10th, 1714, at the age of eighty-one. Like many of those Canadian missionaries he came from Rouen. The French Menology says that " he had the spiritual physiognomy of Brébeuf." For the French there was no one greater than Brébeuf.

PETER MILLET.

FATHER PETER MILLET, though a priest, was for a number of years before his death an Oneida chief, but a chief in chains, though the chains towards the end were only figurative. He received the honor of adoption after having narrowly escaped being burned at the stake. His adventures read like a romance.

The Indian sachem Garagontié had brought him down to Onondaga in 1668, and the warmest friendship began between them. In fact, one of the greatest sorrows the old Indian felt when he thought he was dying was that Tcharonhiagnon, "the one who looks up to heaven," for so Millet was called, would regard him as a hypocrite. Two medicine men had come to the chief's lodge when he was sick, to practise their incantations over him. Being half unconscious, he was unaware of what had occurred, and when Millet entered, the chief's first care was to protest that he had not left the faith. Millet consoled him, and with a little medicine set him on his feet again without an incantation.

He began his work on the New York missions first at Onondaga in 1668, and in 1672 he was sent to Oneida, with which place he was forever after associated. At the very outset he exercised a marvellous influence over his wild people. He could have made them all nominal Christians if he wished; but the delinquencies, especially of the men, were too great, and only a limited number of braves were admitted to baptism. But among them he had occasion to see what wonders divine grace could accomplish in the transformation of brutalized humanity. One warrior, for instance, was so marvellously changed that he packed up his few traps, and with his family made a hermitage in the woods, where the Indians used to gather to hear him explain the truths of Christianity. The corruption of the village was too much for him. Seclusion kept him out of temptation and he won many to the faith.

The conversion of the famous chief Garonhiaé, or Hot Ashes, was perhaps the greatest triumph obtained in Oneida. Hot Ashes had married an excellent squaw, with whom he always lived at peace. They had grown up from childhood together and were inseparable, she always exercising a great control over her hot-tempered consort. On account of some quarrel among the chiefs about moving the village, he left Oneida in a temper, and just then the news came that his brother was killed; by whom nobody knew; but Hot Ashes concluded that it was the French, and so he directed his steps to the St. Lawrence to get somebody's scalp. On his way thither he found that he was mistaken. But while in Montreal, his wife who was already captivated by what she saw in the church, persuaded him to remain and it ended by both becoming Christians and taking up their abode at Caughnawaga; Hot Ashes being made Fourth Captain of the settlement.

At his installation, however, he flared up very fiercely, because of an unintentional affront and for a moment he was a subject of alarm. They had lighted a fire for him, offered him the calumet to smoke, given him presents, but had forgotten the mat, and Father Frémin had a good deal of trouble in cooling down the fiery neophyte. The council had to be summoned again and the initiation repeated.

The news of his conversion caused great excitement, and many of the Oneidas came all the way to Caughnawaga to see him, some of them becoming Christians. He was a strong temperance advocate, for he had witnessed the havoc caused by liquor in the tribes, and he devoted himself to an unrelenting war against drunkenness. It is said of him that on one occasion he came across a number of his tribe in the woods, carousing around a kettle of brandy, and all gloriously drunk. He was invited to join them. He could not reprove them to their face, for there were some old chiefs in the party. So he resorted to a trick. He pretended to be intoxicated and began to cut capers around the kettle, singing and shouting and staggering, and finally upsetting the pot. Every one thought it was an accident and guffawed at his clumsiness, and then rolled over and went to sleep.

He had the gift of eloquence to an unusual degree, and went about everywhere preaching; helping his audience to grasp his meaning by the pictures he always carried with him. He had many imitators in that method of picture-lectures, and conversions multiplied. What was more surprising for a chief, he became extremely charitable and would work for the poor and the sick, carrying their wood, gathering their grain, &c. More than anyone else he deserves the credit of keeping drunkenness out of Caughnawaga, and transgressors felt his heavy hand upon them immediately. One intruder he imprisoned in a pig pen and then drove into the woods. So anxious was he about the Sacraments that when a young brave belonging to his lodge was found poisoned in the woods, he actually fell sick, and was in a delirium all night from sheer worry. He heard two masses every day and never passed the church without entering to pray. He would even abandon the hunt and travel long distances to be present at Christmas and Holy Week.

When war broke out he did not hesitate to pronounce for the French, but his first thought, when he started on the warpath, was to provide himself with a relic from the tomb of Catherine Tegakwitha. He had cured his wife once by applying a coverlet which Catherine had used, and now claimed for himself the protection of the holy maid, who owed him so much, for it was he who at the risk of his life had freed her from captivity.

When the Oneidas lost their principal chief, a deputation

248

was sent to Caughnawaga to ask Hot Ashes to assume the honor. "I will, if you become Christians," he said, "for I do not want to be chief of the slaves of the devil." The reply brought on him a great deal of trouble. His people were incensed and told the Governor that Hot Ashes had some sinister design in staying at Montreal, but the warrior bore it all bravely, assuring his wife he would be vindicated. His prophecy came true.

When he went to join de la Barre at Famine Bay, he took his pictures along with him. Everyone in his cabin had to be faithful at the prayers that were regularly said there, and were compelled to listen to his instructions and study his religious tableaux.

He returned with de la Barre, but went out again with de Denonville against the Senecas. He bade adieu to his wife, telling her to pray for him, for he might never return. His foreboding came true. There were two Caughnawaga Indians killed in that campaign; Hot Ashes was one of them. His adventures in the rescue of Tegakwitha are told in the life of James de Lamberville.

Millet's teaching no doubt had much to do with Hot Ashes' ultimate conversion, for it may be supposed that the missionary's methods appealed to the imperious temper of the chief. Acting on a preconcerted plan, the priests had abandoned the exterior meekness which was so conspicuous in Jogues. They found it to be ineffectual with the Indians, as it was mistaken for cowardice, and so airs of authority and importance were assumed. Millet wore the mask like the rest, and while having a very humble idea of himself, never permitted any rudeness or disrespect. He was particularly domineering with the medicine men and inspired them with terror. He would force his way into their lodges, in the midst of their incantations, and upbraid them with their trickery. Little by little he convinced them of their wickedness or frightened them out of it. Co-operating with Father Pierron, further down the valley, he succeeded in making them abandon the worship of Agreskoué. He presided at all the Indian councils, and opened the proceedings with prayer. His chapel was always thronged. For he had made it as gorgeous as he could, according to Indian ideas. One thing that especially took their fancy was a wampum belt hanging above a Bible and a crucifix, while underneath, in token of subjection were the emblems of idolatry. The Indians grasped the significance of the arrangement. The old bell of the former Onondaga mission was likewise a powerful helper for him, for the savage has a great awe of bells, and quickly obeys their summons. But he had other means of calling them. For while the bell was ringing out its peals, the children were kept parading up and down the streets of the village, singing in alternate refrains: "There is but one God, the Master of Life," and "In Heaven are all good things; in hell fire and endless torments." He was laboring there in 1686 when de Denonville made his foolish attack on the Senecas, and like de Lamberville he was used as a decoy. We have the evidence of it in de Denonville's own hand, for writing to Seignelay in France, he says: "I am going to convoke the Iroquois at Cataroqui; and it is necessary to have a faithful interpreter. As the Recollects, who are chaplains there, do not know the language, I have determined to withdraw them and to put Millet in their place, but I have promised to recall the friars after the conference." He did not even propose to leave Millet at the Fort after using him so vilely. It did not matter to the Governor what happened after his own purpose was accomplished. Happy to co-operate with what he fancied was a convention for a treaty of peace, Millet repaired to Cataroqui. He never dreamed that he was to be associated with the infamous betrayal of his Indian friends. He saw the Iroquois delegates land at Cataroqui, saw them manacled and then sent away to the galleys in France. He knew perfectly well that they could have but one thought with regard to himself; namely, that he was co-operating

NIAGARA.

PETER MILLET.

with de Denonville in this shameful act. His influence with them was gone forever, and his missionary career at an end. Of course, he, like de Lamberville, refused to accompany the French forces in their invasion of the Iroquois territory. That post was assigned to Father Enjalran, who was in the forefront of the fight, looking after the wounded and narrowly escaping death himself. He was struck in the hip by an Indian musket-ball.

A temporary lull in hostilities followed upon this victory of the French; but it is not likely that Millet dared to return to Oneida, as Rochemonteix seems to assume. It would have been inviting death to no purpose. He remained as chaplain at Cataroqui, and when de Lamberville was stricken down with scurvy he took his friend's place at Niagara, arriving there on Good Friday, 1688. It was probably on that day that he erected the wooden cross in the centre of the enclosure, with the inscription: "Christ reigneth, conquereth, commandeth." It was in Latin; but in an abbreviated form, and the letters were rude and unshapely. We have a facsimile of it in Shea's "Colonial Days." It reads: "REGN. VINC. ♥ IMP. CHRS." But it did not remain there long, nor did the fort. On September 15, the palisades were demolished, the French withdrew, and for a time at least, Fort Niagara passed out of history. The garrison made its way to Fort Cataroqui.

The following year marks the beginning of Millet's captivity among his former friends. In June, 1689, while he was engaged in his work as chaplain of the fort, some Iroquois Indians presented themselves at the gate with a flag of truce; informing the garrison that peace had been concluded, and asking that the physician of the post should be permitted to come out to assist some sick and wounded Iroquois, and as there were a number of Christians among them, that Father Millet should accompany him. It was a suspicious invitation, but was accepted; and the priest and doctor walked out of the palisade. A long letter written by

251

Millet at Oneida three years afterwards tells how he fared in his subsequent five years of captivity.   A few extracts will suffice.

" Two of the strongest Indians sprung on me, seized me by the arms, and, taking everything I had, began to abuse me for being opposed to the Iroquois; but an Oneida chief told me not to fear, that the Christians of Oneida would preserve my life.   I needed this comfort, because the English, it was said, had already condemned and burned me in effigy.   When the chief turned away, the others stripped me, leaving me only my trousers.   They then began to maltreat me; some wishing to burn me on the spot; but I was rescued from them, and then others threw me into the water and others again trampled me under foot.   Later on, while they were making an attack on the fort, I was tied to a sapling on the banks of the lake, and afterwards sent with three or four hundred Iroquois to an island two leagues below, to await the army of 1,400 which was expected.   There I was received with great shouts and forced to sing certain words which they made me repeat.   To thank me for the song one of them struck me with his fist near the eye, leaving the mark of his nails and inflicting such pain that I thought it was the stroke of a knife.   I was then brought to the cabins of the Oneidas.   They protected me from further insult, and I sang for them, but it was the *Veni Sancte Spiritus.* From there the army straggled to Otonniata, where a council of war was held, and I was near passing the line, *i.e.,* I was on the point of being immolated as a public victim: for at the suggestion of the English we had been surrendered to the Four Nations, and there was no one to throw into the War Kettle.   The lot was to be cast and would probably have fallen on me; both because putting me to death would have been a signal of irreconcilable war, and because I was held up as a great Iroquois and an English State criminal. . . .   It was decided otherwise.   I was despatched to the camp of the Oneidas and two chiefs and about thirty men were commissioned to conduct me thither, while the army pursued its march to Montreal.

" On my journey I was pretty well treated. They gave me a share of what they had to eat, but they never forgot to put a rope around my neck, feet, hands, and body, lest, as they said, God should inspire me to escape."

He finally arrived at Oneida, where some braves wanted to burn him at the stake; for it was their custom to give that kind of a welcome to the first prisoner of war who was brought into camp. " It was St. Lawrence's eve," he writes, " when I was brought to the council which was to decide my fate, and all morning I had been preparing to die like the holy martyr. The sachems assembled, and one of them, saluting me in Indian fashion, tried three times to strike me in the face, but as my arms were free I thrice parried the blow without reflection." Most of us will pardon the good Father's want of " reflection."

At that moment there entered a chief, the same one who had assured him down at Cataroqui that the Oneidas would protect him. He was the husband of the woman who had befriended Millet as soon as he arrived at Oneida, giving him clothing and affording him the hospitality of her lodge. God rewarded her for her charity, for a few years afterwards when she went to Quebec in the interests of Father Millet, she remained there and became a devout Christian. She had evidently been advising her husband. " The Father is not a prisoner," he said to the assembly, " but a missionary returning to his flock and he must not be harmed." It was a clever ruse, but another orator known for his English proclivities denounced him as a friend of the Governor of Quebec. " I was afraid," writes Millet, " that he was going to advocate burning me. He was fierce at first, but after a while he cooled down, and I was taken to the Council Lodge, and on my way thither had to stand many an assault from drunken Indians, who followed me, and who when shut out of the cabin began to stone it and threaten to set it on fire.

The final decision was not to be given till the return of the war party. Meantime he had the freedom of the village, and although he went from house to house to see the sick, so certain seemed his fate, that the people pointed at him on his rounds as "the dying man who walks." Nor did the warriors who came up from Orange, "a little English town," bring any favorable tidings. Nevertheless, the people would crowd around him to pray, would bring their sick to him, and sometimes carry his mat out in the field where they could listen to his instructions undisturbed.

Finally, the warriors returned from Montreal, and the prospects were gloomy for Millet. One of their chiefs had been killed, and four prisoners had to be burned to atone for it. He with three others sat before the council. His face was painted red and black as a victim, and he heard himself denounced as a traitor who had caused the Onondagas to be seized at Cataroqui. While the trial was going on, Millet was clever enough to hear the confessions of the three unfortunates who were seated next to him. It was an uncomfortable confessional at best and must have been somewhat public for the penitents. Whether they were killed or not we do not know, but Millet escaped. He was given to his Oneida friends, initiated in their tribe, saluted with grandiose speeches, given an Indian name, and he then settled down to missionary work, for how long he did not know. He built a little chapel which he appropriately dedicated to " *Christo Morituro* " (" Christ about to die ") ; and though he could not say Mass, for of course he had nothing with him, continued during the next five years to preach, to teach and to pray.

As we turn over the " Documents pertaining to the Colonial History of New York " we find Millet's name constantly recurring. It is " Millet," " Millet " all the time. The Earl of Bellomont was particularly worried about him, and solemnly recounts a story to the Lords of Trade which he had heard and apparently believed, about an old squaw whom the Jesuits (meaning Millet especially) had taught to poison people as well as to pray. " The Jesuits had furnished her," he says, " with so subtle a poison and taught her a legerdemain in using it; so that whenever she had a mind to poison, she would bring them a cup of water and let drop the poison under her nail (which are always very long, for the Indians never pare 'em) into the cup. This woman was so true a disciple to the Jesuits that she has poisoned a multitude of the Five Nations that were very friendly to us." He then goes on to narrate that " she had poisoned a Protestant Mohawk, and his relatives beat out her brains with a club." So much for Bellomont's credulity.

Nevertheless Millet seems to have been particularly troubled about this accusation of poisoning, and writes to the old Dominie Dellius to complain of it. There are several communications between the priest and the parson which we find in the Colonial Documents, and they show that Dellius, who was at first very friendly, had lost his esteem when he was sent as a delegate with Peter Schuyler to Canada. The parson finally fell into disgrace with Bellomont, who ascribes all sorts of crimes to him, ultimately driving him out of the country, and even complaining to the Home Government that Dellius had acted the part of a traitor when he went to Canada. " I do assure your Lordship he is capable of any mischief whatever." Millet trusted him, however, and we find one letter in which the poor captive says: " I have six Spanish pistoles, given me to assist the poor, the orphans, and the other unhappy wretches of the mission. Be pleased to give them to your Lady that she may buy some shirts, great and small, and some stockings as cheap as possible."

To this letter Dellius replies very coldly, but says at the end: " As for the six Spanish pistoles which you have sent me, my wife has bought twenty-six pairs of shirts and twenty-six pairs of stockings. I have given them all to the messenger that brought the gold and to that lame woman you call your sister. So, Sir, if I can serve you in anything else you need but command. Your humble servant. DELLIUS."

From this letter we get a sidelight upon Father Millet's occupations during his captivity, and at the same time come into possession of the price list for merchandise that prevailed at that time in New York. The money he received was sent by Father de Lamberville, and also by the Superior, Father Dablon or Biblin, as the Dutchmen spelled it. Dablon wrote to Millet and also to Dellius, assuring the latter that whatever disbursements he might make in behalf of the prisoner would be repaid. There is also a communication from Father de Lamberville which begins: " May the Lord have pity on you and send you aid from on high that you may be able with a strong heart and a willing mind to walk day and night in his land, for you became a prisoner on account of your great charity towards the Indians, and for the salvation of souls. For when you were called by them to pray to the Lord for a sick squaw, they took you prisoner, and this is the cause of your captivity.

" We send you by him who is called *l'Outarde* paper and a powder, which when mixed with water will make ink. Thus with the permission of the Indians, you will be able to write to us. We also send you clothes to cover you, and gold coin for the purchase of a woolen or any other cloak or garment that you may need. We have no news except that Dominie Dellius, the minister at Albany, an honest man and well disposed to us, told a French soldier, a prisoner among the Mohawks, that he had seen the letters we wrote to you, and that a bad construction had been put upon them. If you have an opportunity to communicate with him through the Indians, you may assure him that we never entertained any such thoughts, and we abhor crimes of this nature. Should you see him or write to him give him my respects. Although there may be war between the French and English, nevertheless we always entertain the same friendly dispositions towards Dominie Dellius." This is in violent contrast with Bellomont's opinion of the parson.

It is worth noting that the money which finally reached the captive was not employed in procuring " woolen or other garments for himself," but in getting Mrs. Dellius to send him shirts and stockings for the Indians. The " abominable crime " which de Lamberville refers to is of course " the poisoning about which the Earl of Bellomont and Governor Fletcher were in such a panic."

It is very humiliating to admit that the English would have been delighted to see Millet killed. They did their best to get possession of him. We have a letter from Governor Fletcher, July 31, 1693, addressed to the Indians, which says: " I have often told you that the priest Millet will betray all your counsels so long as he lives amongst you, which now plainly appears, for he hath refused to deliver the packet from Canada to be sent unto me *lest the poison be discovered*. If you will cause the old priest Millet with all his papers to be sent unto me, then our peace may not be broken by his means, but flourish while the sun shines," &c. Possibly they thought that anything was fair in war.

War was indeed raging fiercely, and from Mackinac to Acadia, as well as from New York to Quebec, everything was fire and blood. The existence of the French colony was hanging by a thread. They were only 15,000 against 200,000 English, if we count all the colonies, and the Indians were so disgusted by the defeats inflicted on French arms, especially by the massacre at La Chine, that the Ottawas of the West were on the point of making an alliance with the Iroquois, and there was even a likelihood that the old allies of the French, the Hurons, would join the enemy.

Just then Frontenac returned from France for his second term of Governorship. He had with him an Indian chief named Ouréoutaré, one of the victims of Cataroqui, whom de Denonville had sent in chains to France, but who was pardoned, and by dint of flatteries and honors was made to forget his wrongs and even won over to the French cause. By the aid of Ouréouharé and Father Millet, Frontenac hoped to propitiate the Iroquois so as then to be able to set himself to attacking the English; his ultimate object being to capture New York. In propitiating the Iroquois, Millet was to take a prominent part.

A great council met at Onondaga. " There were eighty-four Iroquois chiefs," says Ferland; " and the English and Dutch were represented. Millet, who was an Oneida chief, and Ouréouharé, the Onondaga, both exercised an immense influence with the assembly, but not sufficient to prevail against the Dutch and English, who succeeded in foiling Frontenac's plans. Millet was particularly objectionable to them. " Give us this Jesuit," they said to the Iroquois, " we shall take him to Albany, where he will be prevented from doing you any harm." But the Iroquois in view of a possible future arrangement with Frontenac, were shrewd enough to refuse the offer.

Seeing that peace was impossible, Frontenac addressed himself to the other part of his plan, that of attacking the English on their own ground. The defensive action which he had so far adopted gave him little glory and was rapidly killing off his best men. On that account he organized his triple attack, on Schenectady, Salmon Falls, or Portsmouth, and Casco in Maine. He had been instructed by Louis XIV to attack and capture New York and make de Callières its Governor; the King promising to send plenty of troops for the expedition. But the troops never came; his Majesty having abundance of trouble on his hands in Europe, and the royal injunction about New York was countermanded. On the contrary, orders were sent to make peace with the Iroquois. De Callières persisted. It was useless to attempt to make peace with the Iroquois as long as the English were unchecked, and he explained how easily New York could be taken if the troops were forthcoming. Thus New York might be a French possession to-day if he had been listened

PETER MILLET.

to, but, like many of the French projects, it failed because of the Home Government's unconcern about colonial affairs.

Just at that time Jacob Leisler's assumption of authority as Governor was helping the defencelessness of the place, and the fall of Schenectady is ascribed to the action of his political opponets. Frontenac's victory there was easy. Meantime, with the French storming the gates and the bigotted Leisler raging within the colony, the position of the few Catholics in New York at the time must have been alarming. They were only ten in number and fortunately we have their names. They ought to be preserved. It is a roll of honor. They were Major Antony Brockholes, Thomas Howarding, William Douglas, John Cavelier, Peter Cavelier, John Cooly, John Patte, Christine Lawrence, John Fenny, and Philip Cunningham. Leisler hated the Papists more than he did his political foes.

In the triple invasion made by Frontenac, Millet, of course, was interested on patriotic principles. His correspondence shows he was informed of all that happened, but he was mostly concerned about the detachment that started from Montreal against Schenectady; first, because it was nearest to him, and then because in it were the converted Indians of La Prairie. They were coming down into their own country, and were led by the famous Kryn. After twenty-two days' march in snowshoes they arrived at the palisades, behind which were eighty houses. The inhabitants were all killed or taken prisoners, and the expedition made its way back to Montreal. The other divisions of this army of invasion met with more or less success.

The movement, on the whole, was a failure, inasmuch as nothing more was done against the English, but it had the result of keeping the old allies of the French in their allegiance, and on that account had much to do with Millet's treatment by the Indians and his ultimate release.

While he was at Oneida, he had long talks with Peter Schuyler, the first Mayor of Albany, who had come to induce him to leave the Indians. Millet calls him " Kwiter," not Peter, the Indians not being able to pronounce the labials. The Dutchman's appeals were useless, and he remonstrated at being treated in the same way as old Dominie Dellius, who had been up on the same errand; but the invitations of both Dellius and Schuyler were too much open to suspicion to be accepted.

After Frontenac's victory, all the English colonies combined in a counter attack. Phipps made his attempt at bombarding Quebec with his five pieces of cannon; Governor Winthrop of Connecticut went up the Richelieu, intending to attack Montreal and afterwards Quebec, but had hardly reached Lake George when small-pox broke out among his soldiers and he had to turn back; and finally in the month of August, 1691, " Kwiter " Schuyler invested the fort of La Prairie, where the Christian Indians were gathered. After a two hours' fight, in which the troops from Chambly joined, he was put to flight with the loss of his flags and baggage. Seventeen of his Indians were killed and sixty-five Englishmen, and there was a large number of wounded. Had Schuyler been pursued his corps would have been annihilated.

This failure to exterminate the invaders irritated Frontenac, and he blamed it on the Jesuits, who, he said, were bringing up their converts too meekly. There is considerable controversy on the subject, but it is comprehensible that the Iroquois did not want to kill their friends; which may explain how so many English were slain in that mêlée and so few savages. Charlevoix thinks, however, that it was because of a mistaken order. Millet in his letter of that year shows that he was acquainted with all these happenings, and he records his gratification at the triumph of the French.

The English were beaten for the moment, but the Iroquois were still on the warpath, and Frontenac, in spite of his seventy-six years, was busy pursuing them. " He seized a tomahawk and danced a war dance, to the delight of the

PETER MILLET.

Indians," says Guy Carleton, which may be only a bit of rhetoric for the martial alacrity displayed by the fine old soldier, though he was Gascon enough to cut such capers. Millet kept on inducing the Oneidas to sue for peace. He succeeded at last in getting a deputation to go to Quebec in 1693, and in May of the following year eight envoys from the five cantons presented themselves and asked to make a treaty. "To obtain the peace that you ask," said Frontenac, "it must be with the western Indians, who are our allies, as well as with me, and I insist that Father Millet or someone else should come with you inside of twenty-four days from the time you leave Montreal, and that you bring back all the prisoners you have in your village." In the month of October they returned with Father Millet. Unfortunately peace was not made, but Millet never returned to Oneida. He was at Montreal in 1697 when a band of Oneidas came to live there. Of course they asked for him as their spiritual guide. No doubt he attended to them, but we find him afterwards at Lorette. Charlevoix knew him at Quebec, where he spent his declining years. He died there on the last day of the year in 1708 at the age of seventy-three. He was born at Bourges and had entered the Society November 19, 1635, at the age of twenty.

STEPHEN DE CARHEIL.

W HO has ever heard of Father de Carheil? It would not be rash to answer: very few. Even his biographer, Father Orhand, calls him "the unknown," but he designates him at the same time as "the admirable unknown." De Rochemonteix does not hesitate to describe him as "the most illustrious missionary in the five Iroquois cantons." When one thinks of Jogues, Bressani, Chaumonot, Le Moyne, Ménard and others who were in the Mohawk Valley before him, such a tribute seems like an exaggeration. Like St. James in Spain, de Carheil was illustrious by his failure.

He was a Breton nobleman, and possessed in a marked degree the characteristics of his race. "A little hard," says Dablon, "like the granite of his own Brittany; as an Apostle he was overzealous."

Of course this was not said in depreciation of his worth, for the same writer informed the Provincial that "Fr. de Carheil was a holy man whose apostolic zeal finds that the savages do not correspond to the care he lavishes on them. But possibly he expects too much virtue at the start. At all events, if he does not sanctify the Indians, they are sanctifying him." "We expect great things from this father," Le Mercier wrote to the General of the Society, "because of the rare gifts he has received from God; notably a remarkable grace of prayer, an unusual contempt of everything that does not lead to God, and an incredible zeal in bringing souls to Christ."

The Venerable Mary of the Incarnation, who was a great authority in those days and who still retains her hold in Canada, grows enthusiastic in one of her many letters over "this young man of thirty-five or thereabouts, who is as fervent as possible, and already a great adept in the Iroquois

262

dialects." Finally the Archives of the Society record " his great linguistic powers, his theological knowledge, and note also his unusual tenacity of purpose which is guided by profound experience."

Michelet and Voltaire used to say that the Jesuits set their " stupids " one side and trained them to be missionaries so that the savages could cook and eat them." That certainly was not true of de Carheil. Had he remained in France he would have rivalled Vavasseur, Commire, Jouvency, and La Rue. He was an eminent litterateur, a remarkable philologist, a poet, an orator, a thinker and a writer. His powers as a linguist made him master Huron and Cayuga with extraordinary rapidity, and he has left works in both those languages which are still extant, and held in the highest esteem. The seeker will find them in Carayon's *Documents Inedits.*

His style as a writer is revealed in a letter published by Rochemonteix. It is dated December 3, 1664, and is addressed to the Father General. It is worth quoting, especially in its original Latin:

Reverende Adm. in Xo Pater, P. C.:

Qui dies magno Indiarum apostolo, S. Fr. Xaverio sacer est, is me admonet, ut R. A. Ptem Vestram quam possum vehementissime obtester per amorem Dei Domini Jesu crucifixi, ecclesiae, Societatis, animarum inter barbaros pereuntium, audebo etiam dicere per amorem paternum mei, ut mittat me aliquando ad exteras missiones, praesertim Japonicam, Sinicam, Syriacam, Canadensem; sin minus, in eas omnes, in quas commodum videbitur ad majorem Dei gloriam, sed omnino in aliquam mittat; idque obsecro, quam fieri celerrime poterit, certe ut tardissime, post theologiam, cujus tertium jam annum ingredior. Neque enim vocantem Deum jam ferre amplius possum qui me dies noctesque stimulat ut aliquando proficiscar."

The General must have smiled at this very imperatively submissive letter which says in a way that would not be stopped that "the day sacred to St. Francis Xavier, the great apostle of the Indies, *warns* me to most *vehemently entreat* Your Paternity, for the love of God, of Jesus crucified, of the Church, of the Society, of the souls perishing in savage lands, to send me to the foreign missions, Japan, China, Syria, or Canada . . . And I ask that it be done *as quickly as possible;* certainly, *at the latest* after my theology, the third year of which I now begin. *I cannot stand any longer* the call of God which *urges* me day and night to go."

In spite of all this, he was not allowed to leave France. He was an orator of such exceptional power that much was expected of him in the pulpit, and it was only after two years that, yielding to what Father Oliva called "his *incensissimus zelus,*" which was irresistible, and which had been exerting itself in persistent appeals for eight years, permission was granted, and de Carheil set off post haste for Canada May 12, 1666. He had to stay two years in Quebec, and it was not until 1668 that he entered New York.

He began his work among the Indians as soon as the opportunity presented itself. He appears to have left Quebec in company with Garagontié, who was assiduous in his efforts to obtain missionaries, and who, though an Onondaga himself, persuaded the Cayugas to build a chapel. Thither de Carheil betook himself.

Geographically Cayuga was most attractive, but unfortunately it was peopled by drunken and blood-thirsty savages who were constantly at war with each other or with the French and English, and whose evil propensities were quickened by the liquor which was poured into their country by the Dutch and English. De Carheil found there all the opportunity he wanted for the exercise of his zeal and the practice of sublime virtues. He wandered from wigwam to wigwam, only to be driven out with insults and blows, or trudged weary and hungry after his wild people on their hunting or predatory excursions, often seeing the tomahawk or knife of some angry savage above his head. "We are perpetual victims here," he wrote, "and in hourly peril of being massacred."

These perils and hardships, however, only developed a marvellous patience in this strong, impetuous, and imperious man. Indeed, he was regarded by his brethren as a model of patience and perseverence, so persistent was his pursuit of the souls of those wretched people. But after five years, he broke down and became a shattered, nervous wreck. Unable to recover his strength by earthly means, he betook himself to the shrines of St. Anne de Beaupré, and of Our Lady of Foy, both of which were even in those days places of pious pilgrimage. He was thus New York's first pilgrim to St. Anne's. His prayers were answered and he returned to his post for another eight years of almost hopeless endeavor; insisting upon resuming his work amid the disappointments of his old mission, although Father Raffeix, who had temporarily replaced him, would have gladly held the difficult place. De Carheil was a grateful soul, for we are told that medals of St. Anne are still dug up at Cayuga. He evidently taught that devotion to his neophytes.

It was not so much the personal privations incident to his work as its apparent hopelessness that constituted his trial. The *Relations* tell us very frankly that "for nine consecutive years after de Carheil came to Cayuga, 350 baptisms were all that his heroism could put to his credit. Of these, many were children who died soon after their regeneration, or Huron captives who had felt the influence of Christianity elsewhere." As for the New York Iroquois, they were, at that time at least, impossible to reach. Humiliating as the confession is, it furnishes an answer to the frequently repeated calumny that these early Jesuits baptized their Indians indiscriminately. The very reverse is the case, and only after years of trial would they permit an adult savage to call himself a Christian.

In spite of the appalling contrast between the energy expended and the results achieved, he and his associates kept at their self-imposed task, fighting, as it were, in the dark. Still, the outlook was not altogether without an occasional gleam of hope. There were brilliant examples of Christian virtue, chiefly among the most conspicuous Indians. Over such men de Carheil seems to have exerted an exceptional power.

Into his cabin one day there strode a Cayuga chief. He was no other than the famous Saonchiowonga, who eight years before had appeared at the stockade of Montreal and demanded that the missionaries should renew their attempt to evangelize the tribes. To satisfy him, Le Moyne had gone for the fifth time among the Iroquois. What did Saonchiowonga mean by his abrupt entrance into the missionary's house? He was going to live there, not to dispossess its owner, but to observe him at close quarters and to see if his practice agreed with his preaching. After considerable time he expressed himself satisfied and asked for baptism. Knowing the wily Indian nature, de Carheil still hesitated, but at last consent was given. Saonchiowonga, however, was no ordinary man, and, as in the case of Garagontié, his baptism had to be made an event in the history of the tribe. He was sent to Quebec. Bishop Laval, who had just taken possession of his See, invested the ceremonies with unusual magnificence; the Intendant Talon stood godfather to the neophyte; the crowds of Indians who had come to witness the spectacle were treated with the greatest consideration, and a bounteous feast was spread for them at the expense of the city. Saonchiowonga returned to Cayuga, and by his blameless life and the instructions he gave his people kept up the drooping spirits of the missionaries.

Father de Carheil's difficulties in Cayuga increased as time went on. Drunkenness prevailed there, as at Onondaga, and the scenes enacted in the villages were indescribable. Men would chew off each other's noses and ears and eat them. Murders were the common order of the day. No one's life was safe for an instant. The Indian who owned the lodge where the priest lived was one of the worst of the crew, and over and over again the tomahawk had to be wrested from his hands in his efforts to murder his tenant. Seeing it was no use to remain any longer, de Carheil gave up and travelled over to Onondaga to seek shelter with de Lamberville, who had heard that he was dead, and was amazed to find him dragging himself along the trail, dispirited, sick, and weary.

The news of his ill treatment spread rapidly, and the Onondaga sachems came to console him. " They presented him with a poultice to apply it to the part he felt most sore." The poultice was a wampum belt. " Nothing more humane," writes de Lamberville, "can be imagined than what they said to him." The orator made a speech which was very choice in its language, but as we read it now, not a little amusing, though poor de Carheil scarcely found it so. " I knew not why," said the speaker, " during the past few days the sky was clouded to an extraordinary degree, and the star that gladdens the whole earth hid itself from our eyes. It refused to shine upon the insolence of the drunkards who have insulted you. We grew pale at the description of what had happened to you. We have inveighed against the sellers of brandy, who are the cause of so many evils, and we rejoice that you have found an asylum here. We thought you were dead; our spirits languished in sorrow and resentment, they had sunk to our feet through the weight of sorrow, and now resume their usual place, seeing you sound and unwounded. It is true that your cabin has been pillaged, that your holy house in which you prayed has been profaned. But what has done it? Brandy. Your life has been attempted; what caused that crime? Brandy. Brandy is a pernicious evil which you Europeans have brought us."

He then reminds the priest that things might have been worse, and exhorts him to practise patience.

PIONEER PRIESTS OF NORTH AMERICA.

An attempt was made to reinstate him. He returned, in fact, but conditions grew worse. Ouréouhahé said he could not help it. He was drunk when he acted so, but would not stop drinking. Finally de Carheil abandoned the work, and then a disease, doubtless the consequence of their disorders, attacked the tribe and carried off many victims. Seventeen died in the lodge where he used to live with the drunken chief. Some of the Indians looked upon it as a visitation; others blamed the priest for putting a spell on the place. Thus death was busy when de Carheil went down among the Mohawks, who were better behaved at that time.

There he remained for about a year, and in 1683 we find him at Quebec, after fifteen years of comparatively unsuccessful work in New York.

From Quebec he was sent to Michilimackinac, the gateway of Lake Michigan. At that time it was both a military and trading post, and was occupied by French, Ottawas, and Hurons. The Ottawas and Hurons were separated from each other by a high palisade. They had little mutual intercourse, as they differed in language and religion; the Hurons being largely Christian, the Ottawas, pagan. In the center of the post stood a somewhat elaborate church, and near it the modest slab house of the missionaries, which their enemies said was luxurious. Around were the log cabins of the settlers, and the long, arched-roof constructions of the Indian lodges, some of them as much as 120 feet long and 24 wide, and each sheltering a number of families. Father de Carheil's work was with the Hurons.

The curse of Michilimackinac in those days, as indeed of many another settlement, was the presence of the *coureurs de bois,* wild scapegraces of all classes, who took to the free life of the woods for adventure, and whose sale of liquor, joined to the immorality of their lives, thwarted all the efforts of the missionaries. Under the Commandant Durantaye, the evil was held in check to some extent, but Fron-

tenac removed him and matters grew worse, till Michilimackinac was described as a Sodom; the officers of the
fort being as bad as the *coureurs de bois*. Complaints multiplied so fast that royal orders were issued shutting up the
fort as a trading post and leaving it in charge of a garrison.
The remedy was violent and injudicious.

There was another subject of alarm at that time. Denonville had failed to keep the Iroquois in control and Frontenac, though an old man, had been sent back from France to
avert the crisis which threatened Canada. This was in
1690. Possibly because he was advanced in age he did not
at first display his usual activity, or was not alive to the
gravity of the situation. Not only were the Ottawas, who
had been hitherto allies of the French, about to join the Iroquois, but the tried and faithful Hurons, seeing themselves
unprotected, were on the point of deserting. No one could
perceive this as well as de Carheil, who was in the midst of
both tribes. He put himself in communication with the
Governor, and one of his letters to Frontenac explaining the
situation is the subject of considerable comment by historians. It is more than likely that its contents had something to do with prompting Frontenac to begin the offensive
operations which resulted in the attack on Schenectady,
Casco, and Portsmouth, and in putting a quietus upon the
restless Iroquois, though unfortunately, as the effort was
only spasmodic, it stimulated the English colonies to lay
aside their own differences and unite in a league against
the French. It was the first step towards the English dom-
ination of Canada.

One of the most lax of the commandants at Michilimackinac in enforcing discipline was Cadillac, and though
he was the friend, or rather the worshipper of Frontenac,
he was removed from his post on account of the protests of
the missionaries. He had his revenge in 1701, when he established Fort Pontchartrain, the present Detroit. His
project at first was acceptable to the missionaries, as it

meant another opportunity to get further into the interior, but after he had established himself at Detroit, his real purpose revealed itself. He intended to destroy Michilimackinac by calling every Indian of the Michigan peninsula down to the new foundation. That meant the destruction of all that had been done to Christianize the savages, and hence a royal battle began against Cadillac. De Carheil was his chief opponent, but was beaten. Little by little, every Indian was induced to leave the mission, and in 1705 Cadillac was able to write to France: " There are only 25 Indians left at Michilimackinac. Father de Carheil, who is the missionary there, always remains firm, but I am persuaded that the obdurate old priest will die in his parish without a single parishioner."

"The obdurate old priest" did nothing of the kind. When he saw his mission absolutely deserted he burned all the buildings to save them from desecration by marauders, and returned to Quebec. The act was angrily condemned in France, and he was ordered to return and rebuild. But the order was not insisted on. He returned, however, to Michigan, and labored among the few wandering savages he could find there. It was another of his failures. But he was not alone in his sorrow. Cadillac had destroyed other missions also.

Among the Indians with whom de Carheil came in contact was one whose sombre figure looms large in Canadian history. He was a Huron chief named Kondiaronk, whom the French called " The Rat." Raynal and Charlevoix regard him as one of the most remarkable Indians of North America. Rochemonteix calls him a savage Machiavelli. He deserves all the hard things that can be said of him, at least for the beginning of his career. As he was a bitter and uncompromising foe of the Iroquois, he would hear of no alliance with them. Of course, he was in the fight when Denonville marched against the Senecas, and he saw with pleasure that truce with his foes was made more remote by the foolish act of the Governor. The Iroquois were only provoked to greater reprisals. Aware of his mistake, de Denonville made every effort to patch up a peace, and had begged Father de Lamberville, who was just recovering from a mortal illness, to come to his assistance. Thanks to the influence of the missionary, the Iroquois at last agreed to terms. " The Rat " heard of it. He was down at Cataroqui when the news came. Dissembling his wrath, he pretended to return to Michilimackinac, but instead of that he set out in pursuit of the Iroquois deputies; captured them; murdered some and told the rest that he was acting under orders of the Governor. He purposely allowed a certain number to escape, and they carried the intelligence to their tribes. To add to the confusion " The Rat " presented one of the deputies to the Commandant at the fort, and had him put to death as a spy. The French were thus clearly guilty of treachery in the eyes of the Iroquois. The hatchet was dug up; war raged all along the St. Lawrence. At Lachine alone, 200 people were killed and 120 taken prisoners, most of whom were burned alive. This disaster at Lachine, which is so close to Montreal, almost brought the French into contempt. They could not defend themselves. How could they protect their allies?

It throws light on the methods which had to be employed with those wild men when we find that this wretch, though his treachery was commonly known, was afterwards admitted to the confidence of the French, and promoted to the rank of captain in the army. He was even admitted to the Governor's table. His wit was so keen, and his power of repartee, in which no one was a match for him but the Governor, so remarkable, that these unusual distinctions were willingly accorded to him. He finally came under the influence of de Carheil, and used to say that there were only two clever men among the French, de Carheil and Frontenac. Admiration ripened into friendship, and finally the priest made him a Christian, so fervent, intelligent, and devoted that he often preached to his people and explained the doctrines of the faith. He was fully convinced that Christianity was their only salvation, even in a temporal sense.

When Frontenac withdrew, de Callières, who succeeded him in the Governorship, conceived the plan of uniting all the Indians in a vast federation to support each other as well as their French allies. With their conflicting interests and their inveterate hatred, the scheme seemed impossible of realization, but it was attempted. Messengers were sent in all directions to induce the various tribes to meet the Governor at Montreal. Father Bruyas was despatched to the Iroquois, Enjalran to the Ottawas, and Bigot's help was enlisted with the far-off Abenakis. They all succeeded, and at the end of July, 1701, one thousand Indians met in their canoes on the St. Lawrence, near Montreal.

The great representative of the Hurons was, of course, " The Rat." Everything depended on him. But being a Christian now, he viewed things in a different light. He did not fail his friends. It was the last act, and the most dramatic one, of his eventful career.

On August 1st, while one of the Huron Sachems was talking, " The Rat " was suddenly taken ill. Every one was in consternation, no one more than the Governor. The old Indian had completely collapsed, and anxious efforts were made to revive him. At last he rallied and was placed in an arm chair in the midst of the assembly. He essayed to speak and all listened with breathless attention. He described with modesty, yet with dignity, all the steps he had taken to secure a permanent peace among all the nations; he made them see the necessity, and the advantages accruing to each tribe in particular. Then turning to de Callières he conjured him so to act that no one could ever reproach him with abusing the confidence placed in him.

His voice failing, he ceased to speak, but applause arose from all present. It did not affect him, however, for he

272

was accustomed to receive it even from his opponents.

The Governor pledged his word to be true to the treaty, and at the end of the session, had the old chief carried carefully to the Hôtel Dieu, where he died two hours after midnight in the most Christian sentiments, fortified by the sacraments of the Church. His death caused general sorrow. The body lay in state in an officer's uniform, with side arms, for he held the rank and enjoyed the pay of captain in the French army. The Governor General and Intendant went first to sprinkle the corpse with holy water. The Sieur de Joncaire followed at the head of sixty warriors of Sault St. Louis, all of them weeping for the dead, and "covering him," that is, giving presents to the Hurons, as a tribute to the chief.

His funeral, which took place next day, was as magnificent as it was singular. M. de St. Ours, the ranking captain, marched in front, at the head of sixty men under arms; sixteen Huron braves, attired in long beaver robes, with their faces blackened, followed with guns reversed, marching in squads of four. Then came the clergy with six war-chiefs carrying the bier, which was covered with a pall strewn with flowers. On it lay a chapeau and feather, a gorget and sword. The brothers and children of the deceased were behind it, accompanied by all the chiefs of the nations, while de Vaudreuil, Governor of the city, closed the procession.

At the end of the service, there were two volleys of musketry; a third was given when the body was committed to the earth. The chief was interred in the great church and on the tomb was written the inscription: "Cy git le Rat, *Chef Huron.*" Here lies The Rat, a Huron Chief.

Kondiaronk is the original of the famous "Andario" of La Hontan, de la Barre's and de Denonville's discredited soldier, whose alleged history of Canada made a sensation in Europe by its mockery of religion. He makes Kondiaronk, whom he knew and whom he calls "Andario," discuss the religion, politics, philosophy and social condi-

18   273

tions of civilization, and puts into his mouth words of contempt for them all, contrasting them with the simplicity, innocence and integrity of the simple life of the forest. Of course, it was only a device of the writer to express his own irreligious views. Although the book attracted a great deal of attention at the time, no serious man ever regarded it as worthy of credence. It goes to show, however, the prominence which Kondiaronk enjoyed.

A few years after these events, de Carheil went down to Quebec to prepare for the end, as most of the missionaries did when they escaped the tomahawk. No doubt he stopped at Montreal to pray at the tomb of " The Rat." Soon the priest and the Indian would be together in the happy hunting grounds. Of the once famous monument there is now no recollection; the nuns of Hôtel Dieu having removed to another part of the town.

At Quebec, the old missionary, with his sixty years of heroic labor which had whitened his locks, without, as Charlevoix says, impairing his vigor and vivacity, was a source of happiness and edification for those who were privileged to live with him in the college which was honored by his presence.

His life had been a great one, but Charlevoix rather unkindly says of him: " Nothing shows more clearly that the holiest men, most estimable for personal qualities, are in God's hands mere instruments which he can do without. He had sacrificed the greatest talents which can do honor to a man of his profession, and in the hopes of a fate like that of many of his brethren who had bedewed Canada with their blood, he had employed a kind of violence with his Superiors to secure a mission whose obscurity sheltered him from all ambition and offered him only crosses. There he labored untiringly for more than sixty years. He spoke Huron and Iroquois with as much ease and elegance as his mother tongue. The French and Indians concurred in regarding him as a saint and a genius of the highest order.

STEPHEN DE CARHEIL.

Yet he wrought few conversions. For that he humbled himself before God and this humiliation served to sanctify him more and more. He has often protested to me that he adored the designs of Providence in his regard, convinced that he would have imperilled his salvation by the success which he might have claimed in a more distinguished position, and that this thought consoled him beyond everything for the barrenness of his long and toilsome apostolate." Whereupon the talkative old historian begins to read a homily about the proper dispositions of those who enter upon an evangelical career.

Evidently what troubled Charlevoix was that Father de Carheil had not succeeded in becoming a martyr like Jogues, Brébeuf and the others. But though de Carheil was not a martyr except in desire, he was a great apostle and possibly did not not tell Father Charlevoix all that he had accomplished in New York and Michigan lest there might be written down in *l'Histoire de la Nouvelle France* too much of a eulogy of those glorious sixty years of a splendid and heroic apostolate.

PETER RAFFEIX.

MOST of the old Governors of Quebec took themselves very seriously. Naturally so, for through them, Louis XIV, the *Roi Soleil*, beamed on the western world. Thus the Marquis de Tracy was nothing less than "Viceroy and Commandant of His Majesty's troops in America," though "His Majesty's troops" consisted of just one regiment, the Carignan, and whatever Canadian volunteers wished to enter the ranks. It was not a formidable array, and so the Marquis had to do something to maintain his dignity. Hence he never walked abroad except with a retinue of four or five pages in gorgeous attire and a score or two of soldiers with officers in brilliant uniform. It must have been a curious sight in the then shabby streets of Quebec. Besides the Viceroy, there was also a Governor, who at the time we are speaking of was de Courcelles. As his greatness was eclipsed by the splendor of the Viceroy it may have been a desire to keep up the dignity of his official position that prompted him to organize a punitive expedition to the country of the Iroquois. With sublime contempt of the commonest prudence, he started out in mid-winter. His objective point was Albany, 900 miles away. The snow was deep and the Carignan Regiment was innocent of the art of wearing snowshoes; there were lakes and rivers to cross with constant danger of the ice breaking under their feet; and no one knew the way, though it had been arranged that some Algonquin guides should meet them somewhere on the road. Each man had to carry his own provisions, not even the General being exempt. On they journeyed until they came within 40 miles of Fort Orange without ever seeing an Iroquois except an occasional one skulking in the woods who would try his best to pick off the weary stragglers. Many of the soldiers were frost bitten, others

276

dropped dead from exhaustion; the snow was growing deeper, the forests more impenetrable, and so without having done anything, the gallant de Courcelles determined to go back. " It required French courage, and M. de Courcelles' firmness," say the *Relations,* " to undertake this expedition." After losing sixty men and several officers, and undergoing incredible hardships, the battered soldiers struggled back to Quebec, which they had left with such a flourish of trumpets a month or so before.

Quite in keeping with the judgment that prompted this ridiculous expedition, de Courcelles ascribed its failure to the Jesuits who, he said, had prevented the Algonquin contingent from arriving at the appointed time. As the chaplain of this little snow-shoe army was the Jesuit Father Raffeix, and as the Jesuits would have been the first to be benefited, if this military demonstration had quieted the Iroquois, no one believed the accusation, and after a little while the Governor admitted that he had spoken in his wrath.

The disgrace, of course, had to be obliterated, and so, in July of the same year, Captain Sorel received orders to march against the enemy. He obeyed, but long before he reached the Mohawk, Iroquois envoys met him and pleaded for peace. Everyone knew they did not mean it, but Sorel thought they did, and he marched back with them to Quebec.

No one was satisfied, and consequently, although the season was advanced, de Tracy, the Viceroy, in spite of his age, took the field with 600 soldiers of the Carignan regiment, 600 Canadians and a hundred Hurons and Algonquins, leaving Fort St. Thérèse, at the head of Lake Champlain, September 28. There were four chaplains with this army, among them Father Raffeix, who was thus making his second expedition to New York.

No Iroquois met the invaders. They had deserted their villages and taken to the woods, and all that this great Viceroy did was to give over to the flames the four principal

Mohawk villages, the first of which was Ossernenon, or Auriesville.

We have in the *Relations* a description of its condition at that time, though the account seems rather to apply to the village furthest west, probably Tionnontoguen, but as the arrangements in one were exactly duplicated in the other what was said of Tionnontoguen applies to all the rest. We are told that " it had a triple stockade twenty feet high, each flanked by four bastions. It had a prodigious hoard of provisions, and an abundant supply of water which was kept in bark receptacles. Some old men and women and children still lingered in the village, and the mutilated bodies of two or three savages of another nation who had been partially burned over a slow fire were found there. There were no Indians to fight, so our people were forced to content themselves after erecting the Cross, saying Mass, and chanting the *Te Deum* on that spot, with setting fire to the palisades and cabins and consuming the entire store of Indian corn, beans, and other produce of the country which was found there. This devastation would have the same effect in tranquillizing the savages as a more sanguinary victory." Whether the Cross was erected, Mass celebrated, and the *Te Deum* sung at Ossernenon we cannot be positive, for de Tracy may have been satisfied with one solemn *prise de possession,* but at least one of the chaplains, Father Raffeix, must have been more than happy to find himself in such surroundings, on the very spot consecrated by the blood of his brother in religion, Father Jogues; but as in the case of Father Le Moyne, we find no documents to show that he sought for any mementoes, or endeavored to find any of the relics of Jogues and his companions. After this exploit, de Tracy retraced his steps, for the approaching winter prevented him from venturing any further west, and amid great rejoicings he returned to Quebec. The three expeditions, according to Benj. Sulte, were farcical. But they resulted in a seventeen-year peace with the Iroquois, which was at least something to boast of.

PETER RAFFEIX.

Father Raffeix, of course, went back to Quebec with the troops. He had come out to America along with Bishop Laval in 1663, and had had a wearisome time of it on the four months' journey over the ocean. Forty of the passengers were sick and dying in the ship's hold and ample opportunity was given him to exercise his zeal. He appears to have been destined for the Cayuga mission at the time when the expedition against the Mohawks was organized, but instead of going there was assigned to the chaplaincy of the expedition. It was not until six years afterwards that he was sent to take the place of de Carheil, who was leaving Cayuga in shattered health.

Father Raffeix was enchanted with Cayuga. " It is the fairest country," he says, " that I have seen in America. Its latitude is 42½ degrees, and the variation of the magnetic needle there is scarcely more than ten degrees. It is a tract situated between two lakes and not exceeding four leagues in width, consisting of almost uninterrupted plains with very beautiful woods bordering them.

" Annié, on the other hand, is a very narrow valley, often abounding in stones and always covered with mists. The mountains hemming it in seem to me of very poor soil "— This " Annié " is the part of the Mohawk where he had been with Courcelles and de Tracy. " Oneida and Onondaga," he continues, " also appear to be very rough regions and little adapted to the chase, and the same may be said of Seneca. But around Cayuga there are killed annually more than a thousand deer. Fish—salmon, as well as eels and other kinds—are as plentiful here as at Onondaga. Four leagues from here I saw by the side of a river within a very limited space, eight or ten extremely fine salt springs. Many snares are set for pigeons, from seven to eight hundred being often taken at once. Lake Tiohero, one of the two adjoining our village, is fully fourteen leagues long by two wide. Swans and bustards are very abundant there during the entire winter, and in spring one sees nothing but continual clouds of all sorts of wild fowl. The Oswego River, which flows from the lake, divides in its upper waters into several channels bordered by prairies, and at intervals are very pleasant and somewhat deep inlets which are preserves for the game.

" I find the inhabitants of Cayuga more tractable and less haughty than the Oneidas and Onondagas, and if God had humbled them as He has the Mohawks I believe the faith could be planted there more easily than in any of the other Iroquois Nations. There are estimated to be more than three hundred warriors here, and a prodigious number of little children." However, he does not think " the hour of their conversion has yet arrived, and he tells how he is driven out of their cabins with sticks and stones. On one occasion " the daughter of the family threw a large stone at me without hitting me, however," which is the way with the sex everywhere.

" I introduced singing among the catechumens, adapting thereto various prayers and some hymns in their tongue on the principal mysteries of the faith. On the first day of the year we offered these songs of praise as a New Year's gift to Our Lord and have since continued them with good results, and the great gratification of our savages. I count thirty, children and adults together, to whom God has granted the grace of baptism since Father de Carheil's departure. The idea that the whole nation can be converted at once, or the expectation that Christians can be made by hundreds and thousands in this country is a delusion. Canada is not a land of flowers; to find and pluck an occasional one it is necessary to walk a long distance through thorns and briars."

The observations of Raffeix about the latitude of Cayuga, the declination of the needle, etc., remind us that in the midst of his apostolic labors he was also making scientific observations. In fact we find that he is known to the learned world as a cartographer of some distinction.

BISHOP DE SAINT-VALLIER.

PETER RAFFEIX.

Thus the Catalogue of the Library of Parliament (Toronto, 1858) mentions among the maps in that library, copied in Paris (1852-53), an interesting one by Raffeix, dated 1676, and called " Map of the westernmost parts of Canada." A note by the copyist says: " This map is accompanied by an extensive legend, full of information, especially in regard to the voyages of Father Marquette and Sieur Joliet." By a mistake the name is written *Kaffeix,* instead of Raffeix. On the next page of the Catalogue occurs the notice of a second map, dated 1688, the title of which is the same as that of one in the Bibliothèque Nationale, of Paris, and is ascribed to Raffeix by Sommervogel. It is a map of " Lake Ontario, with the adjacent regions, and especially the five Iroquois nations." Sommervogel mentions another one by Raffeix which is in the library of the Marine Bureau, representing " New France from the Ocean to Lake Erie, and on the south to New England."

Although he wrote to his Superior that persons of exalted virtue could find ample material for the exercise of virtue among the Cayugas, and that faint-hearted people like himself are delighted to find themselves forced by necessity to suffer much to derive their sole consolation from God, and to toil incessantly in self-sanctification, and that therefore he prayed his Reverence to leave him in this happy condition all his life as the greatest favor that could be accorded to him, yet by that time, Father de Carheil had recovered his health and had reclaimed his post of danger among the Cayugas. Consequently Father Raffeix was recalled to Canada. It was then that he suggested founding a settlement at La Prairie for the converted Iroquois, similar to the one which had been established for the converted Hurons at Sillery, further down the St. Lawrence. La Prairie de la Madeleine, as it was known, developed into the present Caughnawaga, where the Indians after several migrations ultimately settled.

It took its name from Jacques de la Ferté, Abbé de la

Madeleine, who was a Canon of the Sainte Chapelle in Paris, and one of the Hundred Associates of the Company of New France. He gave the land, in 1647, to the Jesuits on condition that they would employ such persons as they might judge proper to cultivate the lands, the donor having a share in their prayers and Holy Sacrifices. It was given " in consideration of the assistance their Order had bestowed on the inhabitants of New France and the dangers incurred in bringing the savages to the knowledge of the true God." The Indian settlement was transferred to its present site further up the river, in 1675.

Raffeix remained at La Prairie only a year or so when Father Frémin, at the express desire of de Courcelles, was put in charge of it, Raffeix going to the Senecas. We get only a glimpse of him, here and there, in the general story, but we discover that when La Motte, the Lieutenant of La Salle, went down with Hennepin to ask leave of the Senecas to build Fort Niagara, he met two Jesuits in the village. They were Raffeix and Garnier. Father Morain was at this time somewhere else among the Senecas. Disliking all priests and especially Jesuits, La Motte insisted upon the two missionaries leaving the council. Rather than create any difficulty and no doubt quite willing to leave this swashbuckling envoy to his own devices, they withdrew. La Motte subsequently fell out with La Salle and disappeared from the scene.

Subsequently we find Raffeix as Procurator at Quebec, and Rochemonteix has unearthed a very interesting letter from him which recalls a chapter of extremely turbulent and distressing Canadian history.

After Bishop Laval had resigned his See, the Abbé Jean Baptiste de Saint-Vallier was appointed in his place "to avoid being made a bishop of France." He was clever, having been made a Doctor of the Sorbonne at 19, well connected, pious and zealous. He was almoner of the King and a particular friend of the famous Père La Chaise. Another Jesuit,

PETER RAFFEIX.

Le Valois, directed his conscience. The two Jesuits and the well-known Sulpitian, Tronson, were somewhat concerned about his impetuous zeal as well as his youth, but thought that time would work wonders in him. They were disappointed.

Rome was slow in accepting Laval's resignation. Meantime Saint Vallier went to Quebec as Vicar General. At that time there were 17 secular priests in the diocese and a number of religious communities of men and women. He came as bishop in August, 1688, and for 40 years Canada was in a tumult. Bishop Laval and every one else complained. Even Louis XIV requested the bishop to resign, but the *opinâtre Dauphinois,* as Rochemonteix calls him, refused. Sailing for Canada, after one of his journeys to Europe, he was captured by the English and kept a prisoner for two or three years.

Like everyone else, the Jesuits suffered from the excessive zeal of the bishop. One of his measures especially concerns us. He transformed the famous old Lorette of Father Chaumonot into a parish church, and it is in connection with this action that Father Raffeix, who was in charge of the finances of the Province, writes to the Father General, October 18, 1700: "I, P. Raffeix, priest of the Society of Jesus, having a thorough knowledge of the business matters of the College of Quebec, acquired by 18 continuous years of office as procurator of the same college, and of whatever missions depend on it, declare that the chapel of Lorette, which our Fathers have built for the Huron mission, three leagues from Quebec, of cut stone, as was also the house adjoining, and which from time to time I have had repaired, has cost more than 6,000 livres, French money. This chapel and the adjoining house, the illustrious Bishop of Quebec has expressed the wish that our Fathers should give him for a presbytery and parish church. I wish, also, to note that in the 6,000 livres, French money, I have not included the four acres of cultivated land which the same

283

illustrious bishop desires to take for the use of the parish and parishioners. In testimony of which I have hereunto set my hand and seal, etc."

Father Bouvart, the Superior, made no effort to prevent this transfer, in spite of the protest of all the Fathers, and of many of the laity. His Lordship offered no indemnity, though afterwards he contributed 400 francs. Their pupils in the preparatory college classes were also taken from them and their faculties as confessors of convents were revoked. It is somewhat diverting to hear that they were denounced to the General *Father Gonzales* for teaching the immoral doctrine of *probabilism*.

In his latter days, however, the bishop became more kindly, restored them their faculties, and took a Jesuit confessor, but l'Ancienne Lorette was never given back to its owners. Chaumonot had died seven years before, and it is noteworthy that the bishop was very eager to have some of his relics, for the old founder was looked upon as a saint.

Raffeix died about 24 years after these lamentable events. He was born in Auvergne, 1633, and died in Quebec in 1724, so that he had reached the advanced age of 91. Longevity was very usual with these old heroes who made light of life.

FRANCIS BONIFACE.

IT is not surprising that the mission established on the very spot where Father Jogues was martyred should be conspicuous for the heroic piety of its converts. Piety was, so to say, in the soil, planted there by the blood of its first apostle. In fact the old Jesuits were accustomed to give that explanation of the phenomenon and Father Chauchetière added another: "Was it not these very Mohawks who had gone all the way to Lake Huron to slay Father de Brébeuf? The merits of his sacrifice also must have won great graces for the conversion of those ferocious Mohawks."

The first priest who succeeded in establishing himself there permanently was Father Boniface. It was his only mission in America. He had gone directly to Ossernenon, in 1669, after arriving in Canada, and when his short term of five years was over he went back to Quebec and died. There is absolutely nothing startling or tragic in his life, but it only goes to show that the wonderful transformation so suddenly effected among the Mohawks was not due to natural but to supernatural causes.

He found only about four or five hundred people in the village when he arrived, but a very large part of them seemed to be awaiting his coming, and Ossernenon achieved the glory of being the first regularly established church in the Mohawk valley.

Had we been wanderers in those wilds in 1670, we should have seen the little chapel rising amidst the long-houses of the Mohawks, and within a fervent congregation kneeling before the humble altar devoutly reciting their prayers or chanting in alternate choirs the hymns and canticles of the service. We should have been surprised to see them also just as in a church in Europe, kneeling around the Crib of the Infant Jesus, which the pastor had procured for his

285

chapel, and whose effect on his people he had witnessed with amazement. Even the custom of distributing the *pain benit* at Mass had been introduced from Montreal; a reminder of the love feasts of the early Christians.

Those fervent Mohawks had no false shame about their religion. They paraded it openly, and wore their crosses and medals so that their pagan relatives could see them, and what was more, they flaunted them in the face of the Dutch at Fort Orange, although mocked at for their popish superstition, and even threatened with punishment for displaying the offensive emblems. Nor was it a mere matter of words or an exhibition of dislike that they had to face. One of their great chiefs, Assendasé, by name, so irritated his relatives by his zeal in propagating the faith that he was furiously assaulted by an angry kinsman, who tore the medal from his neck and stood for a moment with uplifted hatchet to cleave his skull. Assendasé looked at him calmly and said, without a tremor: " Strike, I shall be only too happy to die for my faith." He came very near being the first Iroquois martyr.

The Dutch, of course, could not resort to such violent measures, but their contempt was no less galling. Commonly, however, it had no other effect than to confirm the Indians in their faith. It is narrated that on one occasion a strong-minded squaw, angered by the treatment she had received, strode into the Protestant meeting-house at Albany, while service was going on, and in a loud voice recited the prayers she had learned from the Black Gown. Of course, they put her out, but she gloried in her exploit.

One reproach that was hard for the braves to bear was that their faith took away their warlike spirit. Even Frontenac taunted the missionaries with that. But the accusation was altogether undeserved, for the Christian Mohawks, though no longer indulging in their old-time ferocity, were always ready for war, and never failed to distinguish themselves as superb fighters.

286

FRANCIS BONIFACE.

There is one instance, however, at Ossernenon, of a different state of mind on the part of a former warrior who had taken many a scalp and yet who as a Christian refused to fight, without, however, displaying the white feather. War had been declared against the Illinois, and he hesitated about going out. He heard the word: " Coward," and he replied: "You know I am no coward; and I will go to this war, but not to fight, or plunder, or pillage, or kill. My occupation will be to instruct those who wish to hear me, and to prevent all the evil I can. I have witnessed the frightful massacres of children which take place when we make ourselves masters of an enemy's village. I will baptize as many of them as I can and even the adults whom I may be allowed to instruct before you burn them." He spoke to the priest about it and his project was warmly approved. There was one little difficulty, however; it was about the formula of baptism. In Iroquois there is no expression corresponding to the Latin, *in nomine;* so, after learning the Latin form, he set out with the rest of the braves. They reached the Illinois country, and when the fight was on, our brave fellow was always seen in the place of danger, but never killing or scalping or making prisoners. He was running hither and thither, wherever he saw any children. He had, moreover, exacted a promise from the warriors to tell him when they were going to kill any one they had captured, and he seized the few intervening moments to instruct the victim. He sought out the wounded, Illinois and Iroquois alike, and appealed to them to become Christians. That was his only thought. Some of his comrades reported that they saw him baptize as many as ten children in one of the forays. The warriors came back but he was not with them. He was killed by the Illinois when he was out hunting. New York may well be proud of such an aboriginal Christian.

One of the most remarkable of the Ossernenon Indians was the famous chief known as " The Great Mohawk," dubbed by the Dutchmen " Kryn." His wife had become a Christian, and in a towering rage he left her and went away, scarcely knowing whither. Providence directed his steps to Caughnawaga, where he saw his old friends of the warpath transformed into fervent Christians. He remained with them during winter, and one morning Father Boniface heard the shout of Kryn, who was approaching the town. His people hastened to meet him. He was no longer a pagan, and he told them he had left Ossernenon forever. So earnest was his appeal for a reformation of life that when he turned his back on his home forty men and women followed him on the trail to Montreal. Father Boniface, who was then approaching his end, went with them. Frémin made Kryn a chief in Caughnawaga. He accepted the position and no one dared to dispute his authority, though he enforced good behavior with a heavy hand. Very frequently, also, he made apostolic excursions, not only among the Mohawks, but preached the faith to other tribes. When war was proclaimed by Frontenac, Kryn led his Iroquois down into their old home. It was he who was in command of the savage contingent in the attack on Schenectady, and we find in an " *Account of Remarkable Occurrences in Canada,*" by M. de Monseignat, Comptroller General of the Marine in Canada, a very flattering description of our great Indian. The French had originally intended to attack Albany, but Kryn denounced it as madness. When they came to the parting of the ways, where one road led to Corlar (Schenectady), the other to Fort Orange, the Indians, without more ado, started for the former and the French followed. Nine days elapsed before they arrived at the town. During part of the time they were obliged to march up to their knees in water and to break the ice with their feet before they found a solid footing. " They arrived within two leagues of Corlar," says the *Account,* " about four o'clock in the evening, and were harangued by The Great Mohawk. He urged on them all

to perform their duty and to lose all recollections of their
fatigue in the hope of taking ample revenge for the injuries
they had received from the Iroquois, at the solicitation of
the English, and of washing them out in the blood of
traitors.   This savage was, without contradiction, the most
considerable of his tribe, an honest man, as intelligent,
prudent and generous as it was possible to be, and capable
of the grandest undertakings."   Poor Kryn lost his life
in that attack.

He was a relative of the pious Skandegorhaksen, and was
with him on the last hunt when the young brave was taken
ill.   Kryn carried him on his back to the settlement, en-
couraging him as they journeyed painfully along, but listening with delight to the fervent words of the sufferer.   Kryn
told it all when they reached home, and repeated his praises
when they were laying the beloved dead in his grave.

Ossernenon sent many such to Caughnawaga, and deserves all the credit for the good example they gave.   Unfortunately, in an economic point of view, the village suffered in consequence; for their religion was exiling them
from their country; a penalty it often entails.   As many
as a hundred went in a single year.   The priests could not
very well prevent it; in fact they saw many advantages in
the migration, and when reproached with causing the depopulation of the villages, they replied that it was not religion, but vice and war with their train of destructive mal-
adies and want that caused the ruin.   " Become Christians,"
they said, " and your tribe will prosper."

On the other hand, there may have been a homesickness
in this flitting of the Mohawks.   They originally came from
the St. Lawrence.   According to Beauchamp, " this people of the flint, who were called Maquas by the Dutch, and
Mohawks by the English, were probably the inhabitants of
Montreal (Hochelaga), whom Cartier found in 1535.   The
name Canada, then first used by the French, is a Mohawk
word."   Their own tradition points to the St. Lawrence
as the place of their origin.

PIONEER PRIESTS OF NORTH AMERICA.

It must not be inferred, however, that there were no Christians left in Ossernenon. On the contrary, a strong and fervent congregation remained there till the end of the missions, and fulfilled their obligations long after the priests were expelled, just as the Abenakis did up on the Kennebec.

We find a confirmation of this in a curious letter written by " The Rev. Peter Van Driessen to the Very Rev. and Pious and Highly Learned Gentlemen, The Messrs. John Noordbeek, and Leonard Beels, Faithful Ministers of the Gospel at Amsterdam." He addresses them as High Rev. sirs. The letter is found in the *Documentary History of New York.*

The testimony is all the more valuable, as we find this Reverend Peter asking the " High and Rev. Sirs to forward his petition with all submission to the Rev. Bishop of London, with my humble request that you would recommend me *alone* for some salary because of my labors among the Indians, from that renowned English Society for Propagating the Gospel. But the building of churches must not be mentioned to the Bishop as the Indians are immovably attached to us Dutch."

He then goes on to say: " It is indeed true that the enlightening spirit of Christ has now for some time past operated so powerfully among these blind Indians that *they have become very zealous in their attention to prayers, catechetical exercises and singing of Psalms.* The neighboring Christians, living near their castles, from time to time give us assurance of this. *They even hold up these proselytes as examples to their families in order to arouse their children thereby.*"

Whence did this zeal of the Mohawk Indians for religious instruction come? It is almost superfluous to say that it is not to be ascribed to the efforts of the Protestant parsons who succeeded the Jesuits in those fields of missionary work. A glance at the fourth volume of *The Documentary History of the State of New York* will be sufficient to help us to arrive at that conclusion. It teems with letters of the ministers of various sects, all of them addressed to Sir William Johnson, and all discussing the Indian question. The correspondents themselves are not numerous, but their letters are, and we are forced to conclude that whatever virtues Sir William may have lacked, he certainly possessed patience in abundance.

It must be remembered that these anxious parsons never went near the Indians. Old Dominie Dellius, himself, who was the first one appointed by the Government after the destruction of the missions, remained at Fort Orange, and if a squaw wanted her papoose baptized she brought it down there. It is even a question if the good Dominie knew anything of the language of the Indians. He had, as we know, a bad reputation as a land-grabber, and Lord Bellomont, rightly or wrongly, finally drove him out of the country; though, of course, one is not obliged to believe all that Bellomont was moved to say about his enemies. His triumph over the Dominie is only referred to here in order to show that the parson was not worrying excessively about his red men.

Nor, as a matter of fact, were any of the other ministers. Thus a certain Thoroughgood Moore belied his name by waiting a whole year in Albany before beginning his work at Schoharie, and finally he abandoned the task altogether. The ministers found the work too much for them. They could not abide the hardships of real missionary life. Nor would they essay it even when it was made luxurious. Thus, when Bellomont memorialized the Board of Trade " for ministers to instruct the Five Nations and prevent them from the approaches of the French priests and Jesuits, and insisted that they should be men of sober and exemplary lives and good scholars, else they will not be able to instruct the Indians and encounter the Jesuits in point of argument," he also asked for each minister " a salary of £100 a year, a very considerable sum for that period—besides £20 each to furnish their house, and ten or fifteen pounds for books, as well as small presents to the value of ten pounds a year, by which they may retain the good will of the Indians." They are to have, also, a house and chapel at each castle which by computation may cost sixty or eighty pounds a piece." In this memorial we find a most singular provision, viz: that the house and chapel are to be " stockaded round " to defend them against the people they are going to evangelize. The ministers are also to have two servants to attend them. John Chamberlayn, Esq., who protests against such an outlay, writes to the Lords of Trade that " in addition, several other items swell the account so considerably that it can hardly be compassed by any but a royal purse.

In spite of this generous plan, to which was added a promise of a benefice in England after a few years of work in the Indian missions, very few were tempted to offer themselves.

In the *Documents* we find a very valuable memoir of *The Last Missionary of the Mohawks,* which shows that all the good qualities which were found in the few remnants of the old Mohawks left in New York in prerevolutionary times after the Catholic missions were destroyed, must be attributed to the faith planted by the old Catholic teachers of the Gospel.

The *Memoir* is by a Protestant minister, it begins by saying that " the conversion and civilization of the American Indians engaged the attention of Europeans as far back as 1642, when Father Jogues laid down his life on the Mohawk River for the Gospel. The Dutch, who first colonized these parts, did not give the subject much consideration. The clergy at the Manhattans succeeded in teaching one young savage the prayers so that he could repeat the responses in church and could also read and write well. He was then furnished with a Bible and sent to evangelize the heathen. But he pawned the book for brandy, became a thorough beast and did more harm than good."

FRANCIS BONIFACE.

" The Government of New York (the English) did not make any effort to Christianize the Five Nations further than to pay for some time a small salary to the clergyman at Albany *to attend to the wants of such Indians as might apply to him.*" The Rev. Mr. Freeman translated some of the liturgy and passages of the Old and New Testament, but those who professed to be Christians in 1710 are represented as " so ignorant and scandalous they can scarcely be reputed as Christians." In 1712, Mr. Andrews built a chapel at the mouth of the Schoharie, but *soon abandoned the place, so was he the last that resided among them for a great many years;* the Society for Propagation of the Gospel, which sent him out, contenting itself with paying a small stipend to the clergyman at Albany to act as missionary to the Mohawks. *In which capacity he did them very little good.*"

In 1748, three ministers visited successively the tribes on the Mohawk and Susquehanna. These efforts were interrupted by the French war, and not resumed till 1761, when the Rev. Dr. Wheelock endeavored to reclaim the natives from savage life by introducing Indians among them as missionaries and teachers. Dr. Wheelock himself says: " I succeeded in educating 40, but I don't hear of more than half who have preserved their characters unstained, either by a course of intemperance or uncleanness, and some who bid fairest for usefulness have sunk down into as low, savage, and brutish a manner of living as they were in before; and there are some of whom I entertained the hope that they were really subjects of God's grace, who have not wholly kept their garments unspotted among the pots. Six of these who did preserve a good character are now dead."

The last Anglican missionary among the Mohawks was Rev. John Stuart, whose father was a Presbyterian, of *Omagh* (Armagh), Ireland. He established himself at Fort Hunter, in 1770, but not till 1774 was he able to converse with his flock, and " for lack of an interpreter he found great difficulty in conveying to them any distinct ideas on divine subjects, for which cause he could but seldom preach to them. As he left, a year or so after, he certainly exerted very little influence. Service was read at Canajoharie by Paulus Sahonwandi, an Indian schoolmaster, and some idea may be conveyed of the difficulty of imparting elementary instruction to the pupils, from the fact the *teacher had no books and had to teach the alphabet, etc., by means only of little manuscript scraps of paper*. We have a list of the Indian pupils in the school at Fort Hunter in 1769, when Dr. Stuart arrived. They number 30, but from what is reported of the educational facilities afforded one may be excused from taking them into consideration. In 1775 the Revolutionary war began, and as Mr. Stuart was a Tory he was compelled to withdraw. Later on we find him at Cataroqui, in Canada, where the de Lambervilles had labored a hundred years before him. That was all the English Church did for the Mohawks.

Besides this apathy and unconcern, we find as we turn over the records of those days nothing but dissensions, first between the Dutch and English, and then between the various sects of the latter. Thus the Rev. John Jacob Oel writes in Holland-English to Sir William Johnson to complain of " the Bostoniers who in every Castle by choosing uyt two jung boys for to be sent in nieu engelland to be instructed there. Now learning is good, en is most necessary among the haddens; that cannot be contradicted, but y want to know what design it is to introduce their own Presbyteren Church; that can it not be allowed, en as it prejudice our Church en Church ceremonies; en y must maintain and will maintain the Church of our Church so lang y can, en math es en mine little power, etc."

The English ministers had their quarrels, also, and thus there is in 1766, a bitter controversy going on between the Rev. Mr. Chamberlain and the Rev. Mr. Brown, the former saying " it were best to keep from the minds of the Indians

294

Sr *William Johnson Bar*.^t
Major General of the English Forces
in North America.

every notion of any difference or distinction between pro-destant (sic!) Christians lest it bring into contempt and neglect amongst *these ignorant heathens* the whole Christian system." Later on Dr. Brown is scored for trying to prevent the Rev. Hezekiah Calvin from establishing himself at Fort Hunter. Col. Babcock, who wanted to take orders, though he admitted he was very much given to intemperance, but thought he could reform, denounces "the Presbyterians, who are tucking and squeezing in every possible crevice they can, their missionaries among the Indians, who from their solemnity, their ungraceful stiffness, and those recluse, unsociable, dejected airs, which so remarkably distinguish those splenitic and frightened enthusiasts; for while these are continued, piety is quite stripped of its proper ornaments, and assumes the habit of craft, vice, and ill-nature, and is enough to prejudice the Indians against the sublime truths of the Gospel." Of course, the Presbyterians retaliated in kind.

It is rather amusing that all this *odium theologicum* was referred to Sir William Johnson, who is a sort of a lay pope for the contentious parties. Knowing his character, their obsequiousness is rather to be regretted. Meantime he does not hesitate to tell them some wholesome truths as, for instance, that the Indians strongly suspect them of having more thirst for land than thirst for souls, and are "disgusted with them." The principal difficulty, apart from this, he says, in writing to the Rev. Mr. Inglis, is "the want of a thorough knowledge of the genius and disposition of the Indians, and the proper means to be pursued. Secondly, the want of zeal and perseverance which has often rendered many attempts abortive; and where these qualities are found united (as among some of the Dissenters), the possessors are not only deficient in knowledge and capacity, but of a gloomy severity of manners totally disqualifying them for such a task. Thirdly, the want of a suitable fund that may enable the few otherwise fitted for the purpose to attempt it."

PIONEER PRIESTS OF NORTH AMERICA.

The character of one of those engaged in this work may be seen from an elaborate letter to His Excellency. It is from the Rev. Mr. Lappius, and might be consulted as proving the truth of what Sir William says, that many of those engaged in the work were totally unfit. It is dated Canajoharie, December 29, 1763. It is written in a most indescribable jumble of Dutch and English, and is taken up mostly with requests to Sir William for brandy and blankets, and with denunciations of the parson's troublesome neighbors. Those who are in quest of curiosities in literature may find it in the *Documentary History*.

We have gone into this long digression merely to show the lasting influence of the Christian teachings given at Ossernenon by Father Boniface and his few successors. As a matter of fact, however, there were no Mohawks left to evangelize. The rum and powder of the Dutch and English had swept them from the face of the earth. Thus we find in Governor Tryon's report, just prior to the Revolutionary war (1774), the following notice which reads like an inscription on a tombstone:

" The Mohawks, the first in rank of the Six Nation Confederacy, though now much reduced in number, originally occupied the country westward from Albany to the German Flats, a space of about 90 miles, and *had many towns,* but are now reduced to two *villages* on the Mohawk and a *few families at Schoharie,* viz: at Ossernenon. The Lower Mohawks are in number about 185, and the Upper, or those of Canojoharie, 221. This nation hath always been warm in their attachment to the English *and on this account suffered great loss during the late war."*

This was the last of the Mohawks. They had no longer any need of missionaries. They had nearly all been slain or driven to the Far West.

When Father Boniface went back to Quebec in 1674, he was in a dying condition. We are told that when he was in delirium, the Fathers kneeling round his bed besought

FRANCIS BONIFACE.

Father de Brébeuf to restore him to his right mind before he died, and that he recovered immediately. One is prone to ask why they did not invoke the aid of Jogues, with whom Boniface was so closely identified. Possibly because Jogues had already wrought a miracle in restoring a sick nun to health in the Hôtel Dieu. They needed something for de Brébeuf's canonization, but not for Jogues'.

Boniface was succeeded at Ossernenon by Bruyas, who was badly treated by the Dutch; then James de Lamberville came, and finally Vaillant de Gueslis closed his chapel door and went out into the woods as the English troops were approaching the village.

JAMES DE LAMBERVILLE.

A LITTLE above the present town of Fonda, on the hillside that slopes to where the Cayudutta Creek becomes a cascade and tumbles into the Mohawk, there is a deep recess in the midst of a tangle of vines and decaying trees where a little stream of water trickles from the foot of a birch into the creek below. It flows from a source which the tradition of the neighborhood has fixed as Tegakwitha's Spring. There, it is said, the Indian girl who is conspicuous in the history of the Valley used to come to draw water for her wigwam; a difficult operation, even for a sure-footed savage, but next to impossible for a half-blind girl like Tegakwitha. Perhaps it is only a popular fancy.

The basis of this tradition is the belief that the Indian town of Gandaouagé in which Tegakwitha lived, was altogether or in part near the present town of Fonda. This conviction is fortified, if indeed it was not created, by the statement of a certain Wentworth Greenhalgh who made a journey up the valley of the Mohawk, in 1677, and who said that he found all the Mohawk villages on the *north* side of the river. His Report is embodied in the *Documentary History of New York;* but who Greenhalgh is, it is hard to make out. A diligent search through all the great libraries, and inquiries from eminent authorities, have failed to reveal anything of his identity except that he was a fur-trader living at Albany. There is is no record of his having written anything else. His statement, however, seems to have been accepted, not as being conclusive, but as affording a certain amount of probability, and no more.

Morgan, in his great work of *The League of the Iroquois,* also locates Gandaouagé at Fonda, but as the editor of the work, Mr. Lloyd, is continually calling attention to errors made by the author, and as he especially notes some serious geographical misstatements about the very territory around Fonda, his opinion is necessarily deprived of the weight it might otherwise have.

The real authority in the matter is, of course, that of General Clark, who wrote to the author of *The Lily of the Mohawk* as far back as 1885, that " Greenhalgh's description gives sufficient facts to warrant a *reasonable probability* as to the locations of the four principal castles at that date, but it is not absolutely certain." Many years afterwards the same great authority wrote : " The frequent changes of the Mohawk villages and the method of changing makes it impossible to decide with certainty questions about their exact locality. The changes were frequently made gradually from year to year ; the same village having two distinct positions at the same time, sometimes for a year or two and sometimes for three years. The Fathers could not well take note of such changes, and may have given the same name to different sections of the village, though three or four miles apart. Sometimes a fact may be mentioned that makes the location of a certain event absolutely certain, but usually there is an element of uncertainty."

The large-minded tolerance of this distinguished investigator, who has studied the Valley for fifty years, and who still refuses to pronounce positively, is the only reason why any mention is made of suggestions in support of an opposite view. They are advanced merely as a matter of information.

They are, first : Gandaouagé was certainly on the *south* side of the Mohawk in 1667. Father Chauchetière, Tegakwitha's confessor in Canada, writes that after de Tracy's raid in 1666 " the Agniers immediately came, and constructed their old villages, but Gandaouagé was rebuilt at half a league from the old one." Then referring to the arrival of the missionaries, Bruyas and Frémin, in 1667, he says : " As we have already stated, the village of Gandaouagé, where Catherine lived, was quite near the old

299

village where Father Jogues so heroically suffered during thirteen months of his captivity."

Secondly, Fiske, in his *Dutch and Quaker Colonies* (vii, p 55), informs us that eight years later, namely " in 1675, Governor Andros found the first Mohawk Castle on the *west* bank of the Schoharie," and consequently on the *south* side of the Mohawk.

Thirdly, in Vol. LX, of the *Relations,* there is a letter from Father James de Lamberville, who baptized Tegakwitha. It is dated " Gandaouagé, May 6, 1676." He is writing about a sick Indian, and says : " His conversion was a special effect of grace and a particular favor from Father Isaac Jogues, who shed his blood *here,* in God's cause, and who was massacred *here* by the barbarians."

It is true that the original place might have been altogether abandoned and the name given to a village on the other side of the river, but it would be difficult to conceive that of Gandaouagé, which was from the beginning considered to be a sanctuary. The *Relations,* one should fancy, would certainly have noted it.

There remains the other supposition, viz : that there were two sections of Gandaouagé, the old and the new. In such an event, the question would still remain, in which one did Tegakwitha live? Perhaps she lived in both. We shall have to imitate the wisdom of General Clark, who says : " I made up my mind many years ago that Jogues suffered *death* at Ossernenon, and that Tegakwatha *lived* at Gandaouagé." The locality of the first has been settled beyond peradventure by this devoted friend of the missionaries; the second still has an element of uncertainty in it.

The missionary most identified with Gandaouagé was James de Lamberville, the younger brother of the illustrious John de Lamberville, the apostle of the Onondagas. He was born at Rouen, in 1641, and became a Jesuit at the age of twenty. Fourteen years later he set out for Canada, and from that till his death he was laboring in or for the New York missions.

Bruyas and Frémin were the first to arrive, after de Tracy's expedition in 1666. They remained only a day or so, but singularly enough enjoyed the hospitality of the uncle of Tegakwitha. He admitted them to his lodge, though he was hostile to their faith. Father Boniface established the first permanent mission there, and when his health gave out, the indefatigable Bruyas took his place. Finally, came James de Lamberville, who had the happiness of finding and baptizing a saint, the famous Tegakwitha.

She was the daughter of an Algonquin Christian woman who had been captured near Three Rivers, and had been affiliated to the Mohawk tribe. Shortly after the birth of her daughter she died, and the father also disappeared, killed, no doubt, on the warpath. The child was then taken care of by her uncle. When Bruyas and Frémin arrived, in 1667, she was about nine or ten years old. She was very sickly, and smallpox had deeply pitted her face. Besides disfiguring her, it had also impaired her sight, and on that account she rarely left her cabin, and when outside she kept her eyes partially covered to shield them against the glare of the sunlight. She was like a veiled and cloistered nun. Her appearance was quite the reverse of the stately Indian princess, as the sculptor has represented her in the statue at Dunwoodie.

It is very remarkable that this wonderful child escaped the notice of such hunters of souls as Bruyas and Boniface. Possibly the ill-feeling of her uncle and the general irritation of the village about the withdrawal of so many of the converts to Canada, and, perhaps, Tegakwitha's own shyness, prevented her from approaching the priest. She was about eighteen or nineteen years of age when de Lamberville took charge of the mission, and he discovered her by the merest accident.

Going his rounds one day from cabin to cabin, he arrived

301

at Tegakwitha's. She had been disabled by an accident to her foot, and was unable to go out to work in the fields with the other women. The priest was quite unprepared for what happened. He discovered, to his amazement, that from childhood she had been longing to be a Christian. She had even dreamed of becoming a nun in Canada. Her habits of seclusion and her natural propensity had kept her from the degrading amusements of the village, and her disfigurement had been a protection against the advances of suitors; and so she had grown up through her childhood in absolute purity of soul. She was already the Lily of the Mohawk.

Quite taken aback at this revelation, the priest lost no time in instructing her in the faith, but with the caution that characterized the methods of those old missionaries, he was in no haste to baptize her. In fact, in the light of subsequent events, he would appear unaccountably slow. Month after month went by, the neophyte grasping his explanations with a facility and intelligence which could only be explained by the exquisite purity of her soul. Finally, she was publicly baptized, with great solemnity, and took the name of Catherine.

Her profession of faith raised a storm. Persecution of all kinds began. The anger of her uncle displayed itself in ill-usage and abuse, and on one occasion he sent a young brave to her cabin who threatened to kill her. Efforts were made to compel her to marry, and both her virtue and reputation were assailed. These trials continued during two years without disturbing the tranquillity of her soul.

One day three warriors came to the village. They were all converts to the faith. One was the famous Oneida Chief, Hot Ashes; another, an extraordinarily holy Huron from Lorette, and the third, Tegakwitha's brother-in-law; he had married her adopted sister. They had come down to the Mohawk from Canada to preach against intemperance and to explain the doctrines of Christianity. No doubt they had heard from the brother-in-law of Tegakwitha's trials.

TEGAKWITHA.

JAMES DE LAMBERVILLE.

On their arrival, all the people flocked to hear them. Hot Ashes was the principal speaker. He declaimed fiercely against drunkenness and other vices, and then proceeded to enlighten them about the Faith. De Lamberville listened with rapture to their discourse and wondered if their visit would result in Tegakwitha going to Canada with them.

More than likely they had that in view, and they entered into the scheme the more willingly as they were told that her aunts were not averse to her going. The occasion, moreover, was propitious, as the uncle had gone down to the "Flamants," at Fort Orange. So they carefully made their preparations. While Hot Ashes tramped off to Oneida, the other two secretly stowed Tegakwitha away in the canoe, and slipped down the stream.

They had not been gone long when Tegakwitha's cabin was found to be empty, and runners started down to Fort Orange to inform the uncle. In a great rage he loaded his musket with an extra charge of bullets and proceeded up the river to intercept the fugitives. But they, knowing the ways of the savage, hid their canoe in the bushes and waited for him to pass.

They were near Albany by this time, and the brother-in-law proposed to go down to the Fort to procure provisions for the journey. He was hardly out of his concealment when he espied the uncle coming up the stream. Too late to draw back, he coolly faced the enemy, and after exchanging a few words, both proceeded on their way; the old man suspecting nothing. The other reached the Fort, procured his provisions, and returned to laugh over his adventure. All three then hurried away to the north.

But the danger was not yet over. On reaching the village, the uncle found the news to be only too true, and he started across the country after the runaways. They, of course, were on the alert. One of them lagged behind, and as soon as the uncle came in sight, the report of a musket gave Tegakwitha the signal, and she plunged into the bushes. The two braves made no effort to avoid the old man. Coming up to them he found one still engaged in shooting, and the other stretched out on the ground smoking. In a towering rage he asked for Tegakwitha. She was only a few feet from him, and would have been brained if a movement had betrayed her presence. Her protectors answered calmly that they had seen her at Gandaouagé a few days before, and that she was well. Again deceived, he withdrew, possibly thinking that she had gone off in the opposite direction with Hot Ashes.

They were then four days' journey from Lake. George. Fortunately they found a canoe on the shore, so that a delay of two or three days, which might have been fatal, was avoided. Thanking God for the discovery, they launched out on the Lake, and singing hymns and reciting prayers, they made their way to Montreal. For Tegakwitha it was like going to Paradise.

The name Catherine was already in benediction at Caughnawaga. The Erie squaw, Ganneaktena, whom Father Bruyas had converted in Oneida, had made it synonymous in the settlement with every Christian virtue. She had come to Montreal with her husband, over whose fierce temper she exercised a marvellous control, and had induced him to make his home in the new establishment which Father Raffeix was then beginning at La Prairie, further down the river. She was the saint of the mission, for her piety, purity, charity, and patience, and had won the most ardent affection of all the Indians there. She was a devoted mother for them all. She died in 1673, and Catherine Tegakwitha's arrival in 1677 revived the name with which the idea of great holiness was associated.

There was in the settlement at that time another woman, named Anastasia, who had known Catherine at Gandaouagé, and was a friend of her dead mother. They became inseparable companions, Anastasia acting as teacher, and so winning the confidence of the neophyte that it was through her that Father Chauchetière learned all the secrets of the child's soul, and was thus able to compose the exquisite story which he has left us, in quaint old French, of her marvellous growth in the spiritual life.

There was also a third woman, of quite another kind, associated with these two. She was an Oneida, and was called Marie Therèse, and her experiences furnish as wonderful an example of the mercy of God as we can find in the Lives of the Saints. After being baptized in her native village, she fell away from the practice of virtue and took to drink.

Late one autumn she went out to hunt with a party of twelve persons. They were far up the Ottawa, and had been unsuccessful. Hunger overtook them and they began to consider if they should not kill and eat an old man who was with them. Marie Therèse was the only Christian among them, and they consulted her as to what the Christian law said on the subject. The question startled her. If she consented to the murder, they might eat her, and then remorse took possession of her soul. She began to regret that she had not confessed her sins and reformed her life before she had started out on the unfortunate expedition; and she promised God if He would lead her home that she would live another kind of life.

They murdered the old man; and then several others died of exhaustion, and the survivors ate them. They also devoured the decaying carcass of a wolf which they found on the road. Only three out of the twelve were left, and half dead and looking like skeletons, they at last staggered into an Indian village near Montreal. Poor Marie Therèse made her way to Caughnawaga and began a life of the greatest austerity.

Being an Oneida, she had never heard of Tegakwitha, who was a Mohawk, and the entire winter passed without their meeting each other. Their acquaintance began in as picturesque a fashion as one might invent for a novel. It was in the early spring time. They were both looking at a new chapel which was approaching completion, and without speaking to each other, they went in and around it to examine the construction. At last Catherine broke the silence, and inquired about the part that was to be reserved for the women. When she was told, she began to weep and to moan that she did not deserve to go into such a holy place; but should be thrust outside with the dogs, for she had often expelled God from her heart, etc. It was too much for poor Marie Thérèse, the penitent. She, too, began to weep, and together they went to sit down at the foot of a great cross in front of the church and poured out their secrets into each other's souls, promising never to be separated while they lived.

These three women, unknown to their spiritual guide, formed a sort of religious association in order to practice the most terrible austerities, and recite long prayers. They even thought they might dress alike, after the fashion of the nuns at Quebec. They had also picked out the place of their hermitage.

If you stand on the bank of the river where Father Walworth has built a monument in honor of Tegakwitha, whom he loved so much, you see a short distance beyond you an island dark and forbidding, with its dense forests of pines. It is not far from the shore, but between it and the mainland roars a torrent, more angry, it would seem, than the great body of waters which flow on the other side of the island, and it can be seen miles below, lashed into white foam, as the breakers dash down towards Montreal. On this island Tegakwitha and her two companions wanted to establish their dwelling-place. The priest forbade it, for the reason that they would be too much exposed to roaming Indians. But how anyone, savage or civilized, could approach it is a puzzle to the white man, even to-day. He satisfied their devotion to some extent, however, by letting them go to mass at four in the morning. In winter they often tramped through the snow in their bare feet, though the priest was not aware of that, nor did he know of the bloody scourgings they gave each other. He admitted them often to the Holy Table, taught them how to make spiritual communions, to meditate, and the like. Their scruples and delicacy of conscience almost stupefied him. They had found, moreover, a little deserted cabin in a cemetery which they transformed into a sort of convent, going there to meditate, to practice penance, and especially to prepare for confession. Tegakwitha had not much to lament, but it seemed grievous enough to her that she had not been as fervent as she might have been since her conversion; that she had not resisted sufficiently those who had compelled her to work on Sunday at Gandaouagé; that she had not suffered martyrdom instead, and had not a great enough horror for sin, etc.

Even in Caughnawaga, however, although for her it was Paradise, she was called upon to suffer what was worse than martyrdom, an accusation against her chastity, made by an excellent woman, with circumstantial evidence which apparently convinced the priest of her guilt. However, the clouds cleared away after a little while, and her holiness of life shone more brilliantly than before, though she was the only one not to perceive it.

In the month of April, 1680, she died, and the Indians of Caughnawaga have ever since regarded her as a saint. Miracles are reported to have been wrought by her; pilgrimages to her tomb have continued till this very day, and Bishops of the Councils of Baltimore and Quebec have asked for the canonization of this representative of aboriginal New York Indian maidenhood. It is true she died in Canada, but as she had lived two years on the Mohawk after her conversion, and under Father de Lamberville's direction had there made her first steps in the paths of holiness, New York has a right to claim her. Besides, she is the fruit of Father Jogues' martyrdom. She was born and lived in the village where he suffered and was put to death.

De Lamberville continued his work uninterruptedly at Gandaouagé until the English and French began their death struggle for the possession of New York. In 1684, he was summoned to meet Governor de la Barre, who had begun his foolish expedition against the upper Iroquois. The invading army had then reached Galette, the present Ogdensburg, and we find in the Governor's *Memoir,* under the date of August 9th: "I was joined by Father James de Lamberville, whom I ordered to go next day to his brother at Onondaga, with instructions to assure the tribe that I have such regard for their request and for that of the two others that, provided they made a reasonable satisfaction, I preferred to entertain their petition than to go to war." On the 17th of August, John wrote from Onondaga: "Your people brought my brother here with the greatest speed they could. He arrived here with the Sieur Le Duc, at midnight, and having passed all the time till morning in discussing matters, we assembled the sachems and braves at daybreak. We declared your intentions to the Senecas, who left that day to return to their people. The Onondagas have despatched messengers to Oneida, Agnié, and Cayuga, to go to Chouegen (Oswego), to see you and answer your proposals."

After leaving Galette, de la Barre arrived at Famine Bay, which was four leagues from the Onondaga River. Misfortune overtook him, and he no longer talked of satisfaction, but despatched Charles Le Moyne in all haste to ask the de Lambervilles to save him and his army from destruction.

In this correspondence between John de Lamberville and de la Barre, there is question of an Indian named *Grosse Bouche,* or *Grosse Gueule,* the Governor's "Man of Business," against whom the priest warns His Excellency to be on his guard; advising him to reward the savage, "as he is a venal being whom you would do well to keep in pay." In fact, this *Sieur Grande Gueule* pompously called Garangula, is referred to frequently, and we discover him subsequently verifying de Lamberville's description. It was he who spoke insolently to Callières and demanded the acceptance of Dongan's conditions of peace, while protesting that he had always been a friend of the French. One asks in surprise, is this the Big Mouth whom Father Chauchetière holds up as one of the models of Caughnawaga, the famous husband of Catherine Ganneaktena, who rejoiced in the name of Francis Xavier? We are relieved to find that Denonville's evil genius lived on till 1695, whereas his pious namesake died seven years before.

It was in the time that elapsed between the failure of de la Barre and the coming of de Denonville, that James had the happiness of passing a whole year with his brother at Onondaga, during which period they were very successful in their improvised practice of medicine. It was then, also, that James had a fortunate escape from death in their little chapel, when a drunken Indian first shot at him, and then used an iron bar to brain him. As it was midnight and the Indian had been imbibing freely, his failure to take aim with both instruments is explainable, while it shows what a lovable flock these holy men had to work upon.

In 1686, John hastened to Quebec to endeavor to persuade de Denonville not to proceed against the Senecas, leaving James alone at Onondaga. In a letter relative to this interview, de Lamberville says very positively, that the Governor assured him in the most solemn manner that he had no other purpose in view than to make a treaty with the Indians. The horrible treachery is a matter of history.

Where was James while his brother was thus being used as a decoy? Denonville says he had him recalled, leaving John alone in Onondaga. About this time we find a letter from him, written in a jumble of Iroquois, French, and Latin, and addressed to Bruyas, who was in Montreal. In it he says that " Korlar " (the usual name given to the Governor of New York, and in this instance referring to Dongan), " had promised black robes to all the Indians except

309

those of Onondaga." We are left to surmise the reason of this omission of the Onondagas. Was he going to leave the de Lambervilles there? James adds, " *Missionarii vocandi sunt ex Anglia qui erudiant Indos. Gubernator scripsit Anglis de hoc.*" From Onondaga, as far as we can make out, he repaired to Fort Cataroqui, possibly to take his brother's place, as chaplain for the 140 soldiers in that scurvy-stricken station.

Then his life becomes, for a time, uneventful. He is teaching class at Quebec, in 1688. Very likely the work was uncongenial for a man who had been living for years in the forests, for in the following year he is at the Indian settlement at Sault St. Louis, and three years afterwards in the residence at Montreal. In 1701, when Father Bruyas had got the better of Governor Bellomont, and succeeded in inducing the Iroquois to recall the missionaries, James de Lamberville, though well on in life, went back to his Onondagas. But it was only for a while. The English, with their Dutch adherents, were busy endeavoring to detach the Iroquois from their allegiance to the French. By 1709, they had succeeded, and here a shadow falls on the glory of the old missionary. We find a letter from M. de Joncaire to M. de la Fresnière, the King's Commandant at Frontenac, dated June 14, 1709 (Col. Doc. ix, p. 838), which says: "The Rev. Father de Lamberville has placed us in a terrible state of embarrassment by his flight. Yesterday I was leaving for Montreal in the best possible spirits; now I am not certain if I shall ever see you again."

What was the matter? Had the long-tried hero shown the white feather at the last moment? On the contrary, he never faltered for an instant. Such a man as he would never leave his post. The explanation of his action is given in an official letter from Governor Vaudreuil to Pontchartrain, dated some months later (Col. Doc. ix, p. 828), and is as follows: " I informed you of Peter Schuyler's efforts to influence the Indians. Sieur de Joncaire would have thwarted

JAMES DE LAMBERVILLE.

him, but having been absent on a tour to Seneca, whilst waiting for the Onondagas to come down to him, as they had promised, the English sent Abraham Schuyler to Onondaga to sing the war song in the village, and to present the hatchet to the Nations on the part of the Queen of England. Abraham Schuyler managed so well that, having had a long conversation with Father de Lamberville, and having likewise expressed his regret at being obliged to present the hatchet, he persuaded the good Father to come to Montreal to give me an account of what was passing; and as he desired nothing better than to send off Father de Lamberville, of whose influence over the minds of the Onondagas he was aware, he took advantage of his absence, as soon as he saw him depart, to make some drunken Indians set fire to the Father's chapel and house, which he first caused to be pillaged."

Thus, both de Lambervilles were victims of treachery; both were driven out of their missions by conspicuous white men. It is not difficult to understand why it was so hard to convert the Indians.

James, however, had finished his work. He died in the following year. He can be regarded as having died at his post. Charlevoix calls him "one of the holiest missionaries of New France." About the place of his death there is a dispute. Charlevoix makes it occur at Caughnawaga, while Father Germain, the Superior, says he died in Montreal. In the *Elogia defunctorum* Prov. Franciæ (Arch. Rom.) we read that " he was assiduous in crucifying his flesh and in preparing for martyrdom. He slept on the bare ground, and passed whole nights in prayer. The Indians called him *the divine man*. After his death miracles were said to have been performed by touching articles which he had made use of."

JULIEN GARNIER.

JULIEN GARNIER was the Apostle of the Senecas. He was the oldest and the youngest of the New York missionaries. He began his work among the Indians when he was 25, and kept at the task for sixty years. He was the first Jesuit priest ordained in Canada. That was in 1666.

He was born in France, January, 6, 1643, and at the age of seventeen became a Jesuit. Immediately after his noviceship, he was sent to Quebec, and after teaching grammar for three years, studied theology under the famous Jerome Lalemant, and was ordained priest in 1668, leaving immediately afterwards to the Seneca mission, where Father Frémin had already established himself.

The Senecas occupied the Genesee Valley. Their territory extended to the lands of the Onondagas on the east, and to the Cayugas on the south; and all the country west to Niagara; the Eries, or Cats, having been expelled in 1655. They had four large villages which formed the angles of a square. They were called Gaosaehgaah, which was situated on what is now Boughton Hill, south of Victor; Deyudihahdo, about ten miles south of Rochester; Chinoshageh, four miles southeast of Victor; and Deondonseh, five miles south of Avon Springs. The missionaries designated them otherwise. They were respectively Gannagaro, or Gandagaro; Gandachioragou; Gannougaré; and Gannounata. The first of them, Gannagaro, contained about 150 houses and had a population of about two or three thousand, each " long house " containing from six to ten families. About four miles southeast of that town was Gannougaré. There most of the Huron captives lived. The capital was Gandachioragou. In that place Garnier spent twenty years of his life. It was a little north of the present Lima.

JULIEN GARNIER.

Our best information about the Senecas, and, in fact, about the Iroquois in general, comes to us from Father Garnier. Parkman, in his "Jesuits in North America," says: "None of the old writers are so satisfactory as Lafitau. His work *Mœurs des Sauvages Ameriquaïns Comparés aux Mœurs des Premiers Temps* relates chiefly to the Iroquois and Hurons; the basis of his account of the former being his own observations and those of Father Julien Garnier, who was a missionary among them more than sixty years, from his novitiate to his death." Lafitau, himself, says that he studied the character and customs of the Indians, at Caughnawaga, for five years, *et j'y ai surtout profité des lumières et des connaissances d' un ancien missionaire Jesuite, le P. Julien Garnier."*

The Senecas had, of course, come in contact with the missionaries before the advent of Frémin and Garnier. For when Le Moyne was addressing the Iroquois at Onondaga, in 1654, Seneca chiefs were in the assembly. When Dablon, in the following year, descended the St. Lawrence to ask for a colony on Lake Ganentaa, some Seneca sachems went with him, and in 1656, the valiant old Chaumonot was visiting their towns. But twenty years before Le Moyne was holding up his wampum belts in the Long House at Onondaga, and thirty-five years before the arrival of Frémin and Garnier a Seneca brave was baptized in far-away Huronia. His acceptance of the faith was accompanied by the most awful cruelty. It is the first known conversion of a New York Indian.

In 1636, twenty or thirty Iroquois were fishing in Lake Ontario, when they were attacked by a party of Hurons. All escaped, but eight. One was killed, and his head was brought back as a trophy; the other seven were distributed among the various clans; the Seneca being sent to the very village where Brébeuf and his companions were evangelizing the Hurons. The captive was given to a conspicuous chief as a consolation for a brother who had been killed in

war, and he assuaged his grief by dooming his brother's sub-
stitute to be burned to death.   The story of the execution is
told by Father Le Mercier, who was an eye-witness.   It is
too horrible to repeat in its entirety, but some extracts may
be given to show the curious mixture of gentleness and
cruelty which characterized the American savage on such occasions.   It will also give an idea of the kind of monsters the
missionaries had to deal with. It is noteworthy that one of the
Fathers who was instrumental in saving the poor wretch's
soul was the great martyr, Charles Garnier. His namesake,
Julien Garnier, though, as far as we know, not a relative,
was, thirty-five years after that dreadful baptism, to begin a
twenty-year apostolate of incredible danger and hardship in
the very town from which the poor Indian came: Gandachioragou.   Of course, Garnier was familiar with the story,
for it was among the first set down in the famous
Relations.

The Fathers naturally recoiled from being present at this
fiendish execution, but they overcame their dislike and determined to go, hoping that some good might result.

"We reached Arontean," say the *Relations,* "a little
before the prisoner. We saw him coming in the distance.
He was singing, and was surrounded by 30 or 40 savages
who were escorting him. He was dressed in a beautiful
beaver robe, and wore a string of porcelain beads around
his neck, and another in the form of a crown on his head.
A great crowd was present on his arrival. He was made
to sit down at the entrance to the village, and there was a
struggle as to who should make him sing. Up to the hour
of his torment we saw only acts of humanity exercised
toward him, but he had already been roughly handled before his capture. One of his hands was badly bruised by
a stone, and one finger had been violently torn out of the
socket. The thumb and forefinger of the other hand had
been nearly taken off by the blow of a hatchet, and the only
plaster he had was some leaves bound with bark. The

314

joints of his arms were badly burned, and in one of them was a deep cut. We approached to look at him more closely; he raised his eyes and regarded us very attentively, but he did not yet know the happiness that heaven was preparing for him. Father Brébeuf was invited to make him sing, a request which, of course, was refused, but he spoke to the captive of the sorrow we felt for him. Meanwhile they brought him food from all sides—sagamite, squashes, fruits—and treated him only as a brother and a friend. From time to time he was commanded to sing, which he did with great strength of voice, although he seemed to be more than 50 years old, and had hardly been doing anything else than singing since his capture. Then a chief called out, as if making a proclamation, like a town crier in France, and said: ' My nephew; thou hast good reason to sing, for no one is doing thee any harm; behold thyself now among thy kindred and friends.' Good God! What a compliment. All around him were so many butchers. In all the places through which he had passed they had given him a feast. Here they did not fail in this act of courtesy; for a dog was immediately put into the kettle, and before it was half cooked he was brought into the cabin where the people were to gather for the banquet. He told some one to ask Father Superior to follow him and to say that he was very glad to see him. We entered, and we placed ourselves near him, and the Father began to explain to him how it was possible to pass from his present suffering to the happiness of Paradise. Father Garnier and I promised mentally to offer our Masses for him. He listened to our words attentively, was pleased, and repeated what we had said and expressed a great desire to go to heaven. All around listened to us, and even helped out our explanations.

" But let us return to the feast. As soon as the dog was cooked, they took out a large piece of it from the pot and put it in his mouth, for he was unable to use his hands. In fact, his agony was such that he asked to go out to take a little air. His request was readily granted. His hands were unwrapped, and they brought him water to cool them. They were half putrefied and all swarming with worms, a stench arising from them that was insupportable. He begged them to take away the worms, which were gnawing him to the very marrow, and which made him feel the same pain, he said, as if some one had touched him with fire. All was done that could be done to relieve him, but the worms would appear and disappear as soon as we tried to draw them out. Meanwhile he did not cease singing at intervals, and the Indians continued to give him something to eat—fruits, squashes, and the like.

" As the feast was about to begin, the Fathers withdrew, but to their amazement, the prisoner was brought to their cabin, where they began to instruct him, and were not only not interrupted, but listened to by the Indians who thronged around. Christian truth has never been preached in this country on so favorable an occasion, for there were present representatives from all the Huron tribes. The captive was baptized and was called Joseph.

" Then he was taken to a place some leagues off and was made to sing all the way. We followed, and again he was brought to our cabin. He was made to sing and dance a good part of the night. Again there was a chance for instruction, and all listened. In the morning the chief to whom he had been given arrived. Looking pleasantly at the prisoner, he assured him that he desired to save his life, but seeing him so mangled he had determined to kill him, as he would be of no use. 'I am sure,' he said, 'you prefer death. Come, then, nephew, be of good courage; prepare thyself for the evening, and do not be cast down.' 'How shall I die?' 'By fire,' was the answer. 'That is well,' said the captive. While this conversation was going on, a woman brought him food. Her countenance was sad, and tears streamed down her cheeks. The chief also often put his pipe in the prisoner's mouth; wiped off the sweat that poured down his face and cooled him with a fan.

"Then came a feast, and more singing and dancing, and he was brought back to the first village, Father Brébeuf keeping close to him, instructing and exhorting him. When they arrived the sun was setting and we withdrew to the place where the last act of the cruel tragedy was to be performed. It was in the cabin of a great war-chief, which was called 'the cabin of amputated heads.'

"We took a place where we could be near the victim. Towards 8 o'clock, eleven fires were lighted, about three feet from each other. The people assembled immediately; the old men on platforms on either side; the young men below, but so crowded as to be almost piled on top of each other. Cries of joy resounded on all sides. Most of the Indians had firebrands, for before the victim was brought in, the braves were bidden to do their duty, because the Sun and the God of War looked down on them. The chief ordered them to burn only his legs at first, so that he might hold out till daybreak, and commanded them to give up all other amusements.

"He had hardly finished when the victim entered. I leave you to imagine the terror that seized him. The cries redoubled. He is made to sit down upon a mat; his hands are bound; then he rises and makes the round of the cabin, singing and dancing. No one burns him this time. He had no sooner returned to his place than the war-chief took the victim's robe and said: 'Oteiondi will despoil him of the robe which I hold, and the Ataconchronous will cut off his head, which will be given to Ondessoué, along with one arm and the liver to make a feast.'

"After this, he began to walk and run around the fires, each Indian struggling to burn him as he passed. Meanwhile he shrieked like a lost soul, while the whole crowd imitated his cries, or rather smothered them with their horrible shouts. One must be there to see a living picture of

317

hell. The whole cabin appeared as if on fire, and athwart the flames and the dense smoke, these savages crowding upon one another, howling at the top of their voices, with firebrands in their hands, their eyes flashing with rage and fury, seemed like so many demons who would give no respite to the poor wretch. They often stopped him at one end of the cabin; some of them taking his hands and breaking them by sheer force; others pierced his ears with sticks which they left in them; others bound his wrists tightly with cords and then pulled on them fiercely. If he made the round and paused to take breath, he was made to sit upon hot ashes and burning coals. We endured unutterable pain in looking at it. I was reduced to such an extremity that I could hardly nerve myself to look up.

" On the seventh round his strength failed him, and after he had rested a little while on the embers, they tried to make him rise, but he did not stir, when one of these butchers, having applied a brand to his loins, he was seized with a fainting fit, and would never have risen if the young men had been permitted to have their way. They were ordered to cease tormenting him, for it was important that he should see daylight. They lifted him on a mat, most of the fires were extinguished and many of the people went away. They tried to revive him, and at the end of an hour he opened his eyes, and was commanded to sing. He did so in a broken and almost dying voice, but finally he sang so loud that he could be heard outside of the cabin. That brought the young men back, and they began to treat him worse than before.

" One thing, in my opinion, increased his sufferings: the mockery of kindliness and friendship. They scarcely burned him anywhere except on the legs. Some, in applying the firebrands, did not desist until he uttered loud cries; when he ceased shrieking they would begin again, repeating it seven or eight times; holding the fire close to the flesh and blowing on it. Others would bind cords around him and then set them on fire. Some made him put his feet on red hot hatchets, and then pressed down on them. You could hear the flesh hiss and see the smoke rise to the roof of the cabin. One would say to him, ' Come, uncle, where do you wish me to burn you? ' and he would have to indicate a particular spot. ' It is not right,' another would say, ' for my uncle to be cold; I must warm him.' Another would make him a pair of stockings from some old rags, to ease his feet, and then set them on fire, etc.

" Often we would talk to the Indians, and they would stop their torments, and the victim himself would speak on the state of affairs in his own country, doing it as easily and with as composed a countenance as anyone of the assembly. When day dawned they lighted fires outside the village. Father Brébeuf was at his side to encourage him. Then he was made to mount a scaffold, six or seven feet high, and three savages ascended it with him and tied him to an overhanging tree. They began anew to burn him, putting brands on his eyes; hanging hot hatchets on his neck, finally thrusting a torch down his throat. Then they cut him up, piece by piece, and finally struck off his head and tossed it to the crowd, where some one caught it and brought it to the chief. The common people devoured the body."

By this terrible road did the first Seneca Indian enter the Church and heaven. Possibly the missionaries sought out the poor man's family when they entered the Seneca country, to tell the tale of his conversion.

Garnier was unusually young for the dangerous work entrusted to him. But evidently the Superiors took his measure correctly. In the *Journal des PP. Jesuites*—the account which the Minister of the house keeps of current events—we read, under March 13, 1668: " Father Julien Garnier, who is not yet 25 years of age, has just been examined in the whole of Theology, according to the custom of the Society. The four examiners were Fathers Lalemant, Pijart, Dablon, and Pierron "—a board that did not lack distinction. Nine days after we find the note " Father Garnier went on a mission to the Côte de Lauson."

On the 21st of April, it is recorded that " Father Marquette, two men and a young lad, are waiting an opportunity to go to the Ottawa country," an item of whose importance the Minister had then, of course, no suspicion. Right after it is: " Father Julien Garnier and Charles Boquet are to go to assist Father Bruyas at Oneida." " On the 17th of May, Father Garnier left for the Oneida mission." The record is almost military in its brevity.

Evidently Garnier and Boquet went by Lake Champlain and stopped at Ossernenon (Auriesville), for they picked up Bruyas at Tionnontoguen, and the three together went to the Oneida country. Garnier, however, did not remain long at Oneida, for in the *Relations,* of 1666-68, we read: " Father Julien Garnier, who had gone up to Oneida last summer in order to work jointly with Father Bruyas for the salvation of those tribes, saw himself constrained by all motives of charity to devote himself to Onondaga, which is only a short day's journey distant." This change of base by Garnier will explain why Bruyas grew so gloomy when Boquet, although only a trader, went back to Quebec and took with him the famous converts, Catherine and her husband. He then had neither his associate nor his two great converts; and had no one to talk to, for he was ignorant of Oneida.

Garnier was received with enthusiasm at Onondaga. Garagontié, the great chief, built him a chapel, and a few days after went to Quebec and told the Governor what he had done for the missionary. The Governor thanked him, officially, as a great benefactor, and treated him with the most distinguished consideration. It was on this occasion that Garagontié was solemnly baptized.

The first consolation that Father Garnier received at Onondaga was one that often rewards those who have the care of souls. He was for some reason or another on the shores of Lake Ontario, thirty leagues from his mission when he stumbled upon a poor old Iroquois, who was dying. He was a pagan, but was married to a Christian Huron. For two years he was scarcely able to hear or recognize anyone, but all that time his faithful wife patiently nursed him and prayed for him, and occasionally, when he could catch her words, spoke to him about the faith. " I had resolved," she said, to Father Garnier, " to travel fifty leagues to bring a Black Gown, and lo! you have come unexpectedly to us." " For ten years," writes Garnier, " no priest had been there, and for two years the sick man had been kept alive as if by a miracle." Of course, the Father baptized him, and the next day the poor old savage died in the arms of his loving wife.

After a while Father Millet arrived at Onondaga, and matters went well, though the usual Indian horrors were always before them. One of their first experiences was like that which Brébeuf had with the Seneca chief who was burned near Lake Huron, thirty-five years before, only the victim of the tragedy at Onondaga was a poor woman who was going to be burned to death. Garnier led her to his little chapel, and instructed her, while " she listened with admirable gentleness and presence of mind." The account simply says: " The woman came out of the chapel all filled with courage, and made the people admire her firmness in the midst of the fires they had lighted, where her son had just died a blessed death, having been cast into the flames on coming out of baptism." All the details of this fiendish act of burning the mother and child are omitted. In the beginning, these executions were described minutely, but the Fathers had become too accustomed to them now. It was only one of the ordinary events of their life. Only a few days afterwards, another poor squaw was treated in the same way. She was just going up the scaffold to be burned when Garnier arrived. " He had time enough," says the *Relation,* " to instruct and baptize her, and then they began that tragic execution which is the delight of those peoples."

Such occurrences make up the story of Garnier's work at Onondaga, with, however, frequent reminders of the precariousness of his own existence, as when, for instance, an Indian, who one day began to sing that he was going to kill him, because in a public ceremony the priest had refused him something, was only mollified by another savage stepping forward and giving him some trifling present.

After a while de Carheil arrived at Onondaga, and Garnier conducted him to Cayuga, where the great man was to labor so long and unsuccessfully, among the people whom Frémin describes as " breathing only blood and brandy." Father de Carheil had the happiness, however, of baptizing a poor captive squaw, who went at the same time as he did from Onondaga to Cayuga. He saw her burned and eaten. It was his introduction to his flock.

Seeing that comparative tranquillity reigned in the various stations, Frémin determined to convoke all the missionaries at Onondaga to discuss their methods of work. This was the year 1671. They remained there for a week, and when the sessions were ended, he took Garnier with him to the Senecas, for the labor was increasing there. It was near being the end of both of them. On September 7, as " we were calling at Gandagaro, a drunken man seized Father Garnier with one hand and raised the other twice to stab him with a knife, but by good luck, a woman who chanced to be near, took the knife out of his hand and prevented him from carrying his brutality further. I admired on this occasion the firmness and resoluteness of the Father, who did not even change color."

From this very simple account, one would imagine that Garnier was the only one in danger, but we find in Millet's letter from Onondaga, that " although the news had come that Father Garnier had been assassinated, it was only a false alarm with regard to Garnier, but had lacked very little of being true in respect to Father Frémin, who was almost killed by a drunken Indian, and for a long time bore on his face the marks of the Indian's fury." There is a bit of psychological information, also, contained in this account, for it tells us, " the Onondaga is not as savage as the Seneca when he is drunk. He rather strives to caress you, and protests that you don't love him enough." " Three days after our arrival," says Frémin, " Father Garnier took possession of the Mission of Gandachioragou, where there are yet only three or four Christians who make public profession of their faith. He will have the care of this single village—at least for this year—in order that he may have time to learn the language of the country perfectly, and make rules for it, and a dictionary, so as to be able to teach others." Neither he nor Garnier, however, could have had much work among the young men, who were absent, hunting and fighting, for nine months of the year, and prepared themselves for such expeditions by getting drunk one whole month before they set out.

Garnier, however, continued patiently at his task. The four or five Christians whom he found in his village increased in numbers, and his little chapel was soon filled with people, but every now and again the clouds would gather, and the lonely missionary was sure that his end had come. His long prayers at night evoked suspicions, and an old Cayuga chief who was visiting the Senecas had nearly succeeded in making them execute the sentence of death, which they had solemnly passed on him. Then came a fire, which destroyed the village, and destroyed his chapel, but he set to work and rebuilt it. Meantime, the ever-recurring orgies of drunkenness kept him in constant terror, though he records that only one savage, under the influence of liquor, dared to follow him into the chapel, which was his usual refuge when the village was in a riot. But in spite of all this, he writes to his Superior: " I have observed that it is not so much depravity of morals that prevents our savages from being Christians as the prejudices they have about Christianity. I know nearly 200 families among them who maintain inviolate the marriage bond, and rear their children in morality, who keep their daughters from undue freedom of intercourse abroad, and from plunging into riots of sensuality, and who would be inclined to live very Christian lives if they had faith."

In 1673, Garnier probably met La Salle, for the first time. Frontenac had arrived as Governor, and La Salle, who had been rather discredited under Courcelles and Talon, saw his opportunity of achieving distinction. For some time the Iroquois had been crossing Lake Ontario for an occasional fight with their enemies, but chiefly to divert the fur trade of the Northwest to the Iroquois country and down to Fort Orange. La Salle proposed to Frontenac to build a fort at the mouth of the Cataroqui River, to serve as a protection against the Iroquois invasions, and to be at the same time a trading post. Frontenac, who had great projects, but little money to carry them out, readily acquiesced. But the difficulty was to induce the Iroquois to consent. For that purpose, La Salle visited the missionaries, and through their efforts succeeded in getting the necessary permission. If they had foreseen that the ruin of the missions was to be brought about by that fort they would not have been such ready instruments in the hands of La Salle and Frontenac, who hated them cordially. Immediately, La Salle began his preparations, and Fort Cataroqui, which he called Fort Frontenac, rose from the ground to protect the colonists whom he succeeded in gathering around him. He, himself, received from the King many a broad acre and the title of Seigneur.

The Canadian historian, Benj. Sulte, who has no liking for La Salle, thus describes the fort:

" To form an idea of the construction of 1673, it is sufficient to say that they dug a ditch on four sides of a square, and flung the dirt inside the square to raise the level. Large stakes were planted around this level spot, measuring 360 feet, or 90 feet on each face. Inside were the necessary buildings of the fort.

" The cost of the construction amounted to ten or twelve thousand francs, an amount which covered expense of transportation, food, etc. No one was paid any wages, as they were working for the King. From 1673 to 1675, two traders of Montreal were in possession, and had to keep the fort in good condition. They spent in repairs, etc., about 9,000 francs. In 1675, La Salle obtained control of it, promising to reconstruct it in stone, and to keep 20 men in it for two years, and afterwards a garrison like that at Montreal, and to establish colonists in the neighborhood, engaging, also, to pay 10,000 francs to the King and 9,000 to the two traders, he having the monopoly of trade of Lake Ontario and further west, for three years.

" In 1677 the fort was completed. It was six times larger than the old one. On the land side the wall was 498 feet long, 3 feet thick and 15 feet high. It was not finished on the water side as late as 1684."

La Salle pretended that the garrison cost him 18,000 francs a year; and while building the fort he also undertook to build vessels to navigate the lakes, and here, again, he came across Garnier. Cayuga Creek was the place chosen for the shipyard, and thither La Motte, his lieutenant, and the Friar Hennepin betook themselves to get leave from the Senecas. Entering the village of scowling and sullen Indians, La Motte perceived the two Jesuits, Garnier and Raffeix, and instead of greeting them, rose up in the council, which was convened, and demanded their expulsion. The insult was grievous, but, of course, was not resented, as the missionaries were glad to be out of the way of anyone connected with La Salle. Hennepin relates that out of regard for the cloth, he, too, left the assembly; but the good friar's reputation as a story teller is not of the best.

The permission was granted, and the vessel, of 40 or 60 tons burthen—it is not sure which—was launched on Lake Erie. It was called "The Griffin," because that was the device on Frontenac's coat-of-arms, and, moreover, said La Motte, "the Griffin (Frontenac) was going to get ahead of the crows (the Jesuits)." As the Griffin is a feathered beast anything unmannerly might be expected of it. These and other ventures were ruining La Salle. By 1679, he had no money, and his creditors levied on his store of peltries in Fort Frontenac.

In 1679, he started west and lost everything. April 9, 1682, he again set out, and reached the mouth of the Mississippi. A month later his permission to trade expired, and his patron, Frontenac, was recalled to France. His creditors immediately took possession of the fort, whose dimensions they found La Salle had grossly exaggerated. To be as large as he said it was, it would have to include all the structures outside the walls. There were other misrepresentations, they declared, of a similar nature. In 1683, La Salle abandoned the fort and Governor de la Barre took possession, putting in it two traders, Le Bert and La Chesnaye.

The war which broke out in 1684 was not caused by La Salle, as de la Barre feared, but by the two traders, who had ill-treated some Senecas. In retaliation, the Indians seized some goods that were intended for de la Barre, himself, which may explain why that worthy was so intent on war. Possibly he would not have been so zealous for someone else's property. Thus the shadow of the ill-fated fort fell continually across Garnier's pathway. His own Senecas had brought on the war.

Garnier was unable to prevent hostilities. A solemn convocation of military men and ecclesiastics assembled at Quebec and advised the Governor to punish the Senecas. In vain Garnier and de Lamberville pleaded. They represented that reparation could easily be made, and that on the other hand, war meant the ruin of the missions. The whole matter could be arbitrated at the Central Council of Onondaga, but de la Barre's mind was made up. The result is known. De la Barre embarked on his foolish expedition, but never entered the Seneca country. He returned in disgrace to Quebec, and was replaced by Denonville, whose instincts were still more martial and whose orders from the Home Government were peremptory. He arrived at Cataroqui. By that time every missionary except de Lamberville had been recalled, and that ended the twenty years' labor of Garnier in New York. He was not present when the French and Indian army entered the country which he had striven so hard to civilize and convert, and he did not see the desolation, after Denonville had finished his mad march. There were no more Seneca towns. An account of the invasion is found in the *Relations*. It is a letter to Monsieur Cabart de Villermont, who had asked to be informed " of the success of Monsieur, our Governor's expedition against the Iroquois." We read:

" When the army was reviewed on an island near Montreal, it was found to consist of 800 men of the regular troops, and a like number of militia, besides 100 Canadians, for the baggage and canoes, and a hundred others, forming a flying camp. About 300 Christian savages joined the expedition. They started on the 11th of June, and safely passed the rapids. Finally, after much fatigue, and after having had rain and contrary winds nearly every day, they reached Cataroqui. They crossed Lake Ontario on July 5, and arrived at Irondequoit, ten leagues from the Senecas, on the 10th, and were there joined by three or four hundred savages. Leaving 400 men at Irondequoit, they began their march to the enemy's country on the 12th. On the 13th, they passed a dangerous defile, and were attacked by the savages. Astonished at first, they quickly repelled the foe. While this was going on, five or six hundred other Iroquois endeavored to attack our men in the rear, but de

Denonville directed such a heavy fire on them that they were beaten back and fled, but as the roads were bad and the Indians ran like deer to the woods, it was found impossible to pursue them. We had 7 killed and 20 wounded; the enemy, 50 killed and 60 wounded. The army then marched to the first village, which it found deserted and almost reduced to ashes. As our people found no one to fight with, they set to work to burn the corn fields and whatever provisions were stored away. We did likewise with the other villages. As it was by this means that Monsieur de Denonville could do most injury to the Iroquois, he devoted every attention to it. He also thought it of the highest importance to build a fort at the entrance of the Niagara River. As it is only 30 leagues from the Senecas, it would cause alarm to the savages. There he left a garrison of 100 men, and then started for Montreal."

Such was the ridiculous military exploit of the new Governor of Canada. It consisted in destroying cornfields, while it drove the Indians into the hands of the English, and rendered it impossible for a priest to enter the entire territory from Lake Erie to the Hudson for the next 13 years. A letter of de Carheil to the successor of Denonville deals in the most caustic fashion with the disgracefulness of the whole affair, and especially with the humiliating attitude which the French Governor was compelled to assume by entreating Dongan to call off the Iroquois.

After the disaster we find Garnier among the Indians of Lorette and Caughnawaga, but he was a failure, at least in the first place. Poor old Father Chaumonot had lost his hold upon his Indians as the weight of age came upon him, and some one was needed to restore the ancient discipline which had reigned there. Garnier was chosen, but the man who could rule the wild Senecas in their villages was unsuccessful among the civilized Indians of Lorette, and he had to be sent to labor elsewhere.

He was absorbed in various employments until the missions reopened, and in the history of the intervening years we are almost surprised to find quoted in Rochemonteix, a very excellent letter of the rough old missionary, defending the Society against the accusations of fur trading. This particular charge appears to be traceable to Frontenac, who, if he did not originate it, propagated it. He was very unfriendly to the Society, and in this instance vented his spleen because Bishop Laval had forbidden the sale of liquor to the Indians. Not daring to attack the prelate, he satisfied himself by assailing those " who said nothing, but who, he was sure, had prompted the bishop's action."

To the charge of dealing in furs, Garnier simply says: " Yes, the missionaries received some peltries from the Indians, just as they did corn or any other commodity by which the Indians would repay temporal services done to them, and also to contribute to the support of the mission." There was no coin, and people paid in kind in those days; but as for anything like trading, he indignantly denied that the Fathers ever descended to it.

No doubt he was delighted to get out of all the miserable squabbles which were worrying Quebec at that time, and returned with pleasure to his beloved Senecas. That was brought about when, on August 4, 1701, 1,300 Iroquois arrived at Montreal and assented to a treaty of peace, which 38 of their chiefs signed with Callières, the Governor of Canada. The Indians bound themselves to live at peace with the French. James de Lamberville was again at Onondaga, and Garnier among the Senecas, along with Vaillant de Guesles.

If we look at the *N. Y. Colonial Documents,* however, we shall find that the English at Albany and New York were worked up to a religious fury by this proceeding, and availed themselves of every means to drive the missionaries out.

Peter, or Kwiter Schuyler was particularly active and persistent. He began operations as early as 1703. He

329

first convoked an assembly at Onondaga, and then prorogued it to Albany, where in spite of opposition, Father de Geulis and M. de Joncaire forced themselves into the assembly, and brought all Schuyler's fine schemes to naught.

Not deterred by his defeat, however, he dared even to approach the Christian Indians of Caughnawaga, and succeeded in eliciting a promise from them of remaining neutral in case of war, but they were soon won back to their old allegiance. His base trickery with regard to old Father de Lamberville is known. He persuaded the priest to go to Montreal to stop the war, and then induced some drunken savages to plunder the mission church and house and set them on fire. When de Lamberville was out of the way, Schuyler had no difficulty in persuading the Indians to dig up the hatchet. Father Garnier's Senecas, however, remained faithful to the French.

In keeping with his usual methods, Schuyler persuaded Father de Mareuil that his life was no longer safe, and induced him to go to Albany, concealing the fact that the Colonial Government had, on June 29, issued an order for the priest's arrest. Mareuil was so completely deceived that two weeks before, viz: June 16, 1709, he wrote to Father d'Heu, whom he supposed to be still with the Senecas, to accept the same offer from Schuyler, but d'Heu, who was the last one to depart, had followed de Lamberville and Garnier, and escaped to Montreal. Mareuil was kept in custody in Albany until 1710, when he was exchanged for two other prisoners, one of them Schuyler's nephew. He was well-treated, however, and managed meantime to visit New York occasionally, and was a close observer of the preparations that were being made to invade Canada. Like a loyal Frenchman, he, at great risk to himself, informed the French Governor of what was going on and warned him that the first attack would be made at Chambly.

His information was correct. Nicholson led an army of

330

4,000 men towards that place, and de Ramezay was ready to meet him, though with a much inferior force, but Nicholson never arrived. His treacherous Iroquois allies threw a great quantity of skins of slaughtered animals into the River Chicot and, it is said, a thousand men who drank the water fell sick and died. De Mareuil's prophecy was verified. When the treaty was made with the English at Onondaga, he remarked that the Iroquois would not be helpful as allies. The wily savages had determined that neither French nor English should prevail; but that they would stand between both. Poisoning the stream was an example of the methods adopted.

When Garnier returned to Canada for the second time he was sixty-seven years of age. The rest of his days were spent with the Indians in the various settlements along the St. Lawrence. He gave up all active work in 1728, and died at Quebec in 1730.

Of course, the old missionaries did not desert their Indians after the churches were destroyed. The *Colonial Documents* inform us that they made repeated visits to their old homes, often disguised as Indians. They were a continual worry to the English authorities, and though the savages made repeated promises to exclude all " popish priests," they apparently had little scruple about violating their agreement.

The struggle, however, was not yet over, even for permanent establishments. In 1720, the French built a fort at Niagara, and another at Crown Point, on Lake Champlain, in 1734. The Recollects were chaplains there, and no doubt influenced the Indians greatly. Niagara did not last long, but Crown Point continued till 1759. The list of priests who served this latter place is to be found in Shea's *Catholic Church in Colonial Times*.

Meantime, the famous Sulpitian Picquet had established a mission on the site of the present city of Ogdensburg, which he called La Presentation. He expended 30,000 livres on the work, but in 1749 the Mohawks destroyed it. Undismayed, Picquet began again, and in two years had 3,000 Iroquois living in his colony. Sir William Johnson tried to persuade them to withdraw, but they refused. In 1759, however, war swept it out of existence. But all was not yet lost. Just before Picquet's work was destroyed, the Jesuit Father Mark Anthony Gordon, established the present Indian colony of St. Regis, near the Canadian border. At the suppression of the Society it passed out of the control of the Jesuits, but still exists as a mission.

Meantime, a curious chapter of New York Catholic history was beginning. Sir William Johnson, who claimed to be related to the Macdonalds of Scotland, invited them to come over and settle near him in the Mohawk. The Macdonalds were all Catholics, and were, therefore, cordially hated by the Dutchmen down at Schenectady and Albany. With them was a Father McKenna, whose name has nothing Scotch about it. Apart from religious reasons, probably the highland dress, the independent swagger and the handy dirk, added to the feelings of dislike. In fact, a number of the Campbells had come over in 1720, and although they were not Catholics, they found the conditions so unpleasant in the valley that they withdrew to the neighborhood of Saratoga, where they were nearly all massacred by the savages; atoning thus for the massacre of Glencoe, in which they had stained their hands in the blood of the Macdonalds thirty years before.

The Macdonalds continued to live with Sir William Johnson until the Revolution broke out. Being staunch Tories, they declared for the King, and had to surrender to General Schuyler in the early spring of 1776. But being papists and Tories, they felt their position unsafe and they abandoned their homes and fled to Canada. Unfortunately, on their way they met the Catholic Indians of St. Regis, who were on the American side of the quarrel, and although they had been gathered together and Christianized by a Gordon, they did not spare the Scotch fugitives. Those who escaped starvation or the tomahawk reached Montreal with Father McKenna, where the Jesuits took care of them. The Macdonalds are now at Glengarry, and as they look across the river they can see St. Regis, the home of the Catholic Indians who waylaid them in their flight.

By this time, says Gilmary Shea, "the Church in the northern part of the United States, where the French flag had floated, was in a pitiable state. The Indian Catholics in New York, Maine, and Ohio, along with the few French lingering near them, were without a single priest or anything worthy the name of a church. The work of all the years from the visit of Fathers Jogues was recorded rather in the graves of the Faithful Departed than in the living children of the Church and their pastors."

Was it a failure? Possibly it was, though the blame should be put where it belongs. On the other hand, may not the marvellous growth of the Church in New York State have some connection with the heroism of its first priests?

7-29
10-16
10-23
7-31